ArtScroll Series®

Rabbi Nosson Scherman / Rabbi Meir Zlotowitz

General Editors

THE GIFT OF LIFE

WITH HEARTS

Published by
Mesorah Publications, ltd

ספר מתנת חיים

FULL OF FAITH

NSIGHTS INTO TRUST AND EMUNAH

A selection of addresses by

RABBI MATTISYAHU SALOMON

**DAPTED FOR PRINT AND WITH AN INTRODUCTION
BY RABBI YAAKOV YOSEF REINMAN**

FIRST EDITION
First Impression … February 2002

Published and Distributed by
MESORAH PUBLICATIONS, LTD.
4401 Second Avenue / Brooklyn, N.Y 11232

Distributed in Europe by
LEHMANNS
Unit E, Viking Industrial Park
Rolling Mill Road
Jarow, Tyne & Wear, NE32 3DP
England

Distributed in Australia and New Zealand by
GOLDS WORLD OF JUDAICA
3-13 William Street
Balaclava, Melbourne 3183
Victoria, Australia

Distributed in Israel by
SIFRIATI / A. GITLER — BOOKS
6 Hayarkon Street
Bnei Brak 51127

Distributed in South Africa by
KOLLEL BOOKSHOP
Shop 8A Norwood Hypermarket
Norwood 2196, Johannesburg, South Africa

Typography by CompuScribe at ArtScroll Studios, Ltd.

Printed in the United States of America by Noble Book Press Corp.
Bound by Sefercraft, Quality Bookbinders, Ltd., Brooklyn N.Y. 11232

*T*he publishers proudly dedicate this volume to
the Roshei HaYeshivah
of Beth Medrash Govoha

HaGaon HaRav Malkiel Kotler
HaGaon HaRav Yerucham Olshin
HaGaon HaRav Dovid Schustal
HaGaon HaRav Yisroel Neuman
שליט״א

*T*hey have taken their legacy
to progressively greater heights,
nurturing it into America's premier Torah center,
the magnet for the most distinguished b'nai Torah.
With dedication and self-sacrifice,
they have made Lakewood the quintessential עיר התורה.

They embody the lofty ideals and boundless aspirations
of their great forebears,
Maran HaGaon HaRav Aharon Kotler זצוק״ל
and
Maran HaGaon HaRav Shneur Kotler זצוק״ל

The success and health of the Roshei Hayeshivah שליט״א
are the success and health of Klal Yisrael.
May Hashem Yisbarach grant them
continued hatzlachah and good health,
as they raise new generations to the service of ה׳ ותורתו.

ברוכים המקיימים את דברי התורה הזאת

TABLE OF CONTENTS

The Faithful Heart

Upreach, Inreach and Outreach

INTRODUCTION

When Rav Mattisyahu Salomon *shlita* became Mashgiach of the Lakewood Yeshivah a few years ago, I was already a grandfather, and although I still learn in the Yeshivah for a good part of my day, I did not expect that his coming would have a major impact on my life.

I was wrong. I found myself attending his *vaadim* on Chumash in his home and his Monday night *shmuessen* in the Yeshivah, along with my brothers and many other members of the Yeshivah of my own age group. Over the last three years, I have also had the singular privilege of developing a close personal relationship with him, and I am honored to consider myself his *talmid*. I can honestly say that he has changed my life in many ways, and I am forever grateful.

Two years ago, I accepted an invitation to travel to Russia with the Mashgiach — after he promised me that we would learn *Parashas Noach* together on the trip. On our return flight, we sat together for a few hours, and I told him that I believed he had come to Lakewood from England just for my sake. He agreed that it was probably so. I understood, of course, that at the same time he had also come just for the sake of many hundreds of other individuals and just for the sake of the *klal*. I was reminded of the Gemara's statement (*Sanhedrin* 37a) that every person should say, "*Bishvili nivra haolam*; the world was created for me." Every single person, from the greatest to the most humble, is important and worthy enough to have an entire world created for him. The Mashgiach also makes every single person feel important and that it was worthwhile for him to come from England just for that person's sake.

One year ago, Rabbi Nosson Scherman of Mesorah Publications asked me to write a book based on the Mashgiach's *shmuessen* and addresses. Of course, I agreed to do it, but I have to admit that it has been one of the most daunting projects I have ever undertaken.

Speaking and writing are two completely different media, and the transfer from one to the other is often extremely problematic. Great orators — and the Mashgiach certainly ranks high among them — deliver far more than intellectual content. They also connect with their audiences on the emotional and spiritual levels. They touch, they move, they mesmerize, they inspire. Transcripts of the Mashgiach's speeches record only his words, but what about all the rest? What about the charisma, the presence, the gaze, the modulation, the cadence, the pregnant pauses, the passion, the kindliness, the love, the warmth, the sighs and the smiles, the twinkle in the eye, the occasional tremble in the voice, the eyes glistening with tears? All these are missing from the transcripts, and without them the effect is lost.

My task, therefore, was not to edit the transcripts but rather to reproduce the Mashgiach's voice using only the written medium, to use the techniques of the writer to compensate for the techniques and intangibles of the speaker that are inevitably missing in a book. It was to help the reader imagine he is hearing the speaker's voice, even though the words may not be the same. This is always a difficult task, but it is much more so when the assignment is to capture the rich and nuanced textures of the Mashgiach's addresses. This was the challenge facing me.

I have written the book to the best of my abilities, but I still believe it is not possible to reproduce a speaking voice perfectly in print; something is always lost in the translation. I believe that even if the Mashgiach himself had written this book, his voice as a writer would not have been a perfect match to his voice as a speaker. Nonetheless, the Mashgiach was pleased with the results and generous with his encouragement and kind comments, which leads me to suspect that I was successful. It is my hope that readers who have heard him speak will recognize at least an echo of his voice in these pages, and that those readers who have not had the privilege will be drawn to hear him either in person or at least on tape.

The addresses I have selected for the Mashgiach's first appearance in print in the English language are all related to the subject of *emunah* and *bitachon*, trust and faith, as the book's title and subtitle indicate, as well as issues of general inspiration. Some are composites of several addresses, others are abridgements. All were delivered over the last several years in a wide variety of venues, ranging from the hallowed halls of the Yeshivah to conventions and public gatherings to a women's symposium on infertility to an inspirational talk for high school girls. The dates and venues of the Twin Towers addresses (Chapters 11-13) are given in footnotes.

The Mashgiach has also asked me to make an additional clarification. The material on which these addresses are based were developed over many years of study and inevitably include some points and insights drawn from the works of others. It is not expected that sources be identified for every minor point in a public address, but the Mashgiach feels that when it comes to a book, which is a more permanent expression, it is important to try as much as possible to give credit where credit is due. The Mashgiach has provided many original sources for the book, and he acknowledges the contribution of those sources he may have failed to mention.

The Mashgiach has also asked me to make an additional clarification. The materials on which these addresses are based were developed over many years of study and inevitably include some points and insights drawn from the works of others. It is not expected that sources be identified for every minor point in a public address, but the Mashgiach feels that when it comes to a book, which is a more permanent expression, it is important to try as much as possible to give credit where credit is due. The Mashgiach has provided many original sources for the book, and he acknowledges the contribution of those sources he may have failed to mention.

One brief comment on the vocabulary. I simulated the Mashgiach's voice primarily through the form, structure and pace of the writing, but choice of words and phrasing are also distinctive to each voice. Since the Mashgiach is an English speaker with an excellent command of the language, I tried to use only words and phrases that he himself might use. For the purpose of authenticity, I also sprinkled the text with Briticisms such as "straightaway" instead of "immediately" and "in hospital" instead of "in the hospital," but I have to admit that I am not sufficiently well-versed in these differences. If Americanisms have managed to creep into the text, the fault is entirely mine.

I would like to take this opportunity to express my appreciation and gratitude to Rav Aryeh Malkiel Kotler, *shlita*, Rav Yeruchem Olshin, *shlita*, Rav Dovid Schustal, *shlita*, and Rav Yisroel

Neuman, *shlita*, the illustrious *roshei yeshivah* of Beth Medrash Govoha, who have been my good friends since we were *bachurim* together in the *beis midrash*. I thank them for their friendship and kindness over the years and for their wise and inspired leadership of my beloved Yeshivah. On this occasion, I also thank them for their wisdom and foresight in bringing the Mashgiach to Lakewood to assist them in raising up the level of the Yeshivah, the city of Lakewood and the Jewish community at large.

I want to express my appreciation to Rabbi Nosson Scherman for his unwavering courtesy and cooperation. I would like to thank my good friend Rabbi Shlomo Gissinger, who reviewed the manuscript meticulously and offered helpful comments. I would also like to thank Rabbi Sadya Grama, who helped me select the tapes for transcription. A special word of thanks to Mrs. Miriam Hirsch for her intelligence and expertise in the preparation of the transcripts from which I worked. I would also like to acknowledge Rebbetzin Salomon's gracious assistance in this project and her tireless and ceaseless but seldom publicized efforts, day in and day out, to support the Mashgiach in all his work. As always, I am profoundly indebted to my wife Shami for her invaluable contribution to this project as well as everything I have ever undertaken.

In closing, I want to express my humble gratitude to the Creator for granting me the *zechus* to bring the Mashgiach's message to a broader audience. It is a message of faith, hope, encouragement and aspiration, and I am sure it will inspire and uplift many thousands of Jewish hearts and bring them closer to our Father in Heaven. I am grateful that I could have a small share in the accomplishment.

Rosh Chodesh Adar 5762 (2002)   *Yaakov Yosef Reinman*
Lakewood, New Jersey

The Faithful Heart

CHAPTER ONE

Faith and Faithfulness

W hen young people get married, the primary blessing we give them is that they should build "a *bayis ne'eman b'Yisrael*, a faithful home among the Jewish people." This is surely a beautiful blessing, but why is it so fundamental? Why does it take precedence over all other blessings we could give them? We could wish for them to build a home full of Torah, *mitzvos* and good deeds. We could wish for them to build a home in which there will be *yiras Shamayim*, fear of Heaven. Why is faithfulness the bedrock of the Jewish home?

Let us take a look into the Torah in the beginning of the Book of Exodus, where we once again find this extraordinary emphasis on faithfulness. Moses grows up and ventures out from Pharaoh's palace, in which he was reared as an Egyptian prince, and he sets off to investigate the condition of his Jewish brothers and sisters. As he walks through the fields, he catches sight of an Egyptian taskmaster thrashing a Jewish laborer. Moses looks around to make sure no one is watching, then he strikes down the Egyptian and buries the body in the sand.

The next day, he comes across two Jews fighting. "Why do you strike your fellow Jew?" he says to the aggressor.

"Who appointed you an officer and magistrate over us?" the man answers back. "Do you intend to kill me as you killed the Egyptian?"

Frightened, Moses declares (*Exodus* 2:14), "*Achein noda hadavar.* Surely the thing is known."

Which "thing is known"? The simple meaning is that Moses realized that his supposedly secret act had been discovered. The word was out that he had killed the Egyptian, and he was in danger. Rashi also brings a second interpretation from the Midrash. Moses saw in the Jewish aggressor's sarcastic reply that he intended to inform to the Egyptian authorities, as indeed he eventually did. Could it be that there were evil informers among the Jews? Moses was shocked. "Surely the thing is known," he declared. At last I understand why the Jewish people are unworthy of redemption. At last I understand why they are still sitting in exile.

This Midrash is very puzzling. At the lowest point of their bondage in Egypt, the Jewish people had sunk to *mem-tess shaarei tumah,* the forty-ninth level of spiritual defilement. Had they sunk to the last and final level, the damage would have been irreparable. They were so close to utter disaster, and still, Moses did not see their nearly absolute moral corruption as an insurmountable obstacle to redemption. But when he discovered informers among them, it suddenly became clear to him why they were still in exile. Apparently, idolaters could be redeemed, but informers could not.

Why was this so? Why was the presence of informers such a decisive block to redemption, more so than just about the worst spiritual defilement possible?

Every morning, before we pray for our needs, we express our praise and gratitude to God. Among others, we repeat the stirring words of the Levites at the consecration of the Second Temple (*Nehemiah* 9:7-8), "You, O God, are the one and only One; You made the heavens, the upper heavens and all their hosts, the land and all that is upon it, the seas and all they contain, and You sustain all of them; it is to You that the hosts of the heavens bow down. You are the One, O God, that is the Lord, Who chose Abram, brought him forth from Ur Kasdim, changed his name to Abraham and found his heart faithful before You; You forged a covenant with him to give the land of the Canaanites, Hittites, Amorites, Perizites, Jebusites and Girgashites, to give them to his offspring, and You kept Your word, because You are righteous."

If we look closely at these words, we find an unusual point of climax. These two verses are clearly one continuous flow. You, O God, are the one and only, the One Who made heaven and earth, the One before Whom all the hosts of heaven bow down. You, O God, are the selfsame One Who chose Abram and miraculously saved him from the fiery furnace in Ur. And why did You do all this? Because You "found his heart faithful before You." Because he was a *ne'eman*, a faithful man.

How does this soaring, dramatic overture lead to the climactic statement that God "found his heart faithful"?

My *rebbe* R' Elya Lopian, *zt"l*, explains these words with a parable. Imagine seeing a poor beggar walking down the street. He is haggard and hollow-eyed, scruffy, unwashed, bedraggled. Grimy rags hang from his bony frame. Suddenly, he stoops and picks something up from the ground. He looks at it closely, and then he smiles, puts it into his pocket and continues on his way.

Would you wonder about that mysterious item the beggar had picked up and slipped into his pocket? Not very likely. If you had to speculate, you would say it might have been a cigarette butt from which he could squeeze another puff or two. Or perhaps some other item of insignificant value. Whatever it was, you would have no curiosity about it.

But imagine you are watching a king dressed in royal robes walking along a tree-lined boulevard, accompanied by ministers and noblemen. Imagine thousands of people thronging both sides of the boulevard, crying out, "Long live the king! Long live the king!" Suddenly, the king stops, bringing the entire procession to a halt. He stoops and picks something up from the ground. He looks at it closely, then he puts it into his pocket and continues along his way.

Wouldn't you be consumed with curiosity to know what had caught the interest of the king? Wouldn't all the thousands of people watching also be consumed with a similar curiosity? What incredibly precious treasure had the king found that he could not pass by without reaching down and taking it for his own?

Before we speak about Abraham's exceptional qualities, R' Elya concludes, we want to emphasize how extraordinary they are. And so we speak about God's awesome majesty, the unity of His essence, the absolute vastness of His power. This great and omnipotent King, this mighty Master of the Universe, He is the One Who reached down and took Abraham for His own. We are consumed with curiosity. What rare and wondrous quality did Abraham possess that so endeared him to God? Why did God choose Abraham? And the answer is that He "found his heart faithful."

Abraham was famous for his acts of *chessed*, kindness. His *hachnasas orchim*, hospitality, was legendary. Yet faithfulness was the quality that endeared him to God above all else. He chose Abraham because he was a *ne'eman*, a faithful man.

Similarly, God impressed Aaron and Miriam with Moses' greatness as a prophet by saying (*Numbers* 12:7), "*Bechol beisi ne'eman hu.* He is trusted in My entire house." He is a *ne'eman*. He is a faithful servant.

The word *ne'eman*, which appears many times in the Torah, takes on different meanings in different contexts. It can mean trustworthy, faithful, loyal, reliable, responsible, firm, honest. These are all variations and nuances of one overriding quality. A *ne'eman* is steadfast as a rock, unwavering, unfaltering, unswerving. You can count on his support, his loyalty, his word. Above all, you can count on his word.

We find that *ne'eman* is actually used to describe God Himself. The Gemara states (*Shabbos* 119b), "What is the meaning of the word *amen*? Rabbi Chanina said, 'It is the acronym of the words *E-l melech ne'eman*, the Lord, the faithful King.'"

The theme of divine faithfulness is particularly striking in the blessing we say after the Haftarah. "Blessed are You, O God our Lord, King of the Universe, Rock of all worlds, Righteous One of all generations, the faithful Lord Who does as He says, Who speaks and fulfills His word, Whose every word is truth and righteousness. You are the One Who is faithful, O God our Lord, and Your words are trustworthy. Not one of Your words is left behind unfulfilled, for You are the Lord King, faithful and merciful. Blessed are You, the Lord Who is faithful in all His words." God can be trusted to reward virtue and punish sin. He can be trusted to keep His promises. He is absolutely faithful to His word.

Why is this quality so crucial? Why does God value it above all others?

Let us look a little further. We all know that the Jewish people were deemed worthy of redemption because they kept their Hebrew names and spoke the Hebrew language and because they did not become promiscuous. The Midrash Tanchuma (*Numbers* 25:1) adds to the list a little-known fourth reason — because they kept their secrets.

What precisely does this mean? The Midrash explains that God gave Moses a lengthy first message to deliver to the Jewish people when he first returned to Egypt. Among other things, he was to tell them to borrow valuables from their Egyptian neighbors on the eve of the exodus, and he was to assure them that God would compel the Egyptians to surrender these valuables gladly (*Exodus* 3:22). Moses conveyed the entire message as soon as he arrived in Egypt (ibid. 4:30), fully twelve months before the actual exodus. Had word got out that this is what they intended to do, the Egyptians could easily have concealed their valuables deep in the walls of their homes, as the Amorites were to do in Canaan many years later. But word did not get out. For those twelve months, the Jewish people kept the secret faithfully, and in this merit, they were deemed worthy of redemption.

Why was it necessary for them to know for a whole year what they were supposed to do on their last night in Egypt? Why entrust an entire people with such a sensitive secret for twelve long months when they could just as easily have been told only days before the Exodus?

Apparently, God wanted them to demonstrate their trustworthiness by keeping a secret for such a long time. For twelve months, He waited to see if anyone would inform the Egyptians of what the Jewish people were planning to do. For twelve months, He waited to see if they would remain steadfast and faithful. And when they passed the test, He deemed them worthy of redemption.

Again we see how highly God values the quality of faithfulness.

King Solomon declares (*Proverbs* 11:13), "Gossips go about revealing secrets, but those of faithful spirit conceal things." The opposite of a gossip, according to King Solomon, is a faithful person, a *ne'eman*. It follows that the ultimate failing of a gossip is not so much the damage he might cause to others as the corruption of his own character, the destruction of his own faithfulness by acts of betrayal.

Why is faithlessness such a terrible thing? The answer lies in the profound connection between faith and faithfulness.

The heart of the Jewish relationship with God is *emunah*, faith. The Jewish people believe in God. What does that mean? That we believe He exists? Not at all. When the Jewish people saw the sea split open to let them pass in safety and then closed over the heads of their Egyptian pursuers, the Torah tells us (*Exodus* 14:31), "And Israel saw the great hand God laid upon the Egyptians, and the people feared God, and they believed in God and His servant Moses." Under those circumstances, it certainly didn't take much for them to "believe" in the existence of God; it was clear as the day.

So what exactly did they "believe"?

They believed that God would keep His word. They believed that God was trustworthy. They believed that just as He had fulfilled His promise to bring them forth from Egypt and save them from the clutches of their pursuers, He would fulfill every promise He had ever made to their ancestors and would ever make to them. He would lead them through the barren wilds of the desert and watch over them for all eternity. This is the essence of *emunah*, the Jewish faith in God. It is the confident knowledge that God is "the faithful Lord Who does as He says, Who speaks and fulfills His word, Whose every word is truth and righteousness."

Centuries earlier, God had assured the childless Abraham that his offspring would be as numerous as the stars in the heavens above. And the Torah tells us (*Genesis* 15:6) that Abraham "believed in God Who considered this an act of righteousness on his part." Think for a moment. Abraham was in the midst of a prophetic revelation. He was listening to the voice of God. Why then was it considered an act of righteousness for him to "believe in God"? Clearly, this does not mean a belief in the existence of God but in the reliability of His word. When God promised him many descendants, Abraham accepted this as a fact. He believed without a doubt that God "speaks and fulfills His word." This was his act of righteousness.

Jewish faith is the absolute trust in the absolute truth and trustworthiness of God's every word. This level of faith is the foundation that had to be laid before the Jewish people were capable of receiving and embracing God's holy Torah. It is at the core of the covenant between God and Israel.

How do we acquire such transcendent faith in God? How do we take the intellectual belief in the trustworthiness of God's word and implant it so deeply in our hearts that it becomes an absolute reality for us?

The answer lies in the connection between faith and faithfulness. Only a faithful person is capable of absolute faith. Only someone whose own word is inviolate can have faith on both the intellectual and emotional levels. Only a faithful person whose word is an absolute guarantee can accept someone else's word with a confident and serene heart. An unfaithful person, on the other hand, can never have absolute faith. If his own word is not an ironclad guarantee, if it is at all possible that he might not honor an utterance that emerges from his mouth, if his own word is not an absolute fact, an inviolate reality, then how can he have faith in the word of another, even the word of God? If he does not know the meaning of true faithfulness from his own experience, how can he have faith in God's faithfulness?

An unfaithful person may believe that, although he allows himself to take liberties with his word, God would never do such a thing. This is a cold faith, an abstract faith. It does not penetrate to the heart. While he waits for the fulfillment of God's promise, he cannot help but feel apprehensive. He may sing *Ani Maamin* with the most beautiful inspirational melody, "*Ani maamin*! I believe with perfect faith that the Messiah will come!" But deep down, he is not so sure. He does not know the meaning of faithfulness as an absolute reality. He does not feel it. It is not part of his experience.

Even a person who is generally faithful, who keeps his word most of the time, cannot have genuine faith. For him, faithfulness is still not an inviolate reality but a choice. He may choose to keep his word often, he may choose to keep it almost always, but if there is the slightest possibility that he might not keep it, then it all becomes optional and unreliable. Such a person cannot have absolute trust in someone else's promise. He may consider it possible or even extremely likely that the promise will be fulfilled, but he will never accept it in his heart as a hard fact that is solid as a rock.

Absolute faithfulness is the key to absolute faith. God wants us to be faithful people not only because it is the right thing to do but also because if we are not faithful we cannot have faith in Him. Not really. Not the sort of faith that He expects from us.

Twelve months before the exodus, God entrusted the Jewish people with a sensitive secret in order to give them the opportunity to demonstrate their faithfulness. Were they trustworthy? Were they loyal to each other, to their friends, their families, their people? Were they faithful to their word of honor? Were these people capable of entering an everlasting covenant with the Master of the Universe? Were they capable of absolute faith?

Many years before, Moses had discovered evil informers among the Jewish people. Now I understand, he had declared, why the Jewish people are unworthy of redemption. "*Achein noda hadavar!*" If they are unfaithful, how can they have faith? And if they do not have faith, how can they expect to be redeemed? Yes, it is possible for people to be mired in *mem-tess shaarei tumah*, in just about the worst spiritual defilement, and still retain their faith in the Creator. As long as they themselves are faithful people, faith can live in their hearts. But if they are unfaithful, there is no hope for them. God may redeem them, uplift them, purify them, but He will not implant faith in unfaithful hearts. And so the Jewish people continued to languish in exile.

But now Moses returned and entrusted the Jewish people with a secret. This would be the critical test. If the Jewish people kept the secret, if they showed that over the years they had acquired the quality of faithfulness, they would be worthy of redemption. And for twelve long months the entire people remained steadfast in their faithfulness. Millions of people shared a secret, yet no one spoke a word of it. This was steadfast, rock-solid faithfulness, loyalty, truthfulness, honesty, integrity on a vast unprecedented scale. People who exhibited this sort of faithfulness could indeed be expected to stand at Mount Sinai and receive the Torah with perfect faith.

When we give our blessings to a young couple establishing a new home among the Jewish people, we want to make sure that the foundation is rock-solid. We want to wish them the one quality that will make it possible for them to acquire all the other qualities that will make their home a holy place. And so we bless them that they should build a *bayis ne'eman*, a trusted home, a faithful home. If there is faithfulness in their home, there will also be faith, and if there is faith, there will also be Torah, *mitzvos* and good deeds. If the foundation is strong, it will be a *binyan adei ad*. The home will last forever.

CHAPTER TWO

The Way of the Fathers

A mong the Patriarchs of the Jewish people, Isaac is by far the most mysterious. It seems to us that we know a lot about Abraham, the first of our Patriarchs. We know that heroism and courage defined his life, that he stood up in a thoroughly pagan society and proclaimed his loyalty to the one and only God at great risk to his life. We know that Abraham was the epitome of kindness and hospitality, that his door was open to all travelers, that he fed them and served them and brought them closer to the Master of the Universe.

But what do we know about Isaac, the second of our Patriarchs? We know that his father Abraham was prepared to offer him up as a sacrifice to God. We know he dug some wells and had a dispute with the Philistines over them. And we know he mistakenly gave his blessings to Jacob, his second son. But what do we really know about his life? What defined his religious role in the broader context of the Jewish people? What were his thoughts, his feelings, his aspirations, his motivations? How was he like his father Abraham, and how did he differ from him? The Torah does not provide clear answers to these questions, but if we look carefully, we can distinguish the outlines of an extraordinary life.

The key to understanding Isaac's life work is provided to us by his son Jacob. After his flight from his father-in-law Laban's house, when he stood face to face with his father-in-law who had pursued and overtaken him, Jacob declares (*Genesis* 31:42), "Were it not for the Lord of my father, the Lord of Abraham, the One Whom Isaac feared (*pachad*), you would have sent me away empty-handed." Jacob identifies the primary element of Isaac's relationship with God as *pachad*, fear.

This then is the starting point of our search for the hidden Isaac. This is the key, the filter through which we must view Isaac's life if we are to gain an understanding of it. Isaac lived with a higher fear; it was the primary attribute of his *avodas Hashem*, his divine service. What exactly does this mean? And how did it manifest itself in his life? Let us take a new look at some of the episodes we read about in the Torah.

Shortly after Esau sold his birthright to Jacob, we are told (*Genesis* 26:1-2), "And there was a famine in the land, besides the first famine that had occurred in the days of Abraham, and Isaac went to Abimelech, the king of the Philistines, to Gerar. And God appeared to him, and He said, 'Do not go down to Egypt; settle in the land about which I will tell you.'"

For some reason, the Torah tells us that this famine that took place when Isaac's sons were already grown was different from "the first famine that had occurred in the days of Abraham." It was not the same famine, the Torah is telling us. But why does the

Torah find it necessary to make this point? Would we have thought otherwise? Just about a century had already passed since famine had driven Abraham down to Egypt. Why would we think that this famine that Isaac experienced one hundred years later had any connection to that earlier famine?

Let us look a little further. God tells Isaac, "Do not go down to Egypt." Has there been any mention that Isaac intended to go down to Egypt? None at all. And yet God warns him not to go to Egypt. Obviously, God knew what was in Isaac's mind, that he intended to go down to Egypt, and therefore, He commanded him not to go there. But the narrative the Torah presents seems incomplete. Surely, we should have been given some indication of Isaac's intent to go to Egypt, before we are told that God forbade him to do so.

The Ramban offers a wonderful explanation. "It seems to me," he writes, "that when the Torah reports that this famine was 'besides the first famine that had occurred in the days of Abraham,' it means that people still remembered that legendary first famine. They used to talk about that famine and how it forced Abraham to go down to Egypt. Therefore, Isaac wanted to follow in the footsteps of his father and go down there as well. But God told him, 'Do not go down to Egypt.'"

Here we have a sharp glimpse into Isaac's thought processes. There is a severe famine in the land. He is faced with a situation, and he must make decisions. What is he to do? What is the first question he asks himself? Only one thing interests Isaac. Did this happen to my father? And the answer is that it did happen to Abraham. A hundred years ago. Very well, so he comes to the next question. What did my father do? And the answer is that he went down to Egypt. Fine. So now Isaac knows what to do. In times of famine, he has to go down to Egypt. Why? Because that is what Abraham did. Abraham's actions and the precedents he set were Isaac's guidelines in everything he did. What did my father do? I must do the same.

So this is why the Torah tells us about the earlier famine. It is a clue to how Isaac's mind worked. There was a famine in Isaac's days that reminded people of the famine that had occurred in Abraham's time a century earlier. Isaac saw that earlier famine as a precedent, and he considered it his duty to react as his father had done and go to Egypt. The pathways of Isaac's life were charted out for him. If his father had gone, then he must go as well. But God told him that in this case he could not follow in his father's footsteps. After being offered up as a sacrifice, Isaac had become sanctified as an *olah temimah,* an unblemished offering, and it would be inappropriate for him to leave the hallowed ground of Canaan and descend to Egypt.

Let us look a little further "And Isaac returned, and he dug up the wells of water that they had dug in the days of his father Abraham, and which the Philistines had filled after Abraham's death, and he gave them names like the names his father had given them" (*Genesis* 26:18). Isaac is clearly walking in his father's footsteps. He digs up those wells his father had once dug, and he names the wells as his father had once named them. His father's actions are the guideposts of his life.

From this verse, states Rabbeinu Bachya, we derive the instruction of *mesores avos,* following in the traditions of our fathers, for all future generations of the Jewish people. Isaac didn't want to veer even one inch from the path trodden by his father. He dug the same wells and even gave them the same names. Everything had to be exactly the same. On a higher level, explains Rabbeinu Bachya, the wells are more than sources of drinking water. They are symbols for accomplishments in *avodah,* serving God. Isaac's entire life was devoted to *avodah* — in the form established by his father. And that is the lesson he taught us for all generations. How do we perform *avodah?* Exactly as our fathers did.

So here we begin to see the definition of roles between Abraham as Patriarch of the Jewish nation and Isaac as his successor. Abraham, Isaac's great father, blazed the trail; he set the precedents and established the guideposts. Now Isaac's work was to consolidate everything his father had done, to follow precisely in his father's footsteps and thereby establish for all future generations the primacy of tradition.

Isaac had a tradition to follow. God had guided his father Abraham in all his pioneering work and instructed him in every aspect of his *avodah*. Then Abraham had taught all he had learned to his son Isaac. It now became Isaac's life work not to seek new ways and new paths but to follow faithfully on the path trodden by his father. And so he immediately thinks of Egypt when famine comes to the land, and he digs the same wells and gives the same names. And everything else is also the same. Abraham establishes precedent. Isaac establishes tradition.

The Rambam uses a very interesting choice of words to describe the rise of Abraham in a world that had turned to idolatry (*Mishneh Torah, Hilchos Avodah Zarah* 1:2-3). "…And in this manner, the world was careening along until the birth of that pillar of the world, our forefather Abraham. As soon as this personage was weaned, he began (*his'chil*) to cast his mind about while still a child, and he began (*his'chil*) to think day and night… At forty, Abraham recognized his Creator. As soon as he came to this recognition and knowledge, he began (*his'chil*) to ask questions to all the people of Ur Kasdim … And he began (*his'chil*) to let the people know that it was inappropriate to worship any deities other than the Lord of the Universe … And he began (*his'chil*) to stand up and call out in a loud voice to all the world to let them know that there is One Lord Who controls the entire universe, and it is worthwhile to serve Him …"

The word *his'chil*, he began, appears five times in the Rambam's profile of Abraham, because this was the central feature of his character and personality. Abraham was a *mas'chil*, a person who began things. He was a revolutionary, a pioneer. He was the *mas'chil*, the originator and founder of the Jewish people. Abraham was the first in everything he did. He had no father that he could follow, and thus, he was always breaking new ground — with God's guidance, of course.

Isaac was just the opposite. He had the consummate father to follow, and therefore, he did not have to break any new ground. Abraham had taught the ways of God, and Isaac was not going to veer from his teachings even one iota. In fact, the only new ground Isaac broke was to establish that no new ground should be broken, that sons should follow in the footsteps and traditions of their fathers. This is the enduring strength and power of the Jewish people.

When Isaac was forty years old, he married Rebecca, but they didn't have children for many years. Finally, they realized that she was barren. They prayed to God, and He answered Isaac's prayers. Rebecca gave birth to twins, Esau and Jacob. The Torah further tells us (*Genesis* 25:26) that Isaac was sixty years old when his children were born.

Twenty years without children! Why did they wait so long to storm the gates of Heaven with their prayers?

Rashi provides an interesting explanation. Rebecca was born right after the Akeidah, when Isaac was thirty-seven years old. Since he was forty years old when he married her, she was only three years old at the time. Therefore, writes Rashi, "he waited ten years from the time he married her until she reached the age of thirteen, which is the minimum childbearing age. Then he waited hopefully for ten more years, *as his father did for Sarah* [emphasis added]. When she still did not conceive, he realized she was barren and prayed for her. [During all this time, however,] he did not want to marry a *shifchah*, a servant woman, because he had been sanctified on Mount Moriah [at the Akeidah] as an *olah temimah*, an unblemished offering."

Once again, we see very clearly how Isaac follows scrupulously in his father's footsteps. His wife is unable to conceive. A year passes. Two, three, five. Still, Isaac continues to wait patiently and hopefully. Why? Because "his father did for Sarah." Abraham waited ten years after they arrived in the Holy Land for Sarah to conceive. But when she remained childless after ten years, only then did Abraham take action. Isaac also waits ten years before he feels he must do something. He does exactly as his father did.

But not quite. The action Abraham took after ten years of childlessness with Sarah was to take a *shifchah*, Hagar, as a second wife. Rashi must therefore anticipate a question. If Isaac followed his father's ways so precisely, why didn't he also take a servant woman as a second wife after ten childless years with his first wife Rebecca — just as his father did? And Rashi provides the answer. Isaac was an *olah temimah*, and as such, it would be inappropriate for him to marry a servant woman, just as God did not allow him to descend to Egypt during the famine as his father had done. Due to differing circumstances, there are some exceptions to the rules.

But a question still remains. It is quite understandable that a man that has been sanctified as an *olah temimah*, an unblemished offering to God, should not marry a servant woman. It would be beneath him to marry such a lowly woman. But why didn't he marry a noblewoman, a woman of high social stature, a princess of the land? Why should there be a problem with an *olah temimah* having two highborn wives?

Here we see how meticulously Isaac followed in his father's footsteps. He would not make one move without precedent in tradition. Logic certainly dictated that just as Abraham married for a second time when Sarah remained childless after ten years, so should Isaac marry for a second time. And if he couldn't marry a servant woman, why shouldn't he marry a highborn woman? But there was no precedent for such a thing, no tradition. Abraham had married a servant woman, a purchased woman rather than a free woman. There was no precedent for any other option, and Isaac did nothing without precedent. If his father had not taken a free woman as his second wife, neither could he.

This is the characteristic of *pachad*, fear, by which Jacob defines his father Isaac. It is a holy fear, a dread of making the wrong step, of trampling on the hallowed traditions established by his father.

Isaac knew that his father, with God's guidance, had shown the way for his descendants for all future generations. He had established the traditions of the Jewish people. Isaac viewed that process with reverence and awe, and he knew it was his responsibility to establish that reverence and awe of the traditions for the future generations of the Jewish people. He dreaded making a mistake. He did not dare deviate from the tradition in the slightest.

We all know people who are always doing things in a certain way because "*azoi hut mein tatte getuhn,* that is what my father did." For some of these people, this is not a fear of deviating from the tradition. Instead, it is a form of snobbery and arrogance, as if to say, "I am special, because my family has interesting customs." These people, who are always "doing what their fathers did," also do plenty that their fathers didn't do. They just don't mention their fathers while they are doing those things. But those people who are sincere and humble in their adherence to "what my father did" are following in Isaac's footsteps. Isaac had a *pachad,* a fear. Nothing was confirmed in his mind as acceptable unless he had a tradition for it. Isaac did not blaze new trails. Abraham did. Isaac followed tradition.

How did Isaac become an *olah temimah,* an unblemished offering for God? This question brings us back to the Akeidah, the Binding of Isaac, the seminal event in Jewish history that brings merit to the Jewish people for all generations.

In our prayers on Rosh Hashanah, we recall Abraham's great dedication to the word of God at the Akeidah. But the prayer concludes, "*Akeidas Yitzchak lezaro hayom berachamim tizkor.* Remember with mercy on this day the binding of Isaac for the sake of his descendants." The Akeidah was a test for both Abraham and Isaac, and we invoke the merit of both of them in our prayers. But in fact, each of them faced an entirely different ordeal.

Abraham's test was to measure his love and devotion to God against his powerful love for the son he had fathered in his old age. It was a tremendous ordeal for him, and he rose to the challenge with unparalleled faith, courage and spiritual strength. Without hesitation or reservation, he offered up his son as a sacrifice to God with a heart full of joy and faith. This remarkable accomplishment brings merit to the Jewish people for all generations.

But let us consider Isaac's test. What exactly was it? His readiness to give up his life for God? This doesn't seem likely. Of course, it is not a simple thing to risk one's life for a higher ideal, but it is not so great a deed as to bestow merit on future generations for thousands of years. After all, if a person is completely convinced that the purpose of life in this world is to earn a place in *Olam Haba*, the next world, then it puts everything in a different perspective. Faced with a situation in which giving up his life will gain him entry into *Olam Haba*, he will stop and philosophize a bit. How much pain and suffering is involved in giving away your life? There's a moment of pain, intense pain perhaps, and then it's over, and you've earned a guaranteed ticket to *Olam Haba*. It has cost you your life, but you've gained everlasting life in *Olam Haba*. Looking at it logically, it's not an unreasonable or even a very difficult choice, provided you believe with absolute faith that the sacrifice of your life will bring you to *Olam Haba*. Why then is Isaac's test at the Akeidah considered so extraordinary?

The Chasam Sofer answers this question with a brilliant insight. We know that only Moses prophesied with perfect clarity, receiving his messages unfiltered, through an *aspaklaria hame'irah*. All other prophets, including Abraham, received their prophetic communications through an unclear filter, an *aspaklaria she'einah me'irah,* and they were required to decipher the message and interpret it in order to comprehend God's Divine Will. There were many levels of this sort of interpretive prophecy; although all such prophecies required interpretation, some prophets were able to see more clearly than others were.

When God told Abraham to offer up his son as a sacrifice, this prophecy was also delivered through an *aspaklaria she'einah me'irah*, requiring interpretation. Abraham understood that God wanted him to take Isaac to Mount Moriah and offer him up on the altar, and this is what he prepared to do. In his capacity as a prophet of God, Abraham had a right to be confident in the *pis'chon belibo*, in the words of the Ramban, the interpretation in his heart. God gives the prophet the faculties to interpret his visions, and it is his responsibility to use them.

But Isaac had not yet gained the gift of prophecy. God did not speak to him about this critical commandment, only to Abraham. Isaac had to accept his father's word and his father's interpretation of his vision. And based on that, he submitted to being offered up as a sacrifice. He was prepared to give up his life. Isaac's test was *emunas chachamim*, trust in the guidance of the sages. He accepted his father's actions and words without question, without a second thought. When Abraham informed him along the way that there was no lamb for the sacrifice, that he was the lamb to be sacrificed, Isaac did not object. He did not argue. He could have said, "Just a minute! Are you sure you interpreted your prophetic vision correctly? Could it have meant something a little different that would not require my death?" He could have said these things, but he didn't. He didn't even think them. He accepted his father's direction with absolute trust, absolute faith and absolute confidence. This was Isaac's life's work, the establishment of the idea of unquestioning acceptance of tradition and the guidance of the sages, and the Akeidah was his finest hour. On that day, he reached the ultimate in acceptance.

This, concludes the Chasam Sofer, is how we can connect to the merit Isaac gained at the *Akeidah*. When we ourselves live with *emunas chachamim*, when we ourselves live with faith in our traditions, when we ourselves live with the *pachad*, the fear, of deviating one whit from the pathway trodden by our teachers and ancestors, then we can claim for ourselves the merit of Isaac's supreme test. Then we can say on Rosh Hashanah, *"Akeidas Yitzchak lezaro hayom berachamim tizkor.* Remember with mercy on this day the binding of Isaac for the sake of his descendants."

This is what Isaac implanted in the soul of the Jewish people for all generations. New trends, new ideas, new developments, all are suspect at first glance. If there is no precedent for them in our tradition, we must recoil with fear. And then we must turn to our *chachamim,* our revered sages, and ask them if these things are compatible with our tradition. And we must abide by their guidance. This is *emunas chachamim.* This is *pachad.* This is the legacy of Isaac.

CHAPTER THREE

Foresight and Hindsight

The amount of ink the Torah devotes to a story is an important indication of how many vital lessons it holds for all future generations. Moses, of course, gets the most ink in the Torah, because his is the story of the Exodus, the Giving of the Torah and the forty years of instruction and study in the Desert; it covers four of the five Books of the Torah. But let us take a look at the Book of Genesis, the first in the Torah. It begins with the creation of the world and ends with the descent of the Jewish people into Egypt in the prelude to exile and enslavement.

So how is the ink distributed in the Book of Genesis? We find that the Patriarchs get a comparatively short run, but when the

Torah reaches the story of Joseph and his brothers, it elaborates at very great length. It is obvious that the Torah is not speaking about Joseph simply as an individual. Even more, the Torah uses the story of Joseph as a metaphor for the Jewish experience throughout history.

The story of the Jewish people actually begins with Joseph and his brothers, because that is when the Jewish people first came into being. Earlier, there were only the individual patriarchs and matriarchs, but Jacob's twelve sons and his daughter were already a distinct group; they formed the nucleus of a young nation, and their experiences are the first steps in the history of the Jewish people. The patterns of the Jewish experience were established in their lifetimes. By observing and studying the events of their lives, we can identify and appreciate the special divine providence that guides the Jewish people through history

The story of Joseph and his brothers is the story of the Jewish people from the beginning to the end. All the times of our history, the moments of tragedy and the moments of triumph, are somehow represented in this story. They are links attached to the links that came before and follow afterward. Together, these links form a long chain that stretches across the landscape for thousands of years towards a future goal we have not yet seen. Along the way, we pass through stages of sweetness and stages of bitterness, and all of them lead to the one ultimate good.

The early part of the story of Joseph sets the stage for the dramatic events that will chart the course of Jewish history. We read about Jacob's favored treatment of his beloved son Joseph, his pride and joy, the eldest son of his deceased wife Rachel. We read about the resentment of the brothers. We read about the prophetic dreams. And then the story begins.

One day, Jacob sends Joseph out to the pastures to visit his brothers who are tending their father's flocks of sheep. The Torah relates (*Genesis* 37:14), "And [Jacob] said to [Joseph], 'Please go and check on the welfare of your brothers and the welfare of the flocks and report back to me,' and he sent him off from the valley of Hebron (*vayishlachehu me'emek Chevron*)."

Immediately, we are struck by a very strange statement. He sent him off "from the valley of Hebron." What does this mean? There is no such thing as the valley of Hebron. Anyone with a little familiarity with the geography of Israel knows that Hebron is in the mountains. There are no valleys in Hebron. And yet, the Torah states that Jacob sent Joseph off "from the valley of Hebron." Obviously, one cannot translate *vayishlachehu me'emek Chevron* as "he sent him off from the valley of Hebron." What then do these words mean?

In cases such as these, one absolutely cannot budge without the *Torah Sheb'al Peh*, the Oral Torah. Without the tradition, the plain meaning of the words is simply impossible to discern. So we look into Rashi, and based on the Midrash and the Gemara (*Sotah* 11a), he gives us the answer. The words *me'emek Chevron* do not mean "from the valley of Hebron," as one might expect. It means from the *eitzah amukah shel oso tzaddik hakavur b'Chevron*, "the profound plan revealed to the righteous man buried in Hebron," namely Abraham. Here was the beginning of the fulfillment of the *Bris bein HaBesarim*, the Covenant of the Parts.

Many years before, God had said to Abraham (*Genesis* 15:13), "Know full well that your descendants will be strangers in an alien land, and they will enslave them and oppress them for four hundred years. And also the nation that will enslave them I shall judge, and then they will come forth with great wealth." According to our Sages, the words "and also (*vegam*) the nation that will enslave them" are a hint that God also spoke to Abraham about the periods of exile beyond the Egyptian captivity. In the course of this prophecy, God outlined for Abraham the entire future history of the Jewish people — the Exodus, the Conquest of Canaan, the First and Second Temples, the oppression by Babylonians, Medes, Persians, Greeks and Romans — all the way to the arrival of the Messiah in the end of days.

And now the process was starting. Joseph was going out to the fields to visit his brothers, but he would never return. Fate would lead him to Egypt, and the entire family would eventually follow.

Watch what happens, says the Torah in the first words of the episode. *Vayishlachehu me'emek Chevron,* "he sent him off according to the profound plan revealed to the righteous man [Abraham] buried in Hebron." The fulfillment of the prophecy is about to unfold. Pay close attention.

Mistakes characterize the beginning of the story. Jacob peculiarly makes mistakes in his uneven treatment of his sons. Joseph peculiarly makes mistakes in his relationship with his brothers. The brothers peculiarly make mistakes in their evaluation of Joseph. One mistake after the other lead to unexpected developments.

This is the way of Divine providence. God clouds a person's judgment if for no more than a moment, and in that brief befuddlement, he does something out of character. Then he wonders, why did I do that? I'm such a careful person. I'm wiser than that. How could I do such a thing? But only later, with the benefit of hindsight, he understands that God was leading him toward his destiny. This, points out the Ramban, is one of the lessons of the story. People may think they are clever and wise enough to manage their own affairs well, but it is not so. The divine decree will inevitably prevail.

And so the seeds of hatred and strife are sown. The story begins. Jacob sends Joseph to visit his brothers in the fields. Joseph knows he will be in danger, but he obediently tells his father, "*Hineni!* I am ready!" And he goes. Meanwhile, the brothers are plotting against him. They believe he is a *rodef,* a stalker, hounding them and seeking to exclude them from the future of Jewish peoplehood. Fully believing in their own righteousness, they resolve that he deserves to be executed. They look up, and there he is, the hated Joseph, coming toward them from afar. One brother says to the other (*Genesis* 37:19-20), "Behold, here comes the dreamer. Let us kill him now and toss him into one of the pits, then we can say that a wild animal devoured him, and we will see what will become of his dreams."

Listen to these strange words. We will see what will become of his dreams. What do these last words mean? How can they see what will become of his dreams if they plan to kill him right away? What could possibly become of his dreams? What could there be to see?

The Ramban writes that they are being sarcastic, that these are words of cruel mockery. But Rashi does not find this acceptable. These are Jacob's sons, the patriarchs of the future Tribes of Israel. They may decide to condemn Joseph to death for his alleged crimes, but they would not send their brother to his grave with mocking laughter.

Therefore, Rashi gives us a different interpretation, taken from the Midrash (*Tanchuma* 13). "Rabbi Yitzchak explains that this verse cries out, 'Interpret me!' [Actually,] the Holy Spirit is saying these words. They say, 'Let us kill him.' But the verse concludes, 'We will see what will become of his dreams. We will see whose word endures, yours or Mine.' It cannot be that it is the brothers who are saying, 'We will see what will become of his dreams.' Because if they should kill him, there would no longer be any prospect for the fulfillment of the dreams. Then what would there be to see?"

So according to Rashi, God spoke these words. This is very unusual, a rare deviation from the narrative style of the Torah. Except for two or three places, the Torah acts as a neutral narrator, reporting statements and conversations verbatim and giving the account of events without editorial comment, letting us draw our own conclusions. Here, however, God injects His own comment into the narrative right in the middle of the story.

The brothers are getting ready to kill Joseph and get rid of his body, and even before Joseph reaches them, God declares, "You think you will kill him? Well, we will see what will becomes of his dreams. We will see whose plans will be thwarted, yours or Mine. We will see whether or not Joseph will indeed sit on the throne of Egypt and all of you will bow down to him, just as he foresaw in his dream."

Why is it so important to interrupt the story to give us this bit of foreshadowing right now? Why break the narrative pattern of the Torah to remind us that the story will turn out differently from what the brothers are planning?

Because the Torah wants us to read this story with the proper perspective. Don't think you're just reading something that happened to your ancestors many years go. Don't just become enchanted by the story. Read this carefully, with wide-open eyes, because it is your own story, the story of the exile of the Jewish people throughout all the generations.

Watch what is happening, the Master of the Universe is saying to us. Watch carefully. Joseph's dreams were messages from Me. They showed that I planned to put Joseph on the throne. But his brothers have different plans. They are preparing to kill him. It looks very bleak. It seems they are about to finish him off, but "we will see what will become of his dreams." We will see whose designs and plans triumph, theirs or Mine.

And learn from this a lesson for yourselves, says God to us. Who doesn't make plans against the Jewish people? In which generation aren't the enemies of the Jewish people plotting to destroy them? But do not despair. We will see what will become of the dreams. We will see what will become of the prophecies and the promises and the covenants. We will see whose plans win out in the end, theirs or Mine. You will understand everything in hindsight, because you will have seen it. But you should also have the foresight to know that My plan will endure and to recognize My hand in all that you experience.

One of the most fundamental lessons in life emerges from the story of Joseph if we read it with our eyes open, if we see in it not only a moving story but also the signposts for our own lives and the history of the Jewish people. If we absorb this lesson well, we can cope with all times and all situations we encounter in our lives.

The Mishnah tells us (*Berachos* 54a), "A person must bless [God] for the bad just as (*kesheim*) he blesses Him for the good." The

Mishnah does not say that we must bless God not only for the good but for the bad as well. This would imply that there is more reason to bless God for the good than for the bad, although it would still be fitting to bless Him for the bad as well. But this is not what the Mishnah says. It tells us that we must bless God for the bad just as we bless Him for the good. Equally, *kesheim*, just as. They are exactly the same. Strange as it may seem, we must bless God for the bad things that happen with the same appreciation and joy that we would instinctively express for the good things that happen.

How can such a thing be? The Mishnah is not talking to the saintliest people in the generation. It is talking to regular people, to each and every one of us. How can this be expected of ordinary human beings? Does the Torah really expect a person to recite a blessing over an event that he sees as being to his disadvantage? Does the Torah expect a person to recite a blessing over a bitter pill?

But that is exactly the point. There are two kinds of goodness, the goodness that we recognize and the goodness that we accept from God with faith in our hearts, even though it may appear bitter to us. There is only goodness. It is not an easy thing to accomplish, but it is within the capabilities of each of us. We must grasp it with our minds and implant it in our hearts. We have to have faith and confidence that everything is good. Painful situations are a test of our faith, and we have to understand this to the point where we can recite a blessing in those situations with the same enthusiasm we normally associate with happy times.

Still, it seems very difficult to recite a blessing over the bad. That is understandable. So let us consider this logically.

How often does it happen in life that something that seems good does not turn out as well as had been expected? A person opens a business or marries particularly well. He is successful, respected. He becomes wealthy. And everyone thinks this person's life is so wonderful, that everything is just perfect. And then this happens and that happens, and everything begins to fall apart until it all collapses in one big crash. And people nod their heads sagely and say they saw it coming. But not in the beginning. At that time, everyone thought it was wonderful, pure good fortune. We all know such cases. They happen all the time.

We also know of cases where the exact opposite happens. A person is in a miserable situation. Everything is going wrong. His life is bitter and painful. But different things happen, and the bad conditions turn out to be the source of success. The person turns out to be the most fortunate of people. With the benefit of hindsight, everyone suddenly understands how his earlier situation led to his present success. But at the time they pitied him, because they didn't have the foresight to see where he was headed.

So now, knowing that seemingly good things can turn out bad and seemingly bad things can turn out good, what do we think when we see something good happening? Do we say to ourselves, who knows if in the end this will turn out as good as it seems now? Or if we see something bad happening, do we say that it might actually turn out to be quite good? Although we know this is true so very often, we do not say this. Our emotions get in the way. We want the good to continue, so we blind ourselves to the possibility that it may not. And we want the pain to stop, so we ignore the possibility that it may lead to much good.

Our responsibility, therefore, is to crystallize this logic in our minds, to acknowledge the realities that we already know and make them part of our lives. And a sharp look at our history would be extremely helpful.

Imagine for a moment that a story broke in the Jerusalem newspapers today about a sensitive young man, the son of a great sage, who was the apple of his father's eye. The young man sat at his father's feet and drank in every word of wisdom the old man uttered. His father bought him princely clothing in appreciation of his fine qualities, but his brothers became very jealous. They concocted a plan to get rid of him once and for all. They abducted him. He pleaded with them. He begged for his life. "I'm innocent," he screamed in desperation. "Be fair to me. Bring me back to my father, and I will explain everything. Have mercy on me!" But all his pleas fell on deaf ears. The brothers sold him to a band of Arabs who carried him off to Egypt where he disappeared. His old father is brokenhearted and mourns for him every day. The story is reported in newspapers all around the world.

What would you say to such a story? Terrible story! You would be crying before you were halfway through the articles. What a human disaster! What a tragedy!

So why don't we cry when we read the story every year? Why, even little schoolchildren don't get too upset in the early winter, when the story of Joseph is read and retold. And after all, why should we cry? We know the ending, and it turns our beautifully. With hindsight, we know that when Joseph was led away to Egypt, he was really embarking on the journey to the Egyptian throne. He would rise to greatness and fame, and he would feed millions of people during the years of famine. He would bring his entire family down to Egypt and take care of them. This not a story that causes any anguish, but at the time it happened, it seemed a total disaster.

Now let us look at the other side. Imagine again a story in a Jerusalem newspaper. Big banner headlines: Old sage reunited with long-lost son after a separation of twenty-two years. You read the details of the story, and your heart is warmed. After grieving for his lost son for twenty-two years, the old sage discovers that his son is still alive. Furthermore, he learns that his son has risen to the highest circles of power, and he has become the viceroy, the effective ruler of Egypt, second only to Pharaoh himself. His son invites him to come down and join him in Egypt. Moreover, Pharaoh sends special royal chariots to bring him there in a style befitting the viceroy's father. Pharaoh welcomes the old sage with great honor and settles his family in the finest lands of Egypt. The old sage can now live out his final years in tranquility and happiness, reunited with his most beloved son. The royal palace will take care of all his family's needs. How well things have turned out for the old sage. A heartwarming story, you would say as you shed a tear of happiness. What a beautiful ending to such a sad story!

But is it really? We know with hindsight that when Jacob was going down to Egypt and bringing his family with him, he was embarking on the journey into exile in Egypt, a journey of death and bondage and suffering.

What seems to be bad might really be good, and what seems to be good might really be bad. We see it clearly in the story of Joseph. So what are we supposed to do? How do we look at things? The answer is with faith in God's guiding hand, with faith that all He does is goodness in one form or another. We must look closely at the story of Joseph and come away blessing God for the bad just as we bless Him for the good.

Now let us consider an intriguing question. How did Joseph himself cope with his situation? From our vantage point thousands of years in the future, we can see the story in its entire perspective, but Joseph was right in it. He was involved. He was the victim. What went through his mind when the Arabs were carrying him down to Egypt? What emotions gripped his heart when he languished in the Egyptian dungeon? Did he feel despair? Did he have faith? How can we discover what he was feeling?

If we look closely at the events, we notice that Joseph had apparently pleaded desperately with his brothers for his life (42:21), but once the deed was done, we do not hear him utter another word of protest or misery. We see no signs that he was upset or depressed. On the contrary, all indications are that he accepted his fate with deep faith in his heart and a cheerful smile on his lips. If we read well between the lines, and indeed in the lines themselves, it becomes clear that he was in a happy state of mind all along, that he was *besimchah*, full of joy, throughout his ordeal.

Towards the end of the story, Joseph's brothers come and ask his forgiveness. And Joseph responds (*Genesis* 50:20), "You had considered evil with regard to me, but the Lord meant it for the good, in order to do as this day, to sustain numerous people."

What does this mean? According to some commentators, Joseph is telling them that, although they had been motivated by evil designs, it had all been for the good. God had wanted it to happen this way. But the Sforno has a different slant on this statement. Joseph is telling them they are not responsible for what they did. They are not at fault.

"You had considered evil with regard to me," he is saying. You simply made a mistake. You thought I was evil. You thought I meant you harm. With the foolishness of youth, I did certain things and acted in certain ways that caused you to suspect that I was evil, and you reacted accordingly. I really can't blame you. If I was as you suspected, you would have been justified in what you did. I probably would have done the same if I were in your place. So how can I blame you? It wasn't your fault. "But the Lord meant it for the good." Why would such a mistake happen? Only because God wanted it to happen. You were unwitting agents of divine providence.

Earlier, when Joseph had first revealed himself to his brothers, he said a similar thing (*Genesis* 45:8), "And now, it wasn't you that sent me here, but rather, it was the Lord . . ." God had engineered the entire chain of events in order to suit his master plan. You are not responsible for my coming to Egypt. It was God's will that brought me here. And according to Sforno's interpretation, Joseph even absolved them of malicious intent. You never intended to do something wrong. It was a mistake. You thought you were doing the right thing.

Is this really what Joseph believed? Of course, it was. It is forbidden to tell a sinner that what he did was not a sin. It would be considered *chanifah*, insincere flattery. If you see someone commit a sin, you are not supposed to pretend you are being *dan lekaf zechus*, giving the sinner the benefit of the doubt. If you believe he has sinned, you have to rebuke him. That is the *mitzvah* of *tochachah*. Rebuke the sinner. Tell him he did something wrong. Tell him he caused you pain and distress. Tell him he has to repent and change his ways. Don't tell him he shouldn't worry about it. Don't tell him that he did nothing wrong.

Therefore, if Joseph said to his brothers, "You made a mistake; it was all just a misunderstanding engineered by God to further His divine plan," that is what he really believed. That is what he really felt in his heart. Joseph's faith was so deep and so pure that he faced his fate with full acceptance. He struggled to avoid his abduction. He pleaded with his brothers to let him go. Because that is what you are supposed to do when you are in danger. You are supposed to save yourself. But once he saw that his struggles were to no avail, he understood that this is what God wanted, and from that moment on, he was at peace.

How do we know that? Did Joseph really accept his fate straightaway with his heart full of faith? Or did it perhaps take him months or even years to come to terms with his situation?

The evidence shows that it was immediate. Joseph was pulled out of the pit and sold to a caravan of Arabs transporting a load of "spices and perfume" to Egypt. Why do we need to know what they were carrying?

Our Sages explain that Arab caravans normally transported naphtha and other foul-smelling materials, and here was an Arab caravan transporting sweet-smelling spices and perfumes. This was really something extraordinary. Why did this happen?

Because God was being kind to Joseph. The divine master plan may have called for him to be abducted and sold into slavery in Egypt, but there was no need for this *tzaddik*, the righteous Joseph, to be subjected to foul smells while this was taking place. It may have been necessary for him to suffer the pain of separation from his family. It may have been necessary for him to suffer loneliness and isolation in Egypt. But it was not necessary for him to suffer foul odors. And so, in an exquisite gesture of divine love, God sent a caravan laden with spices and perfume instead of naphtha to carry Joseph into captivity. Even when God places the righteous in trying and difficult circumstances, He does so with a loving touch.

This is undoubtedly the very inspiring message the Torah is sending us by informing us that the Arabs were carrying sweet-smelling materials. But I would like to focus on another aspect of this situation. I would like to use it to deduce Joseph's state of mind when he was sold to the Arabs.

Just imagine a person being transported to a concentration camp in a cattle car, Heaven help us. He is squashed together with other people, hungry and thirsty, dirty and lice-ridden, exposed to the elements, terrified for his life, depressed and despondent. And then someone sprinkles a little perfume on his head. Is he going to be interested? Is he going to say, "Ah, a kiss from the Master of the Universe who doesn't want me to suffer one bit more than absolutely necessary"? Is he going to say, "Well, it could have been worse; there could have been bad smells"? Not very likely. The sprinkle of perfume would mean nothing to a person who is depressed and quaking with fear. It would be a waste to sprinkle perfume on his head.

But if God arranged that the caravan should be carrying sweet-smelling substances, it is obvious that Joseph inhaled the sweet smell into his nostrils and was pleased. If so, he must have been in a serene state of mind. The struggle was over, the die was cast. This is what God wanted. Fine. No need to worry. God would take care of him and lead him along the right way. This was acceptance. This was faith. This was peace of mind. This was how Joseph, the tragic victim of abduction, went down to Egypt.

Egypt was probably just about the last place where a righteous young man such as Joseph wanted to find himself, surrounded by immoral idol worshippers on all sides. He is sold as a slave into the house of Potiphar, where he is at the bottom of the ladder of privilege. Everyone else is his superior. He is helpless and alone.

Nonetheless, Joseph does not get depressed. He accepts all that happens with perfect faith, and his fortunes begin to take a turn for the better. The Torah tells us (*Genesis* 39:3-4), "And his master saw that God was with him, and that God brings success to everything he does . . . and he appointed him over his household."

"God was with him," the Midrash explains, means that Joseph constantly spoke about God to those around him. Potiphar used to see Joseph mumbling to himself, and he would ask, "What are you saying there?" And Joseph told him he was thanking the Master of the Universe. When Potiphar praised him for a job well done, Joseph would say, "How would I know how to do a good job? Believe me, I deserve no credit. It is all the Master of the Universe. Thank Him." And people started hearing about the Master of the Universe, something that hadn't happened in Egypt before Joseph arrived. And they came to the realization that there really was a God, and that He was responsible for Joseph's success.

Once again, Joseph teaches us a critical lesson about how to conduct ourselves in exile. Joseph's wonderful attitude and profound faith were closely connected. If we recognize the divine hand in the bitterest exile situations, if we appreciate it and even speak about it to the world, we will inevitably develop a peace of mind and a serenity that will enable us to endure our pain and suffering with an undiminished sense of joy. That is the secret of survival and even success in exile.

The story continues. Joseph rises in Potiphar's household. He holds a position of trust and responsibility. The future seems a little bit brighter. There is some hope. But the situation gets worse before it gets better, as is often the case in the Jewish experience in exile. Potiphar's wife unjustly accuses him of making improper advances, and all of a sudden, he finds himself worse off than ever before. He is tossed into a dungeon, a deep, dark, musty pit.

You can well imagine what the conditions were like in this pit. Any prison today is a five-star hotel compared to a pit dungeon in ancient Egypt. Besides everything else, Joseph suddenly finds himself with the dregs of society, the worst criminals and derelicts in Egypt. Such humiliation, such degradation for an innocent man. Even if he had maintained his good cheer all along, now was the time to get depressed. But Joseph does not get depressed; he withstands this ordeal just as he had withstood all the others. This is again obvious from the events that transpire.

The warden notices that Joseph is an intelligent fellow, and he appoints him to be in charge of the prisoners. It is his responsibility to oversee order and discipline in the pit. One day, Joseph sees two fellows sitting in a corner with long faces. "Why the long faces today?" he asks. As it turns out, these are Pharaoh's baker and wine steward, and this meeting will lead directly to Joseph's release from prison and rise to power.

But let us take a look at this question that he asks the two depressed prisoners. "Why the long faces, my friends?" What kind of a question is this to ask a prisoner in an Egyptian pit dungeon? He is in this nasty dungeon, and he doesn't want to be there. He wants to go home. He has every right to be depressed. What other kind of face should he be wearing if not a long face?

So we see two things from Joseph's question. One, we see that Joseph himself was not at all depressed. He was in good cheer. A depressed person is not disturbed when there are unhappy people around him. On the contrary, he is far more likely to be disturbed if the people around him are smiling happily. One never hears of a depressed person saying to another depressed person, "Tell me, why are you in such a bad mood?" That's the way people are. So if Joseph asked, "Why the long faces?" he must have been in a good mood himself — right there in the dungeon!

But we also see something else. Apparently, these two fellows with the long faces stood out. It was something out of the ordinary, something that required investigation. That means that all the other prisoners in the dungeon were cheerful. The dungeon that was under Joseph's supervision was not a commonplace dungeon. It was a special place. There were no long faces in Joseph's dungeon. Joseph's faith and acceptance were so powerful, and his good cheer was so genuine, that all the people around him were affected. In fact, the prisoners in his charge were in such good spirits that two long faces in the musty pit struck a jarring note, and Joseph had to ask them, "What is this all about? True, you are prisoners in an Egyptian pit dungeon, but why the long faces? Where are the smiles that naturally belong on the faces of people with faith in their hearts?"

The most stunning expression of Joseph's faith, however, appears at the climax of the story. Imagine the scene. Joseph is languishing in the dark, dank pit dungeon when messengers suddenly arrive from the royal palace to bring him straightaway to Pharaoh. They quickly wash, barber and dress him and whisk him off to the palace to interpret the Pharaoh's dream.

Joseph knows he is coming into the presence of a powerful and merciless king, a king who would condemn a royal minister to death for allowing a fly to fall into a cup of wine or a pebble to find its way into a loaf of bread. On this particular day, this cruel king must be in a particularly bad mood, because he has just had a disturbing dream for which he has not yet heard a satisfactory interpretation. He is angry, agitated and extremely dangerous. Joseph must have been terrified.

As soon as he is brought in, Pharaoh says to him, "I have heard that you can interpret dreams." What should Joseph have said to Pharaoh? Perhaps he should have said, "Yes, your majesty." Perhaps he should have simply nodded meekly and bowed his head. But one would think that he certainly should not have had the audacity to contradict Pharaoh. Yet this is exactly what he does.

"*Bil'adai*," he declares. "It is not me. Everything is from God."

Why did he have to respond in this way? At least he could have waited until after he interpreted Pharaoh's dream and calmed him down a bit. Then he could have told him, "By the way, I don't deserve any credit for this interpretation. Everything is from God." But Joseph doesn't wait a moment. As soon as he comes in, with this red-faced despot staring him in the face, he instantly declares that he has no interpretive faculties of his own. Everything is from God.

Here we see the ultimate expression of Joseph's faith. He sees with perfect clarity that the divine hand is guiding everything happening to him, and he has nothing to fear. Therefore, he cannot allow even a moment's misconception among the observers of his interpretation. He will not accept the undeserved credit even for a moment, and as soon as Pharaoh identifies him as an interpreter of dreams, he feels compelled to state the truth.

Moreover, this practice of constantly speaking about God had bolstered his faith in the most difficult circumstances. It had raised him up from abject slavery in Potiphar's house, where people saw that "God was with him," and it had helped him survive in the pit dungeon. When he came before Pharaoh in this state of mind, he was unafraid and at peace with himself. God was with him, and he had nothing to fear.

Indeed, Joseph's strong conviction apparently had a profound effect on Pharaoh and brought him around to his way of thinking, for after the dream is interpreted, Pharaoh tells him (*Genesis* 41:39), "Since the Lord has informed you of this, there is no one as intelligent and wise as you." Pharaoh has apparently been convinced that Joseph's abilities come directly from God. Had Joseph waited to tell him until after the successful interpretation about God's involvement, it is unlikely that Pharaoh would have been won over to his way of thinking. But when Pharaoh saw the fearless, serene, unshakable faith with which Joseph assigned all power to God, he was deeply impressed.

So this is what the lengthy story of Joseph and his brothers teaches us. This is why the Torah devotes so much ink to it. It is the story of our exile, the demonstration that things are not always as they appear to be. And even more important, it is the story of how deep faith can provide a person with peace of mind and indeed joy even during the worst suffering.

It is easy to see the good in everything God does with hindsight. But faithful Jews see it with foresight as well. Faithful Jews know to bless God for the good we cannot see immediately just as we bless Him for the good that is apparent right away. Faithful Jews have the wisdom to recognize that this foresight is the key to true peace of mind.

CHAPTER FOUR

Waiting for the Moment

Before I address the issues and concerns of those who are not blessed with children soon after marriage, I feel I must explain how I can even begin to speak on this subject. The feelings of a childless couple are so complex, the sensitivities so deep, that I would not dare offer words of advice unless I, too, shared the anguish to a certain extent, unless I truly understood what goes through their hearts and minds. Only then could I hope to offer them a measure of encouragement and inspiration. Only then could I hope to lead them higher, to bring them a little closer to God and His infinite kindness.

No, I am not a stranger to this subject. Over the years, I have sat with many couples and listened to them speak. I have shared their expectations and their frustrations, their grief and their joy, their patience and, yes, their moments of panic. I listened and heard and offered whatever I could offer, but most of all, I felt for them and with them. I was there.

In my own family, my daughter and son-in-law — and I along with them — waited a long time for children, over eight years, before God blessed them with triplets. I remember my feelings and thoughts when we were deprived, and I also remember what went through my mind when at long last we were blessed. I tried to articulate these thoughts at the *bris* of two of the triplets, and I would like to begin with them here.

King David says (*Psalms* 71:14), "*Vaani tamid ayacheil, vehosafti al kol tehilasecha.* As for me, I continuously hope, then I add to all Your praises." He doesn't say that he didn't lose hope, but that he continuously hopes. His hope keeps getting stronger and stronger, and this gives him the ability to add on to God's praises. The more he hopes, the more he praises God. What exactly does this mean? How does more hope bring more praise of God?

Let us imagine that a man needs a certain item very urgently, but it can only be purchased by special order. So he places the order with the store and sits back to wait. A week goes by, and the item does not arrive. He waits another week, two weeks, a month, and still no delivery.

Furious, he calls the store manager and complains, "Where is the item I ordered? How long do I have to wait before I finally get it?"

The manager makes his excuses and assures him the delivery will be coming straightaway. Another week passes, and still no delivery. The man is beside himself. He doesn't know what to do. And then, one fine day, when he has just about given up hope, the store's delivery van pulls up in front of his house. The delivery boy brings the package to the front door. It has finally arrived.

How does the man react when he sees the delivery boy holding the package for which he has waited so long? Does he welcome him with a broad smile and an expansive greeting? More likely than not, he vents his anger at the delivery boy, "So you finally brought it, did you? Do you know how long I've waited for this package? Is that what you call service? Is this how you treat all your customers or am I the only one so privileged?" Why the delivery boy deserves such a cold shower is beyond me. He just has the ill fortune of being in the wrong place at the wrong time.

But think about it. When exactly does all the man's anger and frustration come pouring out? At the point of delivery! Just when he holds in his hand the item he needed so badly, this precious item for which he waited and waited, just when he should be dancing with joy, he spills over with mean-spirited rage. And on the poor delivery boy's head, no less.

Am Yisrael kedoshim. We, the holy Jewish people, are not like that in our relationship with God. In fact, we are just the opposite. The longer we wait for the fulfillment of our expectations, the closer we feel to Him. And when it finally happens, when that long-awaited day arrives, we feel only a vast joy and gratitude, so overwhelming that we cannot even find the words to express them.

We wait and we hope, because we know that a Jew who trusts in God must never despair. We reach out with goodness and compassion to others who are similarly or otherwise afflicted so that no one is compelled to keep his or her feelings buried without comfort or relief. We take our personal problems as an opportunity for people to help one another, as a call from Heaven for us to bind ourselves together with love and faith rather than sit in a corner and sulk.

That is how Klal Yisrael is meant to hope — with *emunah* and *bitachon*, with faith and trust in God. Our hope helps us come closer to Him and learn His ways. "*Vaani tamid ayacheil,*" we cry out. "I continuously hope, and then I praise You even more." At that point, when God decides the time is right, we will be ready and standing higher than ever before in our profound appreciation of all His goodness. *Vehosafti al kol tehilasecha*. We will praise Him as never before.

We say in our daily Shemoneh Esrei, "*Refa'einu Hashem veneirafei hoshi'einu venivashei'a*. Heal us, God, so that we may be healed, save us so that we may be saved. *Ki sehilaseinu Atah*. For You are the One we praise." We ask God to send us healing as only He can heal us. We ask Him to save us, to raise us up from the depths and bring us salvation as only He can save us. And then we say, "For You are the One we praise. Because we continuously hoped, because we always knew how good You are, because we were openly waiting for the moment, we will praise You as never before."

But then we come to the close of the blessing, and we find some rather unusual phrasing reminiscent of Rosh Hashanah. "*Ki E-l Melech Rofeh ne'eman verachaman Atah*. For You are the Lord King, a faithful and merciful Healer." When we pray for our livelihood or when we ask God to accept our repentance, we do not refer to Him as the King. Why then do we declare right here, when we ask Him to heal us, that He is the King?

I think it is because medical problems and the feelings of helplessness associated with them remind us more powerfully than anything else that everything is in God's hands, that His is the only true power, that He is the King. Moreover, when we acknowledge that He is King, we also feel committed. If we ask Him to use His power as King to heal us, then we must show Him that we are His servants, His loyal subjects. We must also consider what He wants and expects from us.

After returning from a difficult medical procedure, R' Shmuel Rozovsky, *zt"l*, Rosh Yeshivah of Ponevezh, observed that we speak of God as King in the prayer for healing because only a king can give a reprieve. A doctor can only work within the boundaries of the situation as he finds it, but a king has unlimited power. No matter what situation he encounters, he can change it. No matter how bleak the situation may seem, a king can grant a reprieve.

When we say the word King, that our Sages in their great wisdom inserted into the prayer for healing, we are inspired to think, "Only You, God, are the all-powerful King Who holds our lives in Your hands. Only You can give us a reprieve. Do with us as You deem best."

There is a rule, a very important rule, regarding ordeals and problems that arise from particular situations. More often than not, these are Heaven-sent opportunities that enable us to gain the merit we need to succeed in those very situations.

There is a well-known story in the Gemara (*Shabbos* 156b) about Rabbi Akiva's daughter. On the day of her birth, the stargazers informed Rabbi Akiva that his little girl was destined to die on her wedding day. In those days, there were people who could discern the future and read messages in the stars, and they determined that Rabbi Akiva's daughter would not survive her wedding day.

The years passed. The little girl grew up, and the awful prediction of the stargazers remained a source of worry and heartache. Nonetheless, a suitable match was found for her when she reached marriageable age, and a wedding date was set.

On the night before the wedding, Rabbi Akiva's house was buzzing with work in preparation for the wedding celebration. People were cooking, baking, welcoming guests and rushing to and fro with all sorts of last-minute tasks. The young bride, who would be fasting the next day, was advised to go to bed early. She was given a meal and sent off to a quiet corner of the kitchen where she could eat in peace.

As she sat down to eat, she noticed a poor man standing at the kitchen door. "Please give me something to eat," he called out in a weak voice. "I haven't had anything to eat in a long while, and I'm starving." But in all the hustle and bustle, no one heard him — except for the young bride. She took her meal and gave it to the poor man, and she went off to her room. She undid her hair, which was held together by a long golden pin, before she got into bed. Then she stuck the golden pin into a hole in the wall where she customarily kept it overnight, and she went to sleep.

In the morning, she pulled the pin from the wall to redo her hair, and a deadly but very dead snake came along with it. The pin had pierced the snake's head when she inserted it into the wall the night before. Otherwise, the snake clearly would have bitten and killed her.

The discovery of the dead snake threw the house into an uproar. When Rabbi Akiva heard what had happened, he came running.

"My daughter!" he exclaimed. "What good deed did you do last night that saved your life?"

She told him about the poor man and how she gave away her own meal.

Rabbi Akiva was amazed. He went back to his disciples and taught, "It is written (*Proverbs* 10:2), '*Utzedakah tatzil mimavess.* Charity delivers from death.' Apparently, charity not only protects against a gruesome form of death but even against death itself."

From this story, the Gemara proves that *ein mazal l'Yisrael,* Jewish people are not governed by the astrological signs. Even if the configuration of the stars seem to predict dire consequences, a Jewish person can circumvent his preordained fate, just as Rabbi Akiva's daughter rose above her rendezvous with death through the *mitzvah* of *tzedakah.*

R' Elya Lopian, *zt"l,* pointed out that this Gemara discloses an important secret. Apparently, the Jewish people are indeed subject to the rule of fortune, just as other peoples are. But when misfortune looms over them, God gives them the opportunity to perform one particular *mitzvah* that will gain them a special measure of merit and thus protect them from danger. It was not a coincidence that a poor man appeared at the kitchen door at that particular time on the eve of Rabbi Akiva's daughter's wedding day. God sent him specifically to give her the opportunity to avoid her preordained fate. She rose to the occasion and gave the poor man her own meal, and by doing so, she saved her life. Had she let the opportunity slip by, had she failed to grab onto the lifeline God sent her, she would have been doomed.

At that moment, when a person faces his preordained misfortune, when he is in the greatest danger, when he can only be saved by a special divine protection, at that very moment, God sends him a singular opportunity to earn the protection he so desperately needs. Had Rabbi Akiva's daughter given her meal to a poor man a week earlier, it would not necessarily have saved her from death.

You never know, R' Elya concluded, when those times arrive and what those opportunities are. When a *mitzvah* comes your way, you never know why it came at that particular moment in that particular situation. When someone asks you for a favor and you are inclined to refuse, you never know if perhaps you are not squandering a special opportunity, a gift from God to help you escape some terrible misfortune.

While we are waiting for the moment when God will bless us with a child, we go through many trying times and all sorts of ordeals. And what are they if not opportunities to earn that additional measure of merit that will help us prevail over our situation?

The stress of waiting puts pressure on our relationships. Tempers get short, and we may say things we shouldn't say. Why should it be that at times like these, when we are in such desperate need of divine mercy, we find ourselves dealing with strained relationships? It is clearly a *nisayon*, a test, whose purpose is not to cause us to fall, succumb and give up, Heaven forbid, but to give us an opportunity to grow, to transcend our own nature, to rise to another level.

What does God want from us in this situation? He wants husband and wife to come together, to become closer, to be more caring, more understanding to one another, to refrain from blame and recriminations, to recognize that they can take advantage of the situation to forge an even more powerful bond. If they are successful, if they can rise to a higher level, they can earn the merit that will help them overcome their misfortune.

Yet this is not the only *nisayon*; it is not the only test we face in this situation. Strangely enough, while we anxiously await the moment when we will become parents, we experience difficulties in the fulfillment of the *mitzvah* of *kibud av va'eim*, honoring our own parents. Many sensitive issues arise. How much should they be allowed to be involved? How much should they be told? How should we respond to their questions? How much privacy should we demand for ourselves?

These are difficult questions. We can handle them with wisdom and sensitivity so that we are drawn closer to our parents and they to us, so that we all can rise together as a result of our common ordeal. Or we can cause hurt and pain through insensitivity and selfishness.

God has given us this paradoxical test in this situation as if to say, "So these people want to become father and mother? Let's see how they treat their own fathers and mothers." And if we pass the test, we gain tremendous merit to help us overcome our unfortunate fate. We can then appeal to the ultimate Healer to heal us and to the King to grant us a reprieve.

And then there is the issue of patience. We all know that patience is a virtue, but who really has true patience? There was once an advert for a credit card company that encouraged people to "take the waiting out of wanting." That is the prevalent attitude in contemporary society — no patience, instant gratification. But God puts out an advert with just the opposite message. "Learn how to wait for what you want." What an important lesson this is. What an important virtue. Learn to be patient with God. Learn to be patient with each other. Learn to be patient with yourselves. And on the day your prayers are finally answered, after you have "continuously hoped and added to all the praises of God," you can also praise Him for having given you the wonderful gift of patience.

And if we are speaking about tests, what about all the medical treatments and procedures we have to go through in this situation? We can only endure all these ordeals cheerfully if we look upon them in a positive light, if we make our efforts with the intent to fulfill the great *mitzvah* of *pru urevu*, be fruitful and multiply, which is the first *mitzvah* given to mankind at the very beginning of creation.

Our Sages tells us (*Shabbos* 31a) that one of the first questions we are asked in the afterlife when we come before the Heavenly Court is, "*Asakta befiryah verivyah?* Were you involved with procreation?" We are not asked how many children we had. We are asked if we invested effort into the performance of this *mitzvah*. And who is more involved than those of us who experience difficulties? Who invests more effort into the *mitzvah*? Every telephone call, every appointment, every procedure is another bit of this *eisek*, this involvement.

I would venture to say that with the passage of time this involvement with the *mitzvah* becomes progressively more *lishmah*, purely for the sake of fulfilling God's will, more so than if it had happened naturally and fast. The more difficult it is, the purer the *kavanah*, the intent behind the *mitzvah*, and the greater the ultimate fulfillment. In the end, those who must wait for the *mitzvah* come very close to God, which after all is what life is all about.

This brings us to perhaps the greatest test of all, the one that raises us highest and brings us closest to God if we pass it — prayer. We are all conditioned to pray from a very early age. We know the power of prayer. We know that prayer lifts us up and connects us to God, that prayer is one of the pillars of our spiritual lives. But when we are in desperate straits and cry out to God without a quick response, we can easily become dispirited. We may feel as if our prayers are coming up against a stone wall, and we may lose hope. We may wonder how we can keep repeating the same prayers over and over again so many times when nothing seems to be happening. And we may even, Heaven forbid, waver in our *emunah*, in our faith in God as the merciful Healer, the King.

Think about the *avos* and *imahos*, our great patriarchs and matriarchs. Abraham and Sarah had to wait a long time for Isaac to be born. In fact, all the *avos* had to wait a long time for children. Our Sages wonder (*Yevamos* 64a) why they were all barren to begin with, and they answer that God "desires the prayers of the righteous." It was going to happen in any case, but God wanted all those years of inspired prayer. Those prayers were so precious to Him that He considered it worthwhile to delay the progress of the generations in order to elicit the prayers from the *avos* and *imahos*. And when we find ourselves in a situation where we pray and pray seemingly without a response, we can be sure that God is gathering in every single one of our sincere prayers like a precious jewel and storing it away in His treasurehouse of prayer.

People sometimes fail to grasp this very important concept. They seem to think that a prayer has failed if it does not bring fairly immediate results. Therefore, they often wonder if there is any use in praying for the *Beis HaMikdash*. How, they ask, can we expect God to respond to our prayers when He did not respond to the prayers of the Tanna'im, Amorai'm and all the other great and righteous people that have prayed for the same thing for two thousand years? If those great people pleaded with God for the redemption of the Jewish people and nothing happened, how can little me expect to do any better? Is it possible that I will stand in front of God and say, "*Yibaneh HaMikdash*, let the *Beis HaMikdash* be rebuilt" and suddenly it's going to happen?

But they are missing the point. God has determined the measure of prayer required to bring about the redemption and the reconstruction of the *Beis HaMikdash*. When that measure is filled, it will happen immediately. The exalted prayers of the early generations have gone a long way toward filling the measure. In fact, they have gone most of the way. But there is still a little bit missing, and it is our responsibility to provide those few missing prayers that will fill the cup to overflowing and bring an end to all our suffering.

The stones of the *Kosel HaMaaravi* are a good metaphor for the cumulative effect of our prayers. If we look at the Wall, we see huge, massive stones at the base. A few layers up, the stones are still large but not quite as massive. As we go higher and higher, the stones become smaller and smaller until we get to a few rows of bricks all the way at the top that look like pebbles. The walls of the *Beis HaMikdash* will be rebuilt with prayer. The prayers of the earlier generations laid down the massive stones of the first layers, and each successive generation added its own layers. Now it is our turn, and we are nearing the very top of the walls. Only the few little pebbles that even we can provide are needed to complete the wall, but although they are only pebbles, they are essential. Without them, there is no wall.

Abraham prayed for a son for many years. Twenty years of prayer, thirty, forty, fifty, and still no answer. And then one day, Sarah informed him that she was expecting. What went through Abraham's mind at that moment? Did he think, "Last night's Maariv must have been very good"? Of course not. God "desires the prayers of the righteous." Every one of Abraham's prayers every day of every year was good. More than good. Excellent. Now, the measure was at long last filled.

It is the same with each of us. When we pray to God, we must not be discouraged if we are not answered immediately. Who knows how large a measure of prayer we need in order to achieve our goals? There are different measures for everyone, depending on all kinds of factors. But one thing we do know. Every single one of our prayers goes a distance toward filling our own particular measure. And every single prayer brings us that much closer to God.

Our Sages did give us a hint, however, about how to be successful in our prayers, how to fill up that measure more quickly. We should pray for someone else as well as for ourselves. The Gemara states (*Bava Kamma* 92a), "If a person prays for someone else when he himself has the same need, he will be answered first."

The prayer that clinched the deal, so to speak, for Abraham was the one he offered for the Philistines. When he prayed that an entire city should be healed and be able to conceive once again, that was when he was answered. That was when the measure was filled, and Sarah finally conceived.

Isaac followed his father's example when he had to pray long and hard for children. The Torah tells us (*Genesis* 25:21), "And Isaac pleaded with God concerning his wife, for she was a barren woman." Our Sages inform us that all the *avos* and *imahos* were barren. Isaac himself was also incapable of having children, and yet, he begged God to remove his wife's barrenness. He wasn't thinking about his own needs and feelings but about his wife's aching heart. And that was why his prayers were answered.

We need to learn these lessons well. During times like these, when husband and wife are both suffering from the anxieties of waiting, our first thoughts have to be genuinely for one another. When we pray, we need to worry first about one another and only afterward about ourselves. Such prayers are more powerful. They fill up the measure more quickly.

We have touched here on only a few of the ordeals we face in this and all difficult situations. There are undoubtedly numerous others. The common denominator of all the difficulties we encounter is that they are opportunities for us to gain the merit we need. God has given us challenges, and He wants to see how we react. Do we respond with weakness? Do we succumb to the pressure and become depressed and upset? Or do we rise to the occasion and do the right thing? Do we take advantage of the challenges we face to become better people, higher people, people who are moving ever closer to God?

King David says (*Psalms* 3:9), "*Lashem hayeshuah al amcha birchasecha selah*. Salvation is for God, Your people must bless You forever." Rashi explains, "He is obligated to save His servants and His people, and His people are obligated to bless and thank Him forever."

We pray to God to fulfill His obligation to us, but we cannot forget our obligation to Him. As we "hope continuously" to God, let us consider how much good He has already given us and how much gratitude we already owe Him even though important things are still missing from our lives. Let us not blot out unnecessarily all the sunshine that does stream in through our windows. Let us open our eyes and praise Him. The more we hope, the more we praise, until we have accumulated all the merit we need so that we can someday praise Him with profound understanding for the ultimate fulfillment of our prayers.

.

CHAPTER FIVE

Coping with Tragedy and Joy

Tragedy has become such a commonplace occurrence in our daily lives in America, in Eretz Yisrael and in the rest of the world. Families and communities suffer heartbreaking losses. Children contract dreadful illnesses. Young people die of disease or are killed accidentally. People contend with financial distress and all sorts of other misfortune. And if we stop and think, we see that it is not only in our times. It has always been this way, if not worse. In our times, however, we have higher expectations because of advances in medicine and technology. But tragedies still happen, and we have a hard time coping.

How do we deal with such calamities? How do we cope with these dreadful situations of pain and suffering we witness all around us? What does God want us to think? What does He want us to do?

Let us begin our search for answers in *Sefer HaYashar* (ch. 6), attributed to Rabbeinu Tam, which discusses the factors that can weaken or even sever a person's religious dedication. The sixth factor is life experience.

"The incidents and hardships people experience in their lives," writes Rabbeinu Tam, "such as changes for the bad or even for the good, [are also hindrance to a person's serving God]. A person may suffer distress. He may be promoted to a high position or make a fortune. He may be taken captive or suffer a financial loss. He or a member of his family may fall ill. He may be driven into exile or locked up in prison. One of his friends may die. All these changes and many others like them can sidetrack a person from his religious dedication to the Lord. They can cause him to forget it and remove it from his heart.

"These in particular are the situations that test the judgment of every intelligent person and determine if it is strong or weak. If it is strong, and his faith is enduring, none of these changes will be able to diminish his religious dedication. Just as all the strong winds cannot uproot a large mountain or budge it from its place, so will strong judgment and solid faith be unmoved by all these events.

"A person must be on guard during such times. He must realize that he has entered into a covenant with his Lord on this condition [that he persevere even during such times], that once he took it upon himself to serve Him it is his responsibility to fulfill his vow and uphold his oath. He has to condition his heart to be strong and courageous in order to endure these events. He should think about them before they occur and anticipate that they may happen any day, any hour, any month. He should tell himself that if these events do not happen today, they will happen tomorrow, and if they do not happen tomorrow, they will happen the day after.

"If he does this, if his eyes are open to all possibilities and his heart is prepared for them, the events that befall him will not distract him or cause him to forget his religious dedication. Rather, they will find him fully prepared to deal with them. This is what the righteous do. They are fully aware that the world is a house of hardships. Therefore, their eyes and hearts anticipate that such events may occur at any moment, and when they do occur, these events do not fluster or shock them.

"Such events only shock those who feel assured of their place in the world, who think that no suffering will befall them and that their serenity will never be disturbed. Therefore, when they do occur, contrary to what they had expected, they are shocked, and they lose their composure, their faith and their religious dedication.

"The intelligent person always has to be on guard," concludes Rabbeinu Tam. "He should not put his faith in the goodness of the world, not even for a moment. Rather, he should be aware that hardships might be imminent. If so, he will be successful, and his religious dedication will endure."

People know that bad things or even unexpected good things can happen to anyone at any time, but they don't think about it. And when changes do occur in their lives, when the normal rhythm of their day-to-day existence is disrupted, they are taken by surprise and become confused and disoriented.

These disruptions, explains Rabbeinu Tam, can weaken a person's religious dedication or even destroy it completely. The only way to prevent such a thing from happening is to prepare for these unexpected changes. A person should be aware that life on this earth is stormy. It is a mixture of good and bad. Life provides so much joy and satisfaction, but it is also full of uncertainties, tragedies and misfortune. As long as the Messiah has not yet arrived, this earth will continue to be a "house of hardships." A person should not delude himself into thinking that his life will be secure, serene and placid, because no one has ever had such a life. That is not the human experience. There is no life without its measure of grief.

A person who is mentally and emotionally prepared for the possibility of tragedy is a strong person, so strong that he cannot be weakened by tragedy just as "all the strong winds cannot uproot a large mountain or budge it from its place."

So let us consider some of these ideas. It is worthwhile to think about them, even if doing so may frighten some people or perhaps make them uncomfortable. After all, we are not new to fear; we live in a world of terror, where disaster can strike at any moment. Mature people need to face these possibilities head on rather than live in blissful denial and be shocked should misfortune ever befall them.

Death is one of the inevitabilities of life. No one is spared, not the great nor the humble, not the rich nor the poor, not the mighty nor the weak. Everyone eventually dies. How are we meant to deal with death when it strikes a family member or a friend? What does God want us to think and to feel at such a time?

The Torah states (*Deuteronomy* 14:1-2), "You are children of God your Lord, do not mutilate yourselves (*lo sisgodedu*) or pull out your hair above your eyes [in grief] over the dead. For you are a people consecrated to God your Lord, and God chose you to be His treasured people from among all the peoples on the face of the earth."

It is forbidden to mutilate oneself as an expression of grief over the death of a family member, or anyone else for that matter, in the manner of the pagan nations. Why is it forbidden? Because "you are God's children."

Ibn Ezra explains that we must understand and appreciate that God loves us even more than a father loves his children. And if God really loves us so much, He would surely never do anything to harm us. Therefore, although we cannot understand it, we have to accept that what He did was for the good. Just as a little child accepts everything his father does with full trust even though it may at times be painful, we must accept with equal trust that everything God does is ultimately for the good, no matter how we are affected at the time it happens. Should we grieve excessively over the dead, we would be showing that we think it to be a thoroughly bad thing, and this would in effect be a denial of God's love for us.

Sforno offers a somewhat different interpretation of the connection between our being "God's children" and the prohibition against self-mutilation. "It is inappropriate," he writes, "for you to display extreme anxiety and anguish over the death of a relative when you still have a relative of greater distinction and resourcefulness. [The Torah states that] 'you are God's children,' for He is your Father Who will endure forever. It is, therefore, inappropriate to display anxiety and anguish to an extreme degree over the dead."

A similar idea is expressed in Daas Zekeinim MiBaalei HaTosephos. "'You are children of God your Lord.' Therefore, if your flesh and blood father dies, do not mutilate yourselves. As long as you have a Father Who lives and endures forever, you are not forlorn. Only a pagan who loses his father has good reason to mutilate himself, for he no longer has a father other than the useless wood and stone [idols he worships]." The Rosh gives an almost identical explanation.

The thought that God is our Father, according to these commentators, presents us with two reasons for limiting our grief. First of all, as our Father, He would do nothing to harm us. Therefore, we must accept that what happened is somehow for the good. Furthermore, since we still have our Father with us, we cannot consider ourselves orphans set adrift. We should feel comforted and reassured by His presence, and we should limit our displays of grief.

So we know that because we are "God's children" we should keep our losses in perspective. We should accept that the departure of this particular person at this particular time was in some way for the good. But what about the departed person himself? What about his terrible loss in having his life come to an end? Shouldn't this be a cause for enormous grief?

Not so, says the Torah, because "you are a people consecrated to God." The Ramban explains that as a "holy nation" and "God's treasured people" we can be sure that our souls are indestructible. The soul of every Jew is a divine spark, a part of God Himself, and it lasts for all eternity. Therefore, writes the Ramban, "it is inappropriate for you to mutilate yourselves or tear out your hair over a dead person, even if he died young." The person who died came from the eternal world of souls, and he has returned there. He is now in a better place. The time spent in this stormy world is like the blink of an eye. Then it is over, and the soul returns to its true home in Heaven.

Death is not a tragedy for the departed person "even if he died young." It is only a tragedy for those of us who are left behind, and if we keep in mind that God would never harm "His children," we can also be reassured that it was all for the good in this world as well.

Nonetheless, it is only excessive grief that the Torah prohibits. We must not tear at ourselves, mutilating our flesh and ripping out our hair in exaggerated grief. But a certain amount of ordinary grief is permitted. Even though we know that our loved one has gone on to a better place, and even though we know that even on this earth everything God does is for the good, we are still allowed to weep. "The Torah does not forbid weeping," writes the Ramban, "because it is human nature for friends to be moved to tears when parting from each other even in life."

Weeping is also an expression of pain and sorrow, but it is the pain and sorrow of parting rather than of loss. When people that love each other have been together for a long time, they become close to each other. They enjoy being together, they gain from each other, and they grow together. When they part, each one feels a void in his life, an empty space once occupied by the other. It is painful. And he weeps.

A father and mother send off their son to a *yeshivah* in Israel. They are the ones that encouraged him to go. They helped him choose the *yeshivah*, and they are the ones paying for it. Nevertheless, when they take their son to the airport and say good-bye, they cry. Why do they cry? Isn't everything going exactly as they wanted it to go? Why does a mother cry at her daughter's wedding? Because it is human nature to cry at times of parting with a loved one.

When a loved one dies, it is a moment of parting, not only for a certain period of time but for as long as we live on this earth. This is the pain we are allowed to feel. This is the pain that we are supposed to feel. It is right to feel the loss of a departed loved one, and it is right to give expression to that loss with our tears. But excessive grief? That is forbidden. Did we ever see parents mutilating themselves and tearing out their hair in the airport when they are sending off their children to study in a distant land? Not very likely. Self-mutilation expresses something much deeper than the pain of parting. It expresses shock at the immensity of the tragedy and horror at coming face to face with evil. These have no place at a Jewish death.

The Ohr HaChaim compares death to a father who sent his son to a distant city to buy merchandise. The son spends a lot of time in that city selecting the merchandise that will meet his father's standards. As time passes, the people of the city come to admire and love him. Eventually, the father sends a message to his son summoning him to return. The people are sad to see him leave, but they also know that he will not cease to exist as soon as he leaves the city. On the contrary, they know that he is returning to his father's house, and they are happy for him.

When a person dies, he is returning to his Father in Heaven, to the source of all life. He is returning to a world of eternal life. He is only missing from this fleeting physical world, but he will live forever in the eternal world of souls. Do not mutilate yourselves over his death, says the Torah. Suffer the pain of parting, but do not overstate the tragedy. He is going to a better place. He is fine. You are the one that has suffered a loss. You have a right and a duty to feel the pain of parting, but nothing more.

"Do not feel too sorry," writes Sforno, "about the damage the dead person incurred by his death, 'for you are a holy people,' destined for everlasting life in the next world, whose one moment of *koras ruach*, pleasure, is better than all the life of this world."

In order to describe the good that awaits the person who died, Sforno alludes to the Mishnah (*Avos* 4:17) that "one moment of *koras ruach* in the next world is better than all the life in this world." Obviously, this is a very great good. But if we truly want to get an idea of how vast it really is, we should consider the term *koras ruach*, which the Mishnah uses to describe pleasure. What is its exact meaning? And why is it used in this context?

R' Simchah Zissel, the Alter of Kelm, uses vivid imagery to bring this concept to life. He explains that *koras ruach* means a mere whiff. A man walks by a catering hall where a sumptuous feast is being prepared, perhaps for the wedding of a rich man's daughter. The air is heavy with the scent of the most savory foods and freshly baked breads and pastries. He breathes in the fragrant vapors, and he smiles with contentment. He has not set foot inside the hall. He has gotten only a whiff of the feast, yet he already feels the pleasure.

And what does the Mishnah tell us about this one moment of catching a mere whiff of the next world? That it is "better than all the life of this world." What does that mean? "All the life." That is a very broad statement.

Imagine that a person has many good times in his life, times that brought him joy and satisfaction, times he remembers with profound pleasure. Imagine if he could take all these pleasurable times in his life and compress them into one moment that would capture every bit of the pleasure he experienced during those times.

But wait. That is not all. Imagine if he could compress into that one moment not only all the pleasures of his own life but also all the pleasures of the lives of his family, his friends, his townspeople, all the people of his country, all the people of the world. Incredible. All the pleasures that all these billions of people had experienced in all their lifetimes compressed into that one pleasure-packed moment. And even more. Imagine if he could also compress into that one moment all the pleasures of all the people who had lived in the world from the very beginning of creation when this world came into existence. Imagine if all the myriad pleasures experienced by all the billions of people that ever walked the face of the earth could be packed into that one moment and that he could live that one moment and experience all its pleasures. It is a mind-boggling thought. And the Mishnah tells us that a mere whiff of the next world is better than this near infinity of physical pleasure experienced by the sum total of all the people who ever lived on the face of the earth.

And this is only *koras ruach,* the mere whiff of the next world, a passing whiff from the outside, so to speak. But what about eternal life within the next world? What about "the righteous sitting with their crowns on their heads enjoying the glow of the Divine Presence"? We cannot even begin to create a metaphor to compare this spiritual pleasure with the physical pleasures of this world. The distance is too great even for comparison.

These are the ideas we are meant to learn when we study the prohibition against self-mutilation. These are the thoughts that are meant to go through our minds when we see the dead lying before us and we consider how to express our grief. If we are thus fortified, we do not become flustered and shocked by a close encounter with death. If we are properly prepared to cope with the "house of hardships," as Rabbeinu Tam describes the stormy world within which we live, our faith and religious dedication are strengthened rather than weakened. If we prepare properly, times such as these remind us that we are "God's children" and "a holy people," and we come closer to Him.

The Gemara tells us (*Yevamos* 13b) that it is forbidden to have rabbinical courts following conflicting judicial traditions in the same community. This prohibition is also derived from the words *lo sisgodedu,* do not mutilate yourselves. These words, *lo sisgodedu,* can also be read as *lo saasu agudos agudos*, do not separate your-selves into different factions.

This is very perplexing. There seems to be absolutely no con-nection between these two prohibitions. One is meant to prevent internal dissension among the Jewish people, while the other is meant to prevent excessive expressions of grief over the dead. How can both of these unrelated concepts be derived from the very same word? Moreover, how can a prohibition against fac-tionalism be read into a verse that states explicitly, "Do not muti-late yourselves (*lo sisgodedu*) … over the dead"? No matter how we manipulate and parse the word *sisgodedu*, the Torah states clearly that we are discussing something that is done "over the dead." How then can we say that these words refer to the prohibition against forming factions?

All the more perplexing are the words of the Rambam. He men-tions the prohibition against the pagan practice of self-mutilation in the Laws of Avodah Zarah, where it properly belongs. And then he writes (*Mishneh Torah, Hilchos Avodah Zarah* 12:14), "Included in this prohibition is that there should not be two rab-binical courts in the same city, one of which follows one set of cus-toms while the other follows a different set of customs. Such a thing leads to great strife."

Amazingly, the Rambam writes that the prohibition against forming separate groups is "included" in the basic prohibition against self-mutilation. He also chooses to present the prohibition against factionalism among the laws dealing with idolatry and pagan practices where it does not really belong — unless there is some fundamental connection between factionalism and the pagan practice of self-mutilation.

What is this connection?

In the light of our discussion, we can indeed see a distinct con-nection. How does a Jew deal with a death in the family? Does he allow himself to become depressed? Does he become so despond-ent over the supposed evil that has befallen him that he feels like tearing out his hair and mutilating his flesh as the pagans do? No, says the Torah. During times like these, a Jew bolsters his faith by remembering that we are "God's children" and "a holy nation." More than at other times, he seeks solace in the thought that God is our Father in Heaven and that He loves us more than a mortal father loves his children. The more a Jew thinks about these concepts, the more he recognizes God's fatherly hand in his life, the more he truly perceives God's fatherliness.

The idea that we are "God's children" becomes more of a reality to him than ever before, and so do all its ramifications. If we are really "God's children," then we are all brothers in the deepest sense of the word. Brotherhood among Jewish people is not just an abstract term indicating shared values and ideals, such as the brotherhood of man. We share much more than that. As a "people consecrated to God," we are all brothers, members of one family, because we share a Father in Heaven. Therefore, we must pursue peace and harmony with our brothers, and we are forbidden to allow factionalism, which opens the door to dissension. As the Ritva points out in *Yevamos* (ibid.), the spontaneous grief we experience when the dead lie before us leads us to this inevitable conclusion. For the Jewish people, death gives birth to the greatest appreciation of brotherhood.

The Rambam writes about Jewish brotherhood in the context of the commandment to give charity (*Mishneh Torah, Hilchos Matnas Aniim* 10:2), "All of Israel … are like brothers, as it is written, 'You are children of God your Lord,' and if a brother does not take pity on his brother, who then will take pity on him? To whom should the Jewish poor look for help? To the pagans who despise and persecute them? They have no one to look to for help but their brothers."

How does the Rambam prove that Jews are brothers? Because we are all "God's children." Actually, Jews are described as brothers numerous times earlier in the Torah. It is always "your brother" this and "your brother" that. One cannot go through the

Torah without being fully aware that Jews are considered brothers. Why then did the Rambam have to bring this verse to prove his point? It is because brotherhood is a vague term. It can mean friendship, good will, camaraderie. But if we are indeed "God's children," if we have one Father in Heaven, then we are real brothers, as brotherly as if we had emerged from the same womb. If we are indeed "God's children," then the Rambam is justified in saying, "If a brother does not take pity on his brother, who then will take pity on him?"

So this is where tragic situations lead a Jew who has prepared himself for life in this stormy "house of hardships." His religious dedication does not weaken. It grows stronger. The thoughts that are awakened in his mind and the feelings that spring forth in his heart inspire him and bring him closer to God. His faith grows deeper and stronger. He gains a new awareness of his relationship to his Father in Heaven. He begins to view all other Jewish people as his brothers and sisters in the most profound sense of the words. And he becomes so much more sensitive to them that he can say in all sincerity, "If a brother does not take pity on his brother, who then will take pity on him?"

There is one exception to the rule. Sometimes, the death of a person can be so devastating that no limits are placed on the displays of grief, even though we are "God's children," even though we are a "holy nation."

The Gemara tells us (*Sanhedrin* 68a) that when Rabbi Eliezer died Rabbi Akiva followed the coffin from Caesarea to Lud and was "striking at his flesh until his blood flowed to the ground." One can imagine the force of his self-inflicted blows if he caused himself such heavy bleeding that his blood fell to the ground.

And all the time, continues the Gemara, Rabbi Akiva was bewailing the loss of Rabbi Eliezer. He cried out, "My father, my father, chariot and cavalry of Israel," repeating the words Elisha spoke when his teacher Elijah went up to Heaven in a chariot of fire (II Kings 2:12). "I have so much money, but there is no moneychanger to convert it for me." In other words, as Rashi explains, I have so many Torah questions to ask, and there is no longer anyone who can give me an answer.

After having discussed at such length the prohibition against self-mutilation, our minds immediately turn to the obvious question. How could Rabbi Akiva inflict such bloody wounds on himself? Wasn't this in violation of the prohibition?

The Tosaphists address this question and explain that it was different in Rabbi Akiva's case. He was not expressing his grief over his personal loss. He was beside himself that all his unanswered Torah questions would have to remain unanswered. He was mourning the loss of so much Torah that he could have learned from Rabbi Eliezer. There are no limitations on this type of grief.

The knowledge that we are "God's children" did not limit Rabbi Akiva's grief, especially according to Sforno's interpretation that our loss is not so great as long as we still have our Father in Heaven. But this does not apply to Torah. According to the Gemara (*Bava Metzia* 59b), we have to disregard a Heavenly Voice that offers a Torah opinion, as it written (*Deuteronomy* 30:12), "[The Torah] is not in Heaven." Therefore, when a great sage passes away, we suffer a tremendous loss in Torah, and we cannot console ourselves with the thought that our Father is still with us. Torah is learned only from our teachers, and when they pass away, their Torah is forever lost to us.

If we can digress for just a moment or two, this leads us to a very important observation. Why wait until our Torah scholars pass away to acknowledge how critical they are to us, how truly indispensable? It is far better that we should appreciate them while they are still alive, that we should express our need for them by our prayers for their continued well-being rather than by our tears when they are gone.

Our Sages have instituted a number of prayers on behalf of our Torah scholars. On weekdays, we say the Kaddish d'Rabbanan, the Kaddish for the Rabbis. "Upon Israel, upon their rabbis, upon their disciples, upon all the disciples of their disciples and upon all who are occupied with the Torah in this place and in all places, may there be upon you much peace, grace, kindness, mercy, long life, ample livelihood and deliverance from their Father Who is in Heaven and on earth."

Even on the Sabbath, when we do not pray for our needs, we still say *Yekum Purkan* for Torah scholars. "May salvation arise from Heaven — Grace, kindness, mercy, long life and ample livelihood, heavenly assistance, physical health, good vision, children who are alive and well, children who do not interrupt or withdraw from the words of Torah — for our masters and rabbis, the holy association in the land of Israel and the Diaspora ..."

Some people may be inclined to run through these prayers without really giving the words a second thought. But stop and think for a moment about the Torah scholars, about how important they are in our lives, about how they are the heart and soul of the Jewish people. Think about how you would feel if you were to hear that they are, G-d forbid, no longer with us, and realize that there is something you can do for them right now. You can pray for them. You can plead with God to protect them and shower them with His kindness.

R' Yonasan Eibeschutz in *Yaaros Dvash* writes that when we say the Refa'einu prayer we should pray for the healing of all Jews who are ill as if they were limbs attached to our own bodies whose pain we actually feel. And then he adds a special comment about praying for our Torah scholars.

"It is our obligation," writes R' Yonasan, "to pray for the benefit, welfare and vigor [of Torah scholars], for they are the guardians of Torah and the custodians of the authentic tradition, the Oral Torah, and we depend on them. If we would not have Torah scholars, Heaven forbid, we would not have life itself. Therefore, it is our responsibility to pray to God with all our hearts that they should recover their youthful vigor like eagles, that they should regain the strength to spread their wings and fly like eagles. This is a very great *mitzvah* . . . because it will lead to an increase in the honor of Torah. Indeed, how could a person not yearn for Torah if all Jews would pray for his welfare, good condition and health? Many wealthy people spend a lot of money to have rabbis praying to God for them always, and here all the Jews in the world pray for the Torah scholars. Therefore, we are obliged to pray a lot for them, because we live in their protective shadow."

In our times, when we no longer have towering Torah sages as did generations past, we have to cherish the contribution of each and every Torah scholar in our midst. They are our priceless treasures. We mourn when they are gone, and we should also pray sincerely for their welfare when they are still among us.

Changes in a person's life may upset his equilibrium. In the words of Rabbeinu Tam mentioned earlier, "The incidents and hardships people experience in their lives, such as changes for the bad or even for the good," may cause him to lose his dedication to God.

Not only the tragic occurrences, but even those changes that are for the good, the times of joy and happiness, can cause a person to become estranged from God. A person can become drunk with joy and exhilaration. He can become so completely absorbed in his own enjoyment and pleasure that he forgets his Creator and his purpose in this world.

How are we meant to experience joy? The Gemara gives us very clear guidelines (*Shabbos* 30b). "The Sages originally wanted to suppress the Book of *Koheles* (Ecclesiastes) because its statements contradicted each other ... How were they contradictory? ... It is written (*Ecclesiastes* 8:15), 'And I praised joy.' And it is also written (*Ecclesiastes* 2:2), 'As for joy, what does it accomplish?' There is no contradiction. 'And I praised joy' refers to joy derived from a *mitzvah*. 'As for joy, what does it accomplish?' refers to joy not derived from a *mitzvah*. This teaches you that the Divine Presence does not appear amidst gloom, sloth, merrymaking, rowdiness, small talk or idle chatter, only amidst joy derived from a *mitzvah*."

At first, the Sages saw a contradiction in King Solomon's wise words. Is joy something of substance, something of value, something to be praised? Or is it something fleeting and insubstantial that leaves us wondering what we have accomplished? And the Gemara resolves the contradiction. True joy is derived only from a *mitzvah*. Joy derived from something other than a *mitzvah* is an illusion. It is not really joy.

True joy leads to the appearance of the Divine Presence, says the Gemara, but the Divine Presence does not appear amidst "gloom, sloth, merrymaking, rowdiness, small talk or idle chatter." The Gemara lumps all these things together, because they are all of a kind. Merrymaking and rowdiness are just other forms of gloom. Boisterous, rowdy people may think they are happy and joyous, but they are really depressed. They just make a lot of noise to cover their inner gloom. There is no joy deep inside their hearts and souls, only a dark depression, a lack of direction and purpose in life. And so, afraid to face themselves and the emptiness of their lives, they escape into laughter and chatter. The Divine Presence will not appear among these people, because theirs is not a true joy.

Joy derived from a *mitzvah*, however, is the emotion a person experiences when he comes closer to God. He feels uplifted, sanctified, enriched, and this fills his heart with a boundless joy so profound that, according to the Gemara, it invites the appearance of the Divine Presence.

Let us think about this for a moment. What does the Gemara mean? In what way does joy derived from a *mitzvah* lead to the appearance of the Divine Presence? Actually, it is beyond the capabilities of human beings to perceive the Divine Presence. Yet we say in the Haggadah that *bemora gadol*, in great awe, means *giluy Shechinah*, that the Divine Presence was revealed to the Jewish people at the Splitting of the Sea. How was it revealed to them?

The commentators explain that this refers to divine providence. When the Jewish people saw the wonders God performed on their behalf to rescue them from their Egyptian pursuers, when they saw the "great spectacles," in the words of Targum Onkelos, they felt the close proximity of the Divine Presence. This is the way human beings encounter God. The more a person recognizes the hand of God in everything that happens, the more he has seen God. The more he comes to the realization that everything God does is for his good, for the good of the Jewish people and for the good of all creation, the more his heart fills with the most exquisite joy imaginable. This joy in his heart is his personal revelation of the Divine Presence.

What does a person do when he experiences this joy, when he sees the hand of God with blinding clarity? How is this joy he feels on the inside expressed on the outside? Only by proclaiming to the rest of the world the great truth he has discovered, by showing other people that he is rejoicing in God rather than in his own pleasure, by sharing with all the world his joyous encounter with God.

King David writes of the festivals (*Psalms* 118:24), "*Zeh hayom asah Hashem nagilah venismechah bo.*" This is ordinarily translated as "This is the day God made, let us delight and rejoice in it." But according to Rabbeinu Yonah (*Berachos* 31a), the word *bo* does not refer to the festival but to God. "This is the day God made, let us delight and rejoice in Him." That is true joy. To rejoice over our encounter with God.

Four people are obligated to bring a *korban todah*, a thanksgiving offering — one who recovers from a grave illness, one who crosses the sea, one who crosses the desert and one who is released from captivity. Listen to the words of the psalm related to the thanksgiving offering (*Psalms* 100:1-5), "A melody of thanksgiving, all the earth, greet God with fanfare. Serve God with rejoicing, come before Him with hymns. Know that God is the Lord, He made us, we belong to Him, we are His people, the sheep of His flock. Come into His gates with thanksgiving, into His courtyards with psalms, give praise to Him, bless His Name. For God is good, His kindness lasts forever, His faithfulness endures for all generations."

A man is released from prison. He is overjoyed. He brings a sacrifice to express his joy and thanksgiving, and what does he say? "All the earth, greet God with fanfare." He is the one that has experienced a miracle, not all the earth. Yet he tells all the earth to rejoice. Because that is how he is meant to express his joy. Tell it to the world. You experienced the miracle. You saw God's hand so clearly. You saw the revelation of the Divine Presence. Share it with everyone. Let them know what you know. Let them feel what you feel. That is how true joy is expressed.

The thanksgiving offering has two unusual features. It is the only sacrifice accompanied by forty assorted loaves of bread. Furthermore, unlike other sacrifices in its class, which can be eaten for two days and a night, the thanksgiving offering can only be eaten on the day it is brought and the following night. What is the reason for these unusual conditions?

Sforno offers a beautiful insight (*Leviticus* 7:12). The person bringing the sacrifice and his family cannot possibly consume the entire sacrifice and the forty accompanying breads within the short period of time allowed. Nevertheless, it is strictly forbidden to leave any of it uneaten. So what does he do? He has no choice but to invite all his friends and neighbors to help him finish all the food by daybreak of the following day. This is exactly what the Torah wants.

With so many people gathered around the table, sharing in the sacrifice and the breads, he will tell them all the wondrous details of how God delivered him from danger. "Serve God with rejoicing, come before Him with hymns," he will say to them. "Come into His gates with thanksgiving, into His courtyards with psalms, give praise to Him, bless His Name. For God is good, His kindness lasts forever." This is how joy derived from a *mitzvah* is expressed.

I once heard a rather original interpretation of the Gemara's statement that 'And I praised joy' refers to joy derived from a *mitzvah* while 'As for joy, what does it accomplish?' refers to the joy not derived from a *mitzvah*. I am not sure if this is exactly what the Gemara intended, but there is definitely truth in the idea.

According to this interpretation, the Gemara is referring to the exact same joyous experience. A person celebrates a certain event in his life, and it can go both ways. If he really intends to thank God for his good fortune, it is surely a joy derived from a *mitzvah*. But if he is only giving lip service to God, if his real joy is in his own pleasure and satisfaction, then it is not considered a joy derived from a *mitzvah*. It all depends on what is in his mind and heart at the time.

So how can a person know for certain if his joy is genuinely for the *mitzvah*? How can he know if he is not deluding himself into thinking he has God in mind when he is really thinking only of himself?

These are difficult questions, and the answer becomes clear only after a certain amount of time has elapsed. If he still feels the glow of that joy when he thinks about that celebration, if he is moved to say, "And I praised joy," then he can be sure his joy derived from the *mitzvah*. But suppose he finds it impossible to recapture that elusive joy. Suppose he feels he has gained nothing of lasting value. He cannot even bring those momentary pleasures to mind, and he says, "As for joy, what does it accomplish?" Then he can be sure the wrong thoughts and feelings were at the root of his joy. And he can be sure it was not a joy derived from a *mitzvah*.

May God bless all of us with numerous joyous occasions. But we must always remember that just as we need to prepare ourselves to cope with tragedy, we also need to prepare ourselves to cope with joy. At those moments of supreme joy in our lives, such as when we marry off a child, we can easily fall into the trap of thinking only about the personal pleasure and enjoyment of the moment. We can rejoice in the same way that all parents in the world rejoice at times like these. But it would not be a joy derived from a *mitzvah*. It would not be a genuine joy. It would not lead to the appearance of the Divine Presence.

At times like these, a faithful Jew stops to think about how God has blessed him and showered him with so much goodness. He thinks about how God has given him this child and helped him raise the child through childhood and adolescence, with all the ordeals and obstacles these years present. He thinks about how God has given him the wonderful gifts of life and health so that he can see his child married in his lifetime. He realizes that God has been standing beside him all along, holding his hand and guiding him. And he is so awed and overwhelmed by his encounter with God, by the knowledge that he is standing in the Divine Presence, that his heart fills to bursting with joy. And he begins to dance. And he draws in his friends and his family and every stranger he sees. And he cries out, "Look, my friends. See what God has done. Share my joy." And the joy derived from a *mitzvah* remains in his heart forever.

CHAPTER SIX

Unanswered Prayers

H ow do we feel when we take out the time from our busy schedules to come pray in the synagogue? Do we in some subtle, or perhaps not so subtle way consider it a bit of an imposition? Do we feel as if God should be grateful to us for taking the time out to pay Him a visit? Do we keep looking at our watches if the pace of the prayers is not quite quick enough? Or do we consider it a wonderful opportunity and cherish every moment we are there?

King David declared (*Psalms* 5:7), "As for me, by Your great kindness do I come into Your House." He considered it a great kindness from God that he could come to God's House to pray.

We have to stop and consider when we stand on the threshold of the synagogue what a great privilege it is to have the opportunity to spend a little time praying to God. How fortunate we are when we can come within the holy walls of the synagogue in the presence of God and draw closer to Him. We should think of all the people who cannot come, the sick, the infirm, the home-bound elderly who would gladly give everything to sit in front of the *aron kodesh*, the holy ark of the Torah, with a *siddur* in their hands. We should not take these things for granted. It is only by God's great kindness that we have the time and the ability to approach Him in the synagogue.

So what is this thing called prayer? First and foremost, it is a *mitzvah*, a specific commandment in the Torah, which states (*Deuteronomy* 11:13), "To serve Him with all your hearts." And the Gemara comments (*Taanis* 2a), "What is considered 'serving with the heart'? It is prayer." We do not only pray when we need something or when we feel the urge for spiritual uplift. Prayer is one of our most important daily obligations.

At the same time, prayer does wield enormous power. It could bring us success in all our endeavors, material and spiritual, if only we knew how to pray. But this not a simple thing. We may fulfill our obligation when we pray with concentration and sincerity, but does this allow us to harness the power of prayer? Not necessarily. Let us see why.

The Rambam makes a powerful statement about prayer in the midst of a discussion about repentance (*Mishneh Torah, Hilchos Teshuvah* 2:6). "Even though repentance and prayerful outcries are beneficial for the world," he writes, "they are especially beneficial during the ten days from Rosh Hashanah to Yom Kippur, when they are immediately accepted, as it is written (*Isaiah* 55:6), 'Seek out God when He can be reached.' These things were said with regard to individuals. As for a congregation, whenever they repent and cry out in prayer with full sincerity, they are answered, as it is written (*Deuteronomy* 4:7), 'For which nation is so great a nation that it has a deity close to it as God our Lord is [close to us] when we call out to Him?'"

The Ten Days of Teshuvah, from Rosh Hashanah through Yom Kippur, are the times when God "can be reached." Although we can reach out to God at all times, He is especially accessible to us during these ten days, and prayers offered at this time, explains the Rambam, are "immediately accepted." Very powerful words. If we repent and pray during this time, our prayers rise up to Heaven straightaway. It is something to think about. Moreover, says the Rambam, God is always receptive to a congregation. When ten people get together and pray sincerely, their prayers are always answered, even during the rest of the year. Only an individual needs to rely on the special divine receptiveness of the Ten Days of Teshuvah.

A person is standing in the privacy of his own home, or even walking on the street, and it occurs to him that Yom Kippur is just around the corner. He trembles inside, because he knows how much he needs and how unworthy he is. A thought of repentance flashes through his mind, and he cries out, "Please, God, help me!" This prayer, offered up during the Ten Days of Teshuvah when God "can be reached," goes straight up to Heaven and is "immediately accepted." As for the rest of the year, when a person walks into the synagogue and prays with the whole congregation, his prayers are always accepted.

In his Introduction to *Sefer HaMitzvos*, the Rambam states that the Purim story is proof that the prayers of a whole congregation are accepted. He states that God made us this promise in the Torah, and he quotes this verse, "For which nation is so great a nation that it has a deity close to it as God our Lord is [close to us] when we call out to Him?" When Haman engineered an evil decree against the Jewish people, they came together and sincerely prayed to God, and the situation turned over completely. Everything that had seemed impossible all of a sudden happened. The prayers were "immediately accepted," and so it is always.

But is it really always so? How often do prayers offered up with concentration and sincerity remain unanswered? How often do people facing a crisis, either with their livelihood or their health or their children, run to the synagogue and send their brokenhearted pleas Heavenward, and still things do not get better, even during the Ten Days of Teshuvah, even together with the whole congregation? Why aren't these prayers "immediately accepted"?

There is a baffling Gemara about unanswered prayers (*Rosh Hashanah* 18a). "Rabbi Meir used to say, 'Two people took to bed with the same illness, and similarly, two people were brought to the gallows for the same punishment, one recovered and the other didn't, one was saved and the other wasn't. Why should one recover and the other not? Why should one be saved and the other not? This one prayed and was answered. The other one prayed and was not answered. And why was this one answered and the other not? This one prayed a complete prayer (*tefillah sheleimah*) and the other didn't.'"

What is a "complete prayer"? Rashi says one word, "*Niskaven.*" Ordinarily, one would translate this word as "he concentrated" or "he focused on it." But how can that be?

A man is lying in hospital. The doctor comes in with a grim face and tells him that unfortunately the test results were positive. A dread illness is raging in his body, and there is nothing medicine can do for him. The doctor walks out and the man is left alone to face the Angel of Death. "Help me, God!" he cries out. "I have no one to whom to turn but You. I don't want to die. Please let me see my children grow up. Please let me take care of my family. Don't let my wife become a widow and my children orphans. Please save me!" Can it be that he says these words casually like a man mumbling his prayers because he is in a hurry to get to the office?

A man is standing on the gallows. The executioner puts the noose around his neck and gets ready to open the trapdoor under the condemned man. In another few moments, the condemned man will be swinging from the rope with his neck snapped. In desperation, he cries out to God, "Help me! Save me!" Can there be a more desperate, sincere prayer than his? Can it be that he would not concentrate with every bit of intensity he can muster from his heart and soul?

It is impossible.

And yet, one man prayed a "complete prayer" on his deathbed and the other didn't. One man prayed a "complete prayer" on the gallows and the other didn't. What does this mean?

R' Elya Lopian translates *lo niskaven* in contrast to *niskaven* as "he did not have intent." The patient that died and the condemned man that was executed both prayed "without intent." What does this mean? It means that they didn't believe in the effectiveness of their prayers. They did not have a real intent that their prayers would be answered. They did not expect to succeed.

When the doctor told him that his illness was incurable, he gave up. That's it. It's all over. I'm finished. So why did he pray? Because that is how a Jew reacts. He gets into trouble so he prays. Perhaps it was just a way of gaining merit for his imminent appearance in the Heavenly Court. Perhaps he even thought there was a slight chance it would help. After all, one never knows. But he didn't really believe it. This is not a "complete prayer," and it will not do anything for him.

Sometimes you see people saying Psalms for a sick person, and you see that one of them has tears streaming down his face as he cries out the verses. And you are impressed by the depth of this person praying so powerfully that he is moved to tears. But this may be a mistake. He may be crying because he really doesn't believe the patient will recover — and he is already imagining the funeral!

A real prayer, a "complete prayer," is said with faith and confidence that prayer can heal just as effectively as the latest medications, and even more so. A "complete prayer" is said with faith and confidence that prayer can save a condemned man from the gallows just as effectively as bringing political pressure to bear on the authorities, and even more so. It is said with faith and confidence that the entire world is in God's hands, that He can do whatever He wants to do. God is not restrained by statistics and medical reports. Prayer has the power to accomplish anything, but only as long as the one praying is convinced of it.

A strange thing once happened in the Gateshead Yeshivah. As in all *yeshivos*, there was always great competition for the best *chavrusa*, the study partner for the new semester. Every boy sought to get the best *chavrusa* possible, but not everyone could get what he wanted. One makes the best of it.

There was one particular boy who was not exactly one of the shining stars of the yeshivah. He was a good, serious, hardworking boy, a very nice boy, but of rather average intelligence. His strengths and shortcomings were no secret among the other boys, and one would have expected that he would have to settle for less than the best *chavrusa*. The brightest boys, the most talented and accomplished, the respected stars of the yeshivah were unlikely to consent to be his *chavrusa*. In fact, he would have done well to get at least a good mediocre boy.

For some odd reason, however, this boy always managed to find an excellent *chavrusa*. No one in the administration and staff could understand it. Even the boys that agreed to be his *chavrusa* could not quite explain why they had done so. Of course, the mismatched partnership never lasted for more than one semester. By then the superior *chavrusa* would have had enough and gone on to seek a better one. Nonetheless, to everyone's continuing amazement, this boy would find another top *chavrusa* the following semester. And so on, semester after semester. It was totally baffling.

And then one day at the beginning of a new semester, someone overheard the boy speaking on the hall telephone to his mother.

"Mother," he was saying, "you can stop praying now. I've already got my new *chavrusa*. He is very good. One of the best."

This is what one would call faith and confidence in the power of prayer. And incidentally, it also tells us something about the power of a mother's prayer, but that is a discussion for a different time.

So this is the first point. The Rambam assures us that the prayers of an individual during the Ten Days of Teshuvah and the prayers of the whole congregation at all times are "immediately accepted." But it has to be a "complete prayer," a *tefillah sheleimah*.

Other requirements must also be met before prayers can be "immediately accepted."

Our Sages gave us some famous advice regarding prayer (*Avos* 2:13), "Rabbi Shimon said, 'Pay meticulous attention to the reading of the Shema and the prayers. And when you pray, do not make your prayer routine. Rather, it should be a plea for mercy and favor before [God], as it is written (*Jonah* 4:2), 'For He is a gracious and merciful Lord, slow to anger, extremely kind, and He reconsiders the evil [decrees].'"

Prayer, says Rabbi Shimon, should be "a plea for mercy and favor" before God. It should not be "routine." In other words, we should not consider our prayer a mechanistic method of gaining what we want. We should not come into the synagogue and say a prescribed set of prayers and expect God to grant our request. We should not think that it's a formula, a system, that this is how it works, like putting a coin into a vending machine, pressing the button and waiting for a can to pop out. This is not prayer. When a person prays, says the *Shulchan Aruch*, he has to feel like a beggar standing at the door, making "a plea for mercy and favor." He has to show that he feels dependent on God and that he relies on Him entirely. This is prayer.

And then Rabbi Shimon supports this concept by quoting a verse from the Prophets. "For He is a gracious and merciful Lord, slow to anger, and very kind, and He reconsiders the evil." At first glance, it is rather difficult to see the connection. The prophet is describing the Attributes of God. It doesn't mention a word about prayer. Certainly, no one would argue with Rabbi Shimon's insights into prayer. Nonetheless, we must wonder how he deduced from the words of the prophet that prayer should not be "routine" but rather "a plea for mercy and favor."

Rabbeinu Yonah supplies the answer. "Every person has to plead for his life, because there is no person on earth that never sins... 'For He is a gracious and merciful Lord, slow to anger, extremely kind, and He reconsiders the evil [decrees].' Indeed, every person needs to rely on Heavenly mercy. If things are going well for him, it is only because [God] is slow to anger and forgives him, not because of his righteousness. Therefore, he must plead with Him lest He reconsider His having reconsidered the evil. Perhaps a sin will cause [him to suffer misfortune], because miracles do not happen all the time."

Here is the key. "Every person has to plead for his life," explains Rabbeinu Yonah, "because there is no person on earth that never sins." It is a chilling statement, but an important truth. A person always has to beg for his life, because he is assured of nothing. Who is so righteous that he can say he is guaranteed life and good fortune? No one.

But what if "things are going well for him"? Doesn't this prove that he does deserve his bounty? Not at all. Fortune may be smiling on him. His life may be humming along just beautifully. Things may go well for him for a week, a month, a year, five years, and he gets used to it. He begins to think nothing is going to change. He no longer feels like a beggar standing at the door pleading for mercy and favor when he prays to God. But he is living in a fool's paradise. Everything can change in a moment.

That is how, according to Rabbeinu Yonah, the verse supports Rabbi Shimon's teaching. The prophet describes God as "gracious and merciful, slow to anger, extremely kind" and that He "reconsiders the evil [decrees]." Who can feel assured that God will forever "reconsider the evil" that is coming to him? Maybe He will "reconsider His having reconsidered the evil." Therefore, a person has no choice but to "rely on Heavenly mercy."

Rabbeinu Yonah is in effect saying that we are all living on credit. Our Creditor can call in the loan at any time and force us into bankruptcy in a moment, not only in business but in everything else as well, Heaven forbid. We have no choice but to beg Him for an extension. If we would realize this, that we are not living by our own profits but on credit God has extended to us, we would not be so complacent when we pray. We would grasp that we are in a crisis situation, that our credit line can be closed at any moment, that we have to plead with the Creditor to have mercy and extend us some more credit even though we don't deserve it. If we realized this, we would pray like beggars standing at the door.

I once heard a clever man make an observation along these lines. "Sometimes I see a successful businessman," he told me, "a man blessed with good fortune in every aspect of his life, and I see him praying in the synagogue. And I watch him. The man comes on time, and he says every word with real concentration. I can see it. There's no question about it. And he stands a really long Shemoneh Esrei. And I think to myself that this man is the embodiment of the Mishnah in *Avos*. He is the ideal successful man who realizes that nothing is in his control, that everything he possesses is a gift from God. Despite his success, he is standing like a beggar at the door. It warms my heart to see it.

"And then I meet the man in his office an hour later, and I see a totally different person. I see a ruthless, brutal businessman. For a few dollars profit, he will trample on anyone standing in his way. This has happened more than once, I tell you, and at first, I couldn't understand it. Where was the man who prayed so faithfully and convincingly? Where was the man who realized that all power and success depend on God? Does he think it was his cleverness that made the business deal? Doesn't he know that it is up to God? So why trample on other people in order to make the deal? Does he think God wants him to do this? These questions gnawed at me, until one day the answer struck me.

"This man is definitely praying with concentration and sincerity, but do you know what is going through his mind? He is saying, 'Look, God, I know how to run my business very well, but I have to admit that You are much stronger than I am. If You want to, You can destroy everything I've built up. So I'm praying to You and asking You please not to interfere.' Of course, he doesn't express himself in these words, but this is the thinking at the root of his fervent prayers.

"So this is what he wants from God. This is why he is standing his long Shemoneh Esrei. He is pleading with God not to disturb the well-ordered life he built for himself through his own efforts. He does not really believe that everything comes from God, so if he wants to be successful, he believes he has to trample everyone that gets in his way."

This observation goes to the core of human nature. This is what many people are missing. They don't realize that everything they have is a gift from God. If they understood the working of the world properly, they would say, "God, I know I am totally dependent on You. I know that everything I have is a direct favor from You, pure benevolence, undeserved, an extension of credit to a person who is really not creditworthy. Please, God, I beseech You, let it continue that way, and I will try to do my bit. I'll try to be better. I'll try to be more deserving. I'll try to justify what You are doing for me somewhat. But nothing I can do will ever earn me all the good You have given me. God, I am a miserable beggar standing at Your door. I beg you, give me alms from Your generous hand."

So here is another point to be considered when we speak about the Rambam's assurance that the prayers of an individual during the Ten Days of Teshuvah and the prayers of the whole congregation at all times are "immediately accepted." The prayer has to be a "complete prayer," delivered with faith and confidence in the power of prayer, and it also has to be delivered with humility and the recognition of our total dependence — in the true sense of a beggar standing at the door.

And there is yet another very important point that can determine whether a prayer will be "immediately accepted."

The *Shulchan Aruch* states (*Orach Chaim* 124:7) that when a person talks in the synagogue during *chazaras hashatz* while the *chazzan* is repeating the Shemoneh Esrei, it is such a grave transgression that "*gadol avono mi'neso*, his sin is too great to bear." In other words, his sin is too great to be forgiven, a burden too heavy for God to carry, so to speak.

Nowhere else in the *Shulchan Aruch* does this harsh expression appear, even with regard to the gravest sins. The only place where we find this expression is in the Torah (*Genesis* 4:13), where it appears as a question rather than a statement. Cain has just killed Abel, and God has confronted him with his crime. And Cain says to God, "Is my sin too great to bear?" And God did indeed forgive him. Killing his brother was apparently not a "sin too great to bear." Yet talking in the synagogue during *chazaras hashatz* is too great to bear? How can such a thing be?

Some three hundred and fifty years ago, the Jewish population of Eastern Europe was devastated by Cossack pogroms for two years. These years came to be know as *Tach* (5408/1648) and *Tat* (5409/1649). We do not know for certain how many Jews died in these horrible massacres. Some estimates run as high as the hundreds of thousands. Afterwards, Rav Yom Tov Lippmann Heller, known as the Tosefos Yom Tov, had a dream in which he was told that the reason this calamity befell the Jewish people is that people used to talk in the synagogue during *chazaras hashatz*. He made a great public tumult about it in an attempt to get people to stop doing it. In fact, some *siddurim* have a special *Mi Shebeirach* prayer for those that do not talk in the synagogue during *chazaras hashatz*. It dates from the time of the Tosefos Yom Tov.

How can we understand such a thing? How can it be that so many thousands of people perished because of the sin of talking in the synagogue during *chazaras hashatz*?

Without question, the problem here is not the seriousness of the sin. Talking in the synagogue during *chazaras hashatz* is certainly a serious sin, but there are sins that are considerably more serious. The problem is something else entirely.

What do you think happened when the Cossack massacres began? What do you think the people of a town or village did when they saw Cossacks thundering towards them on their big horses? They ran to the synagogues and prayed desperately to God. They prayed "complete prayers" with faith and confidence in the power of their prayers to save them. And they prayed without arrogance and complacency like "beggars standing at the door." But it was to no avail. Their prayers were not "immediately accepted." Why? Because God said, "When you came to the synagogue during the good times, you sat there talking with your friends and neighbors during *chazaras hashatz*, as if this were not a holy place. You made a mockery of the prayers directed to Me. Now you come to pray? Now you come to say *Avinu Malkeinu*, Our Father, Our King? If I am a Father, where is My honor? If I am a King, where is My reverence? (*Shemos Rabbah* 46:4) Did you consider me your Father and your King when you sat and chatted in My Presence during the good times? It is too late. Your prayers are not accepted."

That is why talking in the synagogue during *chazaras hashatz* is a "sin too great to bear." It is the height of negligence. Talking in the synagogue neutralizes the most potent defensive weapon in the Jewish armory, which is prayer. And then when calamities loom, Heaven forbid, when we suddenly realize we are in a crisis situation and we turn to God with faith and sincerity, it is too late. The power of prayer has been forfeited, and we are left defenseless.

If we look closely at the language of the Rambam, we find that he always groups *teshuvah* and *tefillah*, repentance and prayer. These two go together. Why? Because when we get ready to pray, if we want our prayers to be effective, we must first clear our record.

We have to express our regret for talking in the synagogue, if we ever did it. We must express our regret for offering up "incomplete prayers" devoid of faith and confidence that God listens to our prayers and responds to them. We must express our regret for all those times we prayed without proper humility and subservience, like prosperous householders rather than beggars standing at the door. And we also have to express our determination to improve in the future. Our repentance is not expedient. It is not meant just to make today's prayers effective. It has to be a full repentance. Only then can we begin to pray. Only after we ask forgiveness for our neglect and abuse of prayer can we expect God to accept our prayers.

If we really believed that "by Your great kindness do I come into Your House," we would appreciate all the wonderful opportunities God has given us to come close to Him and be uplifted. We express to Him our deepest gratitude for the opportunity to enter the portals of the synagogue and ask Him for all the good things, material and spiritual, we want Him to provide for us. During the Ten Days of Teshuvah, we would be beside ourselves with joy that God has given us the opportunity to "seek Him out when He can be reached."

The shortest line in the *Avinu Malkeinu* prayer is "*kasveinu besefer zechuyos,* inscribe us in the Book of Merits." Most people fly right through it. They concentrate when they ask for good health and when they ask for prosperity, but the book of merits? They don't even give it a second thought. But perhaps we should.

What does this mean, inscribe us in the book of merits? Either we have the merits or we don't. If we have earned the merits, He will undoubtedly enter them into our account even without our asking for it. And if we have not earned the merits, what do we expect Him to do for us? Enter a few extra ones in our account that we haven't earned? Are we asking Him to fiddle with the accounts?

R' Daniel Movshovitz of Kelm proposed quite an original explanation. Every Rosh Hashanah, God not only determines how much a person will earn but also how many opportunities he will have to perform *mitzvos*. How many opportunities will he be given to perform a *mitzvah* and thereby build his share in *Olam Haba*, the next world, the eternal world, the only really meaningful world? So we beg of Him, "Inscribe us in the book of merits. Give us the opportunities to gain merits of eternal value. We are ready and willing to do the job."

This is one of the most important parts of the judgment passed on each individual on Rosh Hashanah, and we have to beg for our share of opportunities like beggars standing at the door, hungry for these priceless opportunities. And we have to do it with "complete prayers," confident that if we pray for them, God will give them to us.

R' Elya Lopian once spoke at length about that part of the Selichos in which we speak to the *machnisei rachamim*, the Heavenly messengers "who bring in our prayers." We ask them to bring our prayers to the Master of Mercy. He asked, who are these Heavenly messengers? And he explained that when someone comes to the door and asks us for a charitable contribution, he may very well be one of these Heavenly messengers.

In fact, the Gemara brings a number of instances where people were saved from death in the nick of time because they performed a *mitzvah* at the very moment they were meant to die. God granted them the opportunity to perform a *mitzvah* at that critical moment, and they had the good sense to take advantage of it. But if God had not sent them this opportunity with a Heavenly messenger, they would never have gained that extra bit of credit that meant the difference between life and death.

This what we ask for when we say, "Inscribe us in the book of merits." Give us the opportunities to gain merit. It is not up to us, but to You. Give us the ability, the means and, above all, the opportunities to accumulate merit. Give us the opportunities to come to the synagogue with health and vigor and the wisdom to stand like beggars at the door and offer up our "complete prayers" to You.

During the war years, the Mirrer Yeshivah escaped to Shanghai, China; it was the only yeshivah to remain intact. The whole world was in flames, and the men in the yeshivah knew that their families at home in Europe were in the gravest danger. When Yom Kippur came, one can well imagine the mood of the yeshivah and the intensity of the prayers.

Shanghai is a humid place, and on that Yom Kippur, it was so suffocatingly hot, so hot that the men, perspiring profusely, prayed in their shirtsleeves, a liberty unheard of in the strict decorum of the Mirrer Yeshivah. People fainted from the heat and exhaustion, but the prayers continued with undiminished intensity. So much was at stake.

Against the eastern wall in the front of the yeshivah stood R' Chatzkel Levenstein, the Mashgiach, in his long black caftan and his *tallis* over his head, impervious to the heat and humidity. As was his custom every Yom Kippur, he took a very long time with each Shemoneh Esrei, concentrating on every word with all his strength, as if he bore the weight of the entire Jewish people on his frail shoulders. And so he spent just about the entire day standing, going from one Shemoneh Esrei almost directly into the next.

The men of the yeshivah were very moved by the sight of the holy sage, their revered and beloved spiritual leader, praying with such intensity and so oblivious of his surroundings, and they wanted to do something for him, something that would mean a lot to him. And so they had an idea.

After Maariv was over, R' Chatzkel was, of course, still saying the Shemoneh Esrei, and everyone knew that it would be a while before he finished. They decided to say the Havdalah quickly, have a bite just to break their fast and come back to the *beis midrash* to learn. When R' Chatzkel finished his Shemoneh Esrei, he would turn around and see the whole yeshivah learning the holy Torah, and he would be pleased.

A few minutes after all the students were in place, R' Chatzkel turned around and saw them, and he smiled with pure delight. With tears in his eyes, he addressed his beloved students.

"My precious children," he began, "Let me tell you something. I felt that the prayers of the yeshivah this Yom Kippur were higher and purer than those of any year before. And the repentance was sincere and complete. It was a very special day, an extraordinary day. But I know that some of you are thinking to yourselves that this moment of inspiration will pass. Tomorrow will not be Yom Kippur, and we will slip back from this high place onto which we have climbed today. So did we accomplish? What was the use? Let me tell you a story.

"There was once a man who built himself a beautiful mansion, a real palace. It took a long time to build, and he decided to make a celebration in honor of the completion of the construction, during which he himself would place an extravagant ornament on the pinnacle of the roof. He invited all his friends and family to participate, and in full view of them all, he climbed up to the roof to affix the ornament to his mansion. Just then, a sudden gust of wind blew him off the roof. He dropped the ornament and tumbled to the ground. Dazed and rolling around in agony, he cried out, '*Oy*, my mansion has fallen down. My mansion has fallen down. All my work was for nothing.' His friends and family rushed over and reassured him, 'Your mansion hasn't fallen down. You have. You may have broken bones. You may have to go to hospital. But when you recover, the mansion will still be there. You'll be able to go into it. It hasn't fallen down."

"My dear children, we built a mansion this Yom Kippur. Every prayer we offered up is like a different room, and all together we have constructed a beautiful mansion. If tomorrow we feel that we've lost some of our inspiration, I want you to know that the mansion has not fallen down. It will be we who have fallen down. The mansion will still be standing. It will stand forever. One day, we will enter that mansion once again. When and how, that depends on us, but the mansion will always be there waiting for us. It will be there forever."

R' Chatzkel's words of encouragement to his students in the heat of a world war are an important lesson to all of us. When we stand in the synagogue and prepare to pray to God, the thought can sometimes be so intimidating that we may lose heart. We know that it will take so much emotional and spiritual effort to reach the highest level of prayer to which we aspire. Who knows if we will be successful? And even if we are, will we be able to maintain ourselves on that high level? Or will we fall back to earth, so to speak? And if we do, is all the effort worthwhile?

The answer is, yes, most definitely yes. All the effort is indeed very worthwhile, because every transcendent prayer builds us a beautiful mansion. And no matter what happens, that mansion will endure forever.

CHAPTER SEVEN

Faith vs. Effort

Success is a goal to which virtually all people aspire, although different people define success differently. Some may aspire to financial or social success, others to creative or intellectual success, and yet others to spiritual success. But all have in common the desire to be successful. How does a person become successful?

The Torah teaches us to have *emunah* and *bitachon*, faith and trust, in God to provide all our needs, because He controls the entire world. If He chooses to give, we have. Otherwise, we do not have. Success comes from God alone. At the same time, we must also make *hishtadlus*, a bona fide effort to achieve our goals.

We cannot simply sit back and say to God, "All right, send me my monthly check." We must make an effort to earn it, and then God will send it to us.

Why do we need to combine faith with effort? And if we do, what exactly is the proper balance between them? How much faith must we put into our effort and how much effort into our faith?

Faith comes naturally to all people. Every person bases his life on faith and trust. Otherwise, how would he step onto a plane or take a morsel of food into his mouth? How does he know that the pilot is properly trained to fly the plane? How does he know that all the parts of the plane are in working order? How does he know the food in his mouth is not poisoned? Obviously, a person could not exist without faith. The question is where he invests his natural faith. Does he have faith in other people? Does he have faith in his own abilities? Or does he have faith in God?

The Jewish people have faith in God. We know that everything is in God's hands and that the efforts of people are really ineffectual without God's help. But what does it mean to have faith in God? Does it mean to have faith that He will do for us whatever we want done? If we have faith that God will make us rich, does that mean that He will make us rich? If we have faith that God will heal us, does that mean that He will heal us? Can we control God with our faith?

Not at all. Having faith is to believe that everything He chooses to do is good and just and that He can do whatever He wishes in all circumstances and situations. A man is sick, and the doctors tell him he has only a ten-percent chance of survival. Statistically speaking, the man is doomed. It is a virtual certainty that he will die. But the faithful Jew knows that God is not bound by statistics. The faithful Jew knows that his chances of survival do not depend on statistics but on his finding favor with God. If he prays for a cure, if others pray for him, if he can accumulate merit in other ways, God may heal him even if he has only a ten-percent chance of survival. But if he lacks the merit, a ninety-percent chance of survival may not save him. The faithful Jew knows that his life down to its most minuscule details is completely and exclusively in God's hands.

If so, why do we need to make any efforts on our own behalf? Why not just let God do whatever He wants to do since we have no real power to affect our own fortunes?

Actually, effort also comes naturally to a person. It is the way people are constructed. The lower forms of life such as plants exist without making any effort. Everything happens by itself. Air flows in, rain falls from the sky, nutrients rise through the roots, and the plant lives — even though it has made no effort toward its survival. Animals and birds, however, need to make an effort to survive. They forage for food and seek shelter from the elements. For whatever reason, God chose to make this the nature of the higher forms of life.

Human beings also exist only by exerting an effort. They cannot expect to live like plants standing in the garden. They have to lift the food and put it into their mouths. Only small babies and invalids do not sit and stand and walk and dress themselves. All fully functioning human beings exert an effort in their day-to-day existence. But how much effort? Animals and birds do not work from nine in the morning to five in the afternoon and overtime during tax season. God "provides food for the beast, for young ravens that cry out" (*Psalms* 147:9). Only people have to invest such an enormously complex and sophisticated effort in their livelihood and sheer existence. Why is this so?

The *Chovos HaLevavos* gives two reasons. One is *bechinah*, testing. The process of *hishtadlus*, effort, provides the setting for the performance of *mitzvos*. There are laws and commandments that apply to every step in a person's efforts to exist; plowing, reaping, buying, selling, everything a person does in pursuit of his livelihood is governed, regulated and restricted by the *mitzvos* of the Torah. Everything provides him with an opportunity to demonstrate his loyalty and obedience to God. There is also a particular test here to a person's faith. A person of insufficient faith might perceive a conflict between the fulfillment of *mitzvos* and his efforts to earn a livelihood. Since *mitzvos* often restrict his freedom in the marketplace, he might see them as an interference, an obstacle to prosperity, and be tempted to transgress from time to time. A truly faithful person, however, understands that prosperity comes only from God's generous hand; he will never disregard a *mitzvah* for the sake of personal gain.

The second reason is *yegiah*, toil. If a person did not have to spend so much time and energy in pursuit of his livelihood, he would be at the mercy of the *yetzer hara*, the evil inclination. A person is naturally inclined to gratify his physical drives and desires, and it is only through a great effort that he can overcome them and resist sin. A person who works hard or is otherwise occupied in some aspect of *hishtadlus* usually doesn't have the time or the opportunity to sin. By the time he comes home, he is quite exhausted. The *yetzer hara* finds him sitting in a chair, his eyes drooping, his feet feeling like lead, and begins to entice him with all sorts of inappropriate suggestions. And it is a struggle. Should he listen to the *yetzer hara* or not? Hopefully, he will be able to resist. "I'm too tired," he will tell the *yetzer hara*, "and besides, it is not allowed." His exhaustion will allow him to see clearly and differentiate right from wrong. But what if he were free all day? What if the *yetzer hara* could follow him wherever he goes and constantly whisper invitations in his ear? It would be practically impossible to resist. "Work," says the Mishnah (*Avos* 2:2), "makes one forget sin."

Therefore, concludes the *Chovos HaLevavos*, a person who attains a high level of righteousness no longer needs so much *hishtadlus*. First of all, he has already shown his loyalty and obedience to God by the exemplary life he has led. Furthermore, his strong attachment to the Torah gives him much greater control over his *yetzer hara*, and he is not as vulnerable as other people are.

In addition to these two fundamental reasons, R' Eliyahu Dessler, in *Michtav Me'Eliyahu*, offers yet another. Effort also serves to give the appearance that a person's livelihood is the result of natural processes. We find throughout the Torah that God clothes miracles in natural causes as much as possible. For example, the wind blew all night before the splitting of the Sea of Reeds (*Exodus* 14:21), although it could easily have been split simply by Moses raising his staff. If a person would earn his livelihood with no effort other than prayer, it would be an unmistakable miracle. Therefore, we clothe our faith in the illusion of effort.

This then is why we have to make an effort and cannot rely completely on faith. We do not have to exert an effort because God needs our assistance. God is perfectly capable of giving us all that we need, just as He provides food for the ravens. We have to exert an effort in order to perform all sorts of *mitzvos* that we wouldn't have the opportunity to encounter otherwise. We have to exert an effort in order to have a fighting chance in the battle against the *yetzer hara*. In other words, we have to exert an effort in order to accumulate the merit we need to gain God's blessings. We have to have faith that all blessings are in God's hands alone, and we have to make the effort so that we will become purified and worthy of receiving those blessings.

We should put no faith in our efforts, because our efforts are not the direct cause of our blessings. But we should put a lot of effort into our faith, because faith and closeness to God are the true sources of all the blessings we receive in life.

How can we test ourselves, in an honest moment, if we indeed have the proper perspective on faith and effort? How can we tell if we really believe that effort is only secondary to faith? We tell by the way we balance prayer and effort.

Sometimes, a man runs into the synagogue, says his prayers quickly, and then he is out the door, in a big rush to get to the office. If he had a major business meeting with an important prospective client in the morning, of course, he would not be in such a rush to bring the meeting to a close and get back to the office. He would understand that the meeting is more critical to his success than any tasks waiting for him back at the office. But he has no patience for the prayers. Obviously, he considers his efforts to be the primary cause of his success. He relies on his own efforts, but he also goes to the synagogue to show God that He also plays some role in the business. So he gives a passing thought to his upcoming business meeting during Shemoneh Esrei at the appropriate blessing, and even while he is asking God to help him at the meeting, he is also considering different ways to persuade the prospective client to sign on with him.

This man has supreme faith in his own efforts. He expects that his talents and cleverness will bring him success. But being a good and faithful Jew, he also believes that he could use a boost from God. A little help from Heaven is always welcome, especially when you're dealing with a reluctant but very important client. It does not occur to him that all his efforts have nothing to do with his success. It does not occur to him that the time spent in serious prayer is far more crucial to his success than any business meeting he may have on his schedule.

The man that has real faith, however, will invest all his efforts in his prayers. He understands that blessings come directly from God, that his efforts are no more than an obligation, a condition for success rather than a means to achieve success. He prays with all his heart, because he knows that this is the only effective way of achieving success. He understands that the most important effort is sincere prayer.

Then an interesting thing happens. As he concentrates more and more on his prayers, he draws ever closer to God. His faith becomes deeper and more textured, and he gains an even clearer understanding of the true nature of the world. He realizes more than ever that it is his prayer rather than his efforts that bring him success. He prays with more concentration and faith than he ever did before — which brings him to an even deeper faith in God. The cycle draws him higher and higher, bringing him the material and spiritual success that he needs to accomplish his purpose in life.

This same cycle works in the opposite direction as well. The person who invests his faith in his own efforts does not really have time for prayer. He rushes through his prayers and runs to his meeting. If the meeting does not go well, he tells himself he was not sufficiently prepared. So he prepares better for the next meeting. He regretfully has to cancel his Gemara class the night before the meeting, because he has too much paperwork to do. He stays up late until all his work is done. Finally, he falls into bed and gets a few hours' sleep. He comes bleary-eyed to the synagogue the next morning, stumbles through the prayers with less concentration than ever, jacks himself up with a few cups of strong coffee, and he is off to the meeting, perhaps with a quick word to God, "Please help me make this work." Then he finds himself struggling, and he cannot understand why it is so. It does not occur to him that he has misplaced his faith and misdirected his efforts.

The Gemara (*Bava Basra* 123a) discusses Jacob's special bequest to his son Joseph of those lands that he had "taken from the Amorites with my sword (*becharbi*) and my bow (*uvekashti*)" (*Genesis* 48:22). Can these words, asks the Gemara, be taken literally? Doesn't the Psalmist state (*Psalms* 44:7), "For I do not trust in my bow, nor does my sword save me?" Rather, explains the Gemara, when Jacob spoke of "my sword," he meant his prayer, and when he spoke of "my bow," he meant his entreaties.

This is more than just a metaphor. Targum Onkelos actually translates the words *becharbi uvekashti* as *bitzlosi uv'va'usi*, my prayer and my entreaties. The sword and bow and the prayer and entreaties are one and the same. Jacob actually did wrest the land from the Amorites with his sword and bow. That was his effort. But he understood that effort is not what is important. It was the prayer behind it that won him the land. Outwardly, it may have appeared that Jacob excelled as a great swordsman, a master archer, but Jacob knew the truth. He excelled as a man of faith, a man who understood that his swordsmanship was effective and his arrows flew true only because of his prayer. The physical sword and bow were a mere formality, a fulfillment of his obligation to make an effort and a means of concealing the miraculous nature of his conquest. The real sword and bow, the real weapons of conquest were Jacob's prayers and entreaties.

The connection between faith and prayer is very profound. It is not simply that a person who has faith understands that he must pray to achieve success. The effectiveness of prayer derives from the very essence of faith. The greater the faith, the more effective the prayer. Why is this so?

Let us consider for a moment why prayer should help at all. A person is having difficulty earning a livelihood. He does not have enough money for his expenses, and he is sliding into debt. If this is happening, God clearly has ordained that it should be so. What good then is it for a person to plead with God for a reprieve?

The commentators explain that it is impossible for a person to persuade God to change His mind. After all, how could such a thing be? A person cries out to God, "I know that my fortunes are in Your hands. I know that my business is failing because You want it to fail. Please let me make a decent living." What does this person expect from God? Does he expect God to say, "All right, you seem like a nice fellow, so I'll disregard My earlier plans and give you what you want"? It doesn't make sense. Now if a person were to repent and make a renewed commitment to Torah study and *mitzvos*, we can see how that would be effective. But prayer alone? Why should it work?

The answer is that prayers do not change God's mind, they change the one who prays. A person who really embraces prayer with full seriousness enters the cycle of prayer and faith and becomes transformed. The more he prays, the greater his faith, the more worthy he is of God's blessings.

When a person stands before God with humility and faith and pleads for his livelihood, God listens. "Yesterday you didn't recognize that health, wealth and happiness come from Me," says God. "Yesterday you thought you were a tough guy who could accomplish anything he set his mind to do. You had such over-whelming faith in yourself and your skills and talents, so I decreed that you should be completely on your own. If you have faith in yourself, prosper or suffer by it alone. But now you stand before Me with a contrite heart. Now you are ashamed of your foolish-ness, of your former arrogance. Now you are a different person. You are no longer that arrogant man from whom I turned away yesterday. You are My faithful son, and I will give you what you need. Yesterday's decree does not apply to you."

The more we pray, the greater our faith, the more clearly we see God's hand in everything, the worthier we are of receiving God's blessings, the more we invest our efforts in prayer. This is the cycle of prayer and faith.

So this is the system. It is a process of growth that requires time and patience. It starts with being a bit more aware of what we say when we pray, of concentrating on the words and their meaning. It starts with giving priority to the prayers and not rushing through them. Little by little, it will dawn on us with a sense of reality that we are standing face to face with the King of Kings, the Master of the Universe, and we will tremble with awe and rever-ence. It will dawn on us how powerless we are and how insignifi-cant are our efforts, and we will realize that the keys to all we desire are right here where we stand and that everything else is an illusion. This is the discovery of faith. This is the road to success.

CHAPTER EIGHT

Darkness Before Dawn

It seems that in recent years we have seen a great increase in suffering among the Jewish people. We hear so many stories about families with all sorts of problems, struggles with earning a livelihood, health problems, broken homes, wayward teenagers, handicapped children, young mothers and fathers dying of dread illnesses. The list just goes on and on, and every day, it seems to get longer. And we cannot help wondering why these things are happening to these poor, innocent families. What have they done wrong? Why do they deserve this sort of misery?

In truth, we can never really understand how God runs the world. He has numerous intricate designs and purposes, and everything He does fits into this vast divine plan. But still, we cannot help but wonder why at this stage of our exile we are seeing such an increase in suffering in the ordinary walks of life. These are not the consequences of war or some other major catastrophe. Suffering and tragedy have become the commonplace feature of everyday life. Why is this so, and what can we do about it? Let us look into the Torah for the answer.

A very strange and totally unexpected thing happens when God sends Moses down to Egypt to bring the Jewish people out of bondage. Everything seems to be in place for the great liberation. God has chosen Moses to be the redeemer of the Jewish people and given him his exact instructions. He has also given Moses the secret sign that will convince the Jewish elders that he is the genuine messenger of God. He comes to the elders, gives them his sign and delivers his message of redemption. They accept him as the Jewish redeemer. It is time to go to Pharaoh and demand the release of the Jewish people. It is time to say, "Let my people go!"

The story is building to a climax. Moses, Aaron and the elders set off for the royal palace. Hopes are high. Hearts are pounding. God has heard the prayers of the Jewish people. After centuries of enslavement, the final redemption is at hand.

But this is not exactly what happened. In fact, the opposite took place. The Torah tells us (*Exodus* 5:1-8), "And then Moses and Aaron came and said to Pharaoh, 'So said God ...' And the King of Egypt said to them, 'Why should you, Moses and Aaron, disturb the people from their affairs? Go take care of your own tasks.' And Pharaoh said, 'Behold, the people of the land are now numerous, and you are keeping them from their tasks.' And on that day, Pharaoh commanded the taskmasters of the people and their [Jewish] supervisors (*shotrim*), saying, 'You shall no longer give straw to the people to make bricks, as you did yesterday and the day before. They shall go and collect straw themselves. Yet you shall demand of them the number of bricks they have been making yesterday and the day before, do not reduce it, for they are becoming indifferent, therefore they shout, saying, "Let us go sacrifice to our Lord." Let the workload on the men be made heavier, and let them be occupied with it, then they won't be distracted by foolish things.'"

What has happened here? Instead of redemption and liberation, the enslavement gets even worse. The people are no longer supplied with straw, and nonetheless, they are expected to produce the same number of bricks. Jewish misery reaches new depths. Why should such a thing happen just when the end of the exile seems to be in their grasp?

And this is not the end of it. The Egyptian taskmasters warn them that they must produce the same number of bricks as before. The people struggle desperately under the new, impossible regulations, and of course, they fail to reach their quotas. If they could barely meet their quotas when straw was supplied to them, how could they possibly meet their quotas when they had to collect their own straw? The Egyptian taskmasters are furious, as we read (ibid. 5:14), "And the [Jewish] supervisors of the people of Israel (*shotrim*), those whom Pharaoh's taskmasters had appointed over them, were beaten, saying, 'Why haven't you completed your quota to make bricks as you did three days ago, neither yesterday nor today?'" The Jewish supervisors complain to Pharaoh, but it is useless.

Some of the people then turn on Moses and Aaron and lash out at them. Why did they have to come and make trouble? Why did they have to cause Pharaoh to become even more antagonistic to the Jewish people? Why did they have to give him a weapon to use against them?

Moses is stung by the unexpected developments. He had thought he was coming to alleviate the situation of the Jewish people, and instead, he only made matters worse. He cannot bear the thought of all the pain he has caused his Jewish brothers and sisters, and he complains to God (ibid. 5:22-23), "My Master, why have You ill-treated this people? Why have You sent me?

From the time I have come to Pharaoh to speak in Your Name, he has ill-treated this people, and I have not performed any rescue for Your people." And God tells him (ibid. 5:24), "Now you shall see what I am about to do to Pharaoh ..."

Why did God have to do it this way? Why did He have to create such misery in the Jewish condition and confusion in the Jewish mind? If He wanted to strike Pharaoh with the spectacular plagues, He could have simply hardened Pharaoh's heart to Moses' demand, as He indeed did later on. Pharaoh could have refused to release the Jewish people, and the plagues would have begun. Why did He allow Pharaoh to increase the misery of the bondage at this very moment when He had already sent Moses to redeem and liberate them? Why did such a deep darkness have to descend on the Jewish people just when they had seen the first glimmers of the light of freedom?

There is another enigmatic verse in this episode. After the supervisors are beaten for failing to fill the daily quota of bricks, they complain to Pharaoh, but he arrogantly dismisses them. And then we read (ibid. 5:19), "And the supervisors (*shotrim*) of the people of Israel saw them in evil (*bara*), saying, 'You shall not reduce the number of your bricks day in and day out.'" What exactly does "[they] saw them in evil" mean? What did they see?

So Rashi explains that they saw the evil and the suffering that had befallen the oppressed Jewish laborers when the taskmasters had said, "You shall not reduce the number of your bricks day in and day out." In other words, the Torah is showing us the Jewish supervisors' inner feelings, that they shared the misery of their brothers. But if so, this verse is really out of place. It should have been told to us before, when the Jewish laborers were subjected to Pharaoh's new cruel and unreasonable regulations, not after the whole story has already taken place. We are left in puzzlement. What is the special significance of this cryptic statement?

How can people bring an end to their suffering in all circumstances? What can they do to extricate themselves from unbearable situations? Of course, they can always do more *mitzvos* and good deeds and accumulate merit in their favor. But what if their merits are insufficient? What if the gap is simply too great? Is there another way out of suffering? Is there a short cut, so to speak?

R' Elya Lopian explains that there is another way. The key is in the Gemara (*Shabbos* 151b), "*Kol hamerachem al habrios merachamim alav min hashamayim.* Heaven is merciful to all those who are merciful to other people. *Kol she'eino merachem al habrios ein merachamim alav min hashamayim.* Heaven is not merciful to those who are not merciful to other people." God has Thirteen Attributes of Mercy, and we can activate some of them for our favor. We can arouse God's merciful response toward us, and the way to do it is by being merciful to other people.

God responds to us *middah keneged middah*, measure for measure. If God sees us emulating His ways, if He sees us fulfilling the *mitzvah* of loving others as we do ourselves, then He responds to us in the same way. If we are kind and merciful to other people, even if they are undeserving, then God is kind and merciful to us, even if we are undeserving.

This is a hard and fast rule, and it works both ways. "Heaven is merciful to all those who are merciful to other people." All those who are merciful, all of them, are treated mercifully, measure for measure, even if they don't deserve it. And conversely, "Heaven is not merciful to those who are not merciful to other people." Those oblivious to the suffering of others deprive themselves of Heavenly mercy, measure for measure, even if they have accumulated enough merits to deserve it.

The primary role of merits is to earn reward in *Olam Haba*, in the next world. In this world, they can alleviate suffering only when the sufferer does not face situations where he can help others. If he does face such situations, his response will determine how God treats him. If he is merciful to others, God will be merciful to him. If he turns his back on others that he could have helped, God will ignore him as well.

In this light, explains R' Elya Lopian, we can understand what happened when Moses first went down to Egypt. The appointed time of redemption had arrived, but there was a problem. The Jewish people did not deserve to be redeemed. Mired in *mem-tess shaarei tumah*, in the penultimate level of spiritual defilement, they simply did not have enough merit to bring an end to their suffering. And yet God wanted to redeem them. But He couldn't just forfeit all the standards and rules by which people are released from dire situations. There had to be a rationale.

We find during the period of the Judges that God delivered the Jewish people from calamity with the attribute of extreme empathy (*Judges* 10:16), "*Vatiktzar nafsho ba'amal Yisrael*. And He could not bear the distress of Israel." God says that He feels so close to the Jewish people that He feels their pain and cannot bear it, so to speak. This attribute could activate the redemption, but the Jewish people would have to do something to activate this attribute. If they could show extreme empathy for each other, then God would show extreme empathy for them. If Jews could show that they felt the pain of other Jewish people as if it were their own, if they could show that they found this pain unbearable, then God would feel their pain and also find it unbearable, so to speak. And the redemption would follow, even if the Jewish people hadn't earned it with their merits.

So what did God do? He engineered a situation for the Jewish people in which they would have the opportunity to respond to each other with this transcendent extreme empathy. He caused the bondage in Egypt to become that much darker and the experience that much bitterer. He caused the suffering to increase to unbearable proportions. And He did all of this for only one reason: so that among the Jewish people there should emerge those individuals who would rise to a higher level of sensitivity, those individuals who would feel the suffering of their brothers to the very core of their beings and find it unbearable, those individuals who would show how they felt by their actions and words. And indeed, these individuals did emerge, and through their spiritual heroism, they facilitated the redemption of the entire people.

Who were these heroic individuals?

They were the *shotrim*, Jewish supervisors of the laborers.

The Torah tells us that the *shotrim* "were beaten" when the people failed to meet their brickmaking quotas. But the story is not so simple. The Midrash explains that the Egyptian taskmasters did not really hold the *shotrim* responsible for the failure of the laborers to meet their quotas. Rather, the responsibility fell on each laborer. If he failed to make the number of bricks expected of him, he was to be beaten. If his shortfall was small, he was to receive a small beating. If his shortfall was large, he was to be beaten severely. That was the Egyptian policy. That was how they expected to discipline the Jewish laborers and ensure that they produced what was expected of them, regardless of how unreasonable the expectation.

When the Egyptian taskmasters came to inspect the brick production of a particular labor battalion, they would calculate the brick production target based on the number of laborers in the battalion. If there was a shortfall, they would ask the *shotrim* for a report detailing the brick production of each laborer under their supervision. Based on this information, they would decide what level of punishment each man had earned.

But the *shotrim* refused to do it. They "saw [the Jewish people] in evil" circumstances. They "saw the evil and the suffering that had befallen the oppressed Jewish laborers," as Rashi explains. They felt in their own hearts the anguish and suffering of their Jewish brothers who were being driven beyond the limits of human endurance, and they could not bear to watch them suffer one iota more. They could not bear to stand by and let their oppressed brothers be beaten brutally for failing to meet the ridiculous Egyptian quotas. And so the Midrash tells us that they said, "Better we should be beaten than they should be beaten."

These gallant *shotrim* refused to turn over to the Egyptian taskmasters the list of each laborer's production. "Do with us as you wish," they said defiantly, "but we will not give you the list. It's enough that our brothers suffer from the backbreaking work. We cannot let them be beaten as well. We are prepared to accept the punishment in their stead."

And so the *shotrim* were beaten. Willingly, they took upon their own shoulders the whiplashes intended for the shoulders of their Jewish brothers. And by this act of extreme empathy, by showing that they felt the pain of their brothers and found it unbearable, they activated the Almighty's attribute of extreme empathy and set the redemption in motion.

This, explains R' Elya Lopian, is what God meant when He said, "Now you shall see what I am about to do to Pharaoh . . ." The description of the feelings of the *shotrim* is not just incidental information. Rather, those feelings are the direct triggers of the redemption. Now that the *shotrim* have "seen [the Jewish people] in evil," now that they have felt as if they themselves were trapped in these desperate, unbearable, evil conditions, now that they have shown such extreme empathy toward their brothers who are suffering, now that they have activated My own extreme empathy toward the Jewish people, now the time has finally come. Now you shall see what I am about to do to Pharaoh. Now you shall see the redemption of the Jewish people even though they haven't earned it through their own merits.

From time to time, during the various exiles of the Jewish people, there have been periods of deep darkness, of exceedingly terrible suffering. And if we look back, we see that these usually took place right before periods of redemption. People refer to these times as the deeper darkness that comes before the dawn. But why should it be this way? Why should there be periods of such intense darkness before the dawn of redemption?

The Jewish *shotrim* of Egypt provide us with the answer. It is that very darkness that brings the dawn. When God wants to redeem us but finds insufficient merit to justify a redemption, He intensifies the darkness. As the suffering of the Jewish people reaches unbearable levels, certain people rise to the occasion. They feel for each other. They bear the burdens of their suffering brothers, and they move heaven and earth to help them. And this extreme empathy brings the dawn of redemption for the entire Jewish people.

The times in which we live certainly qualify as a period of intense darkness. The Jewish nation as a whole finds itself in a precarious position, under attack from all sides, persecuted, abused, maligned. Blood flows on the holy soil, and there is no end in sight. In Jewish homes in all parts of the globe, there is also an unusual amount of suffering. All around us we see heartbreak and heartbreak and more heartbreak.

I do not believe that all of this misery is being visited upon us in order to exact punishment for sins and transgressions. I believe that it is rather to bring us to reach up to God with higher levels of prayer and to reach out to our fellow Jews with higher levels of compassion.

Our generation has apparently not accumulated enough merit to earn redemption. But we are nonetheless in the final days of our long and bitter exile. We are finally on the threshold of redemption, but we lack the merit to actually make it happen. But God wants it to happen. Destiny has brought us to our appointed time, to the last moments before the dawn, but how shall we move forward? How shall we cross the final barrier between oppression and liberation?

God has given us the key. He has darkened our world, sending down so much suffering that we cannot help but see it everywhere we turn. But suffering is not always a punishment. It can also signal the opening of the *shaarei rachamim*, the gates of mercy, and it is important that those of us who suffer accept their lot with trust and faith. As for the rest of us, this is our opportunity to respond to our suffering brothers as the *shotrim* responded to the suffering of the oppressed laborers in Egypt. This is our opportunity to rise above our safe and comfortable little corners and truly feel for our brothers and sisters who live with hunger, pain, anxiety and sorrow. This is our opportunity to experience and express extreme empathy, to show that we hurt and weep with our people, that their pain and grief are our own. If we do this, then God will also bring to bear, *middah keneged middah*, measure for measure, His own attribute of extreme empathy and send us the final redemption speedily and in our days.

CHAPTER NINE

Stop the Robbery

There are many commandments in the Torah, many things we are supposed to do and many we are forbidden to do, and it is sometimes difficult to determine the level of importance the Sages assign to each of these commandments. So we have to look into the sayings of the Sages and the prayers they formulated in order to find the answers. Most instructive are the prayers of Rosh Hashanah and Yom Kippur.

We know, of course, that we cannot transgress a commandment in the Torah, but what exactly is the philosophical rationale for this? There are two schools of thought.

According to one view, when God tells us to do a *mitzvah*, He is like a doctor prescribing a medication for a patient. God in His infinite wisdom understands that the patient — us, in this case — will benefit from doing the *mitzvah*; he will accomplish great things in the spiritual world. In the mystical imagery of the Kabbalah, when a person performs a *mitzvah*, he is in effect "building cities and great edifices in the eternal world of the spirit," and when he sins he wreaks terrible, terrible destruction in the higher, spiritual worlds.

If so, God and humankind have a doctor-patient relationship. When you ask a patient why he is taking a certain medication, he will say, "Doctor's orders." So why is he obeying these "orders"? Has the doctor threatened to send him off to prison if he disobeys? The doctor has simply given him his instructions and left, and still, the patient feels compelled to obey. Why? Because he knows it is for his own good. If he obeys the doctor he will recover, but if he doesn't obey he will cause himself irreparable harm. This self-interest is sufficient motivation for obedience.

Self-interest is also the motivation for obedience to God. He constructed the world, and He knows exactly how it works, and in the Torah, He has given us His prescriptions for living. If we obey Him, we will produce these great spiritual edifices from which we will derive benefit for all eternity, and if we disobey, we will cause destruction and be forced to endure the most dreadful consequences in this world and the next. This is undoubtedly an excellent motivation for obedience.

According to a different school of thought, God and humankind have a king-servant relationship. The world belongs to the King, and the servant only exists at the sufferance of the King. The servant is obliged to satisfy every one of the King's wishes and demands without question or explanation. Disobedience runs the risk of severe punishment or even worse. Therefore, when God commands us to do *mitzvos*, the explanation and motivation are irrelevant to us. As servants, we are obliged to obey.

If a king tells his servant to stand on his head, the servant will instantly do so. He has no choice. Should someone ask him why he is standing on his head, he will say, "Why? I don't know why. Because the king told me to stand on my head. If it's a choice between standing on my head and losing my head, I'd rather keep my head, even if I have to stand on it." If a doctor tells his patient to stand on his head, the patient will also do it. But when he is asked why he is doing it, he will say, "Because it is good for me. My doctor told me to do it twice a day for three or four minutes at a time. I think it is supposed to improve my blood circulation." A completely different approach to obedience.

These are the two opposing views, and the general consensus is that both are valid. God is certainly King of the Universe, Master of our fate, and we owe Him absolute obedience. The question of how our obedience or disobedience will affect our personal condition is not a consideration. At the same time, it is also a good idea to do as God tells us, because He means our own good. God is perfect; nothing we can do will bring Him any benefit. The benefits of obedience affect only us, as do the consequences of disobedience.

The Viduy, the confession of our sins that we say so often on Yom Kippur, begins with three statements. "*Ashamnu*. We were guilty. *Bagadnu*. We rebelled. *Gazalnu*. We robbed."

The word *ashamnu*, according to the Vilna Gaon, is more accurately translated as "we destroyed," related to the word *shemamah*. As such, it refers to the doctor-patient relationship that exists between God and us. We are making a general acknowledgment that through our misdeeds we have wreaked havoc in the higher worlds. We confess to having sown destruction when we transgressed. With the next statement, *bagadnu*, "we rebelled," we are also making a general acknowledgment about our disobedience. We confess that we rebelled and thereby violated the king-servant relationship that demanded absolute obedience. With the third statement, we begin to get into specifics. And what do we say? "*Gazalnu*. We robbed."

Robbery apparently heads the list of the transgressions we must confess on Yom Kippur. Why is this such a critical transgression? But first let us ask a more basic question. What does it have to do with most of us? Are we robbers? Do we break into other people's houses or hold them up in the street and take their wallets?

Actually, most of us are treading very close to the edge of robbery. In fact, the Gemara states (*Bava Basra* 165a) that most people step over the line and are guilty of robbery in one form or another. This is, of course, not a reason to feel complacent, to think that we're no worse than other people are. On the contrary, it is a reason for alarm. If this transgression is so widespread that most people are guilty of it, how much more vigilant and circumspect do we have to be to avoid falling into the trap. If the danger is so great, then the precautions must be equally great.

So why is robbery such a prevalent transgression? In what way are so many supposedly honest people guilty of it?

When the Torah forbids *gezel*, robbery, it is not only referring to burglars and highwaymen, where the robber removes property from the owner's possession and takes it into his own possession. There are also other, more subtle forms of *gezel* that are equally forbidden under this general transgression.

One of these alternate forms of *gezel* is called *oshek*, which means withholding someone else's rightful property. If someone lent you an object or asked you to watch it for him for a while and you deny having it, that is *oshek*. If someone lent you money and you deny it or if you are late in paying it back, that is also *oshek*, unless the lender gives you an extension. If you bought a product in a store on credit and do not pay your bill, that is also *oshek*, unless the storekeeper gives you an extension. If you are late with your rent payment, that is also *oshek*, unless the landlord gives you an extension.

Another form of *gezel* is causing damage to other people's property. The Torah deals extensively with the amount and form of payment for every conceivable type of damage — from the person causing the damage himself to damage caused by his animals, property, fires or obstacles. But no specific *mitzvah* in the Torah specifically defines causing monetary damage to another person's property as a transgression of Torah law. *Rabbeinu Yonah* contends that all forms of damage are included in the general prohibition of *gezel*. When you cause someone damage you are removing from him a portion of the value of his property, and this is considered *gezel*. It doesn't matter if you put it into your own pocket. If you remove it from another person's pocket, it is *gezel*.

And how about a worker who does not deliver a full day's work for a full day's pay? The Gemara says that a worker is exempt from saying the Shema, because he is obligated to his employer who is paying him for his time. So what if someone goes to his job and takes his paycheck but spends some time conversing with his fellow workers or making personal telephone calls, not to mention if he takes office supplies home for personal use? Isn't this absolute *gezel*?

And what if a young man is learning in yeshivah and takes a *kollel* check or support from his family but comes late to yeshivah or misses days altogether? And what if he wastes much of his time talking to his friends about all sorts of nonsense when he should be learning Torah? Isn't this absolute *gezel*? How careful we have to be.

Here is another common pitfall. People like to be independent. They don't want to feel beholden to others, so they don't accept charity or gifts. A person doesn't want to live off charity; this is very commendable. A person refuses gifts from other people; this is also very commendable. The Torah says (*Proverbs* 15:27), "*Sonei matanos yichyeh*. One who loathes gifts will live long." Turning down gifts is certainly a noble gesture. So how does this person who needs money but refuses charity and gifts survive? He borrows money and tries to make it on his own.

Now, this is all good and well if he fully expects to be able to repay the money he borrows. But what if he doesn't know how he will repay it? Or worse yet, what if he never really intended to repay it? Then all his noble gestures are worthless, because he has become a thief. Far better that he should live off charity or the generosity of friends and family than to take money under false pretenses.

The Psalmist declares (37:21), "*Loveh rasha velo yeshalem.* The villain borrows but does not repay." Borrowing with no concrete plan of repayment is the height of villainy, the most insidious, underhanded form of *gezel.* The borrower presents himself to the lender as a trustworthy person. He assures him that his money is secure, that it will be paid back on time. But once the money is in his pocket, he no longer thinks about the lender's concerns, only his own. The money is now in his pocket, and the lender can wave good-bye to it. So this villain has managed to extract the lender's money through subterfuge. He did not break into his house nor did he point a pistol at him, but he robbed him nonetheless.

And here is yet another common pitfall. Our Sages say (*Berachos* 8a), "One who lives by his own efforts is greater than one who fears Heaven." Based on this statement, some people claim it is better to go into business than to learn Torah while being supported by others. Rather than stay in *kollel*, they want to "live by their own efforts." Many if not most of these people really mean this sincerely; they much prefer to live by their own efforts. There are some people, however, who are just using this argument as an excuse to demean *kollel* people.

The Chofetz Chaim has a way of calling their bluff. What do you mean, says the Chofetz Chaim, when you say you "live by your own efforts"? A person can only be considered to "live by his own efforts" if he can account for every penny that has come into his hands. If even a single penny is the product of less than perfect honesty and perfect integrity in business, he absolutely cannot be considered a person who "lives by his own efforts." He is living off someone else's money. And if he enjoys those ill-gotten gains, he is much worse than is the person supported by others while learning Torah. At least, the one learning Torah got the money with permission and, in exchange, is sharing the merits of his Torah study with his supporters. But the less than perfectly honest businessman is taking money from others without permission. He is also being supported by other people, but against their will. He is no better than a thief.

All this is what we should have in mind when we stand on Yom Kippur and say, "*Gazalnu*. We have robbed." We should not say it by rote as part of the liturgy, as if it doesn't really relate to us. It very much relates to each of us. If the Gemara states that most people fall into the trap of *gezel*, this should be of major concern to us. Were we successful in avoiding the prohibition of *gezel*? Did we meet all our financial obligations on time? Did we request extensions of the repayment schedule when we could not pay on time? Did we deliver full value for any monies we received? Did we cause anyone damage in any way or form?

We have to prepare for this confession of "*gazalnu*" long before Yom Kippur, because it is ineffectual unless we first fulfill our obligations to the victims of our *gezel*. We have to pay back all monies we owe, and we have to make restitution for all damages we caused. Even if we only caused a slight damage, even if it is only a pennyworth, it is considered as grave a transgression of the prohibition of *gezel* as if we had caused huge damage; *gezel* is *gezel*, no matter how great or how minor. And repayment is not enough. We also have to beg the victim's forgiveness. Only then can we come before the Master of the Universe on Yom Kippur, confess our transgressions and ask for His forgiveness as well.

The Chofetz Chaim finds another powerful indication of the overriding importance of avoiding *gezel* elsewhere in the Yom Kippur prayers. Yom Kippur, he points out, is "the last day with a connection to the previous year." Although we know that the last day before Rosh Hashanah was the last calendar day of the previous year, the days after Rosh Hashanah until and including Yom Kippur are nonetheless connected to the previous year. In other words, if an average person should die two days after Rosh Hashanah, the judgment that decreed his death was not issued two days earlier but fully a year earlier. Since judgment is sealed on Yom Kippur, the cycle of judgment is from Yom Kippur to Yom Kippur.

Furthermore, writes the Chofetz Chaim, Yom Kippur is "also the best day of the entire year, for on this day our sins are forgiven." The most important prayer of Yom Kippur is the Neelah prayer, the "climax of all the awesome prayers," because this is the time of last resort. The Heavenly portals are closing, the day is waning, and these last desperate moments we offer up our final Yom Kippur prayer. What do we say? "*Atah nosein yad* . . . You give Your hand to sinners, and Your right hand is extended to receive those who repent. And You have taught us, O God our Lord, to confess all our sins before You, so that we will desist from the *oshek* in our hands . . ."

Listen to these words. God is actually stretching out His hand, so to speak, and saying to the sinner, "Take hold of My hand, and I'll pull you out." Who can refuse such an offer? And in order to be pulled out, God has "taught us to confess all our sins." And why? So that "we will desist from the *oshek* in our hands." So that we will repay the monies we owe and make restitution for the damages we have caused. This is the terrible crime that Yom Kippur allows us to correct. How clear it is, concludes the Chofetz Chaim, that it would be devastating to leave Yom Kippur with the taint of *gezel* still on our hands.

So why indeed is the prohibition against *gezel* of such prime importance?

If we dig down to the roots of *oshek* and *gezel*, we find the twin evils of *sheker* and *mirmah*, falsehood and deception. Truth would prevent a person from taking property that is not his or talking another person into lending him money when he has no serious intention of repaying it. Falsehood and deception are the ideas, the concepts, while *oshek* and *gezel* are the deeds that result. If a person were not inclined to falsehood, if he were not a dishonest person, he could not do these things.

Falsehood, the absence of the attribute of truth, is a sign of extreme corruption. The *Sefer HaChinuch* uses strong language to describe it (§ 74). "It is well known," he writes, "that everyone considers falsehood abominable and shameful. Nothing is more despicable. Misfortune and curses are found in the homes of those who love it. God is the Lord of Truth, and everything about Him is truth. Therefore, blessing can be found only among those who resemble Him in their behavior, who are truthful just as He is truthful. But those whose behavior is the opposite of His good traits, specifically those who embrace falsehood and are thereby the exact opposite of His traits, will not receive the blessings of joy, peace and pleasure, which are among [God's] traits. Instead the Lord gives an evil person a portion of worries, quarrels and pain.

"Therefore," concludes the *Chinuch*, "the Torah uses an expression to characterize the prohibition against falsehood that it does not use to characterize any other prohibition elsewhere in the Torah. The Torah states, '*Mi'devar sheker tirchak*. Keep your distance from false words.' Stay far away from falsehood, because it is so despicable."

Throughout the Ten Days of Repentance, we beseech God to have mercy on us. We repeatedly refer to His attribute of truth and ask Him to judge us with that very attribute and bless us with a good new year. But if we are guilty of *oshek* and *gezel*, if we ourselves epitomize the attribute of falsehood, then we are the exact opposites of God. How then can we brazenly ask Him to bless us? God looks down upon us and says, "Who is this person that is asking for a judgment of truth? He doesn't even begin to know the meaning of truth."

On Yom Kippur, we beseech God to inscribe us in "the book of life, blessing, peace and a good livelihood." We acknowledge that all these things are in His control. Whether or not we earn a decent livelihood in the coming year depends solely on Him, and in the light of our recognition of His absolute power, we ask Him to provide a decent livelihood for our families and ourselves. What kind of hypocrisy is it then to go out and cheat and swindle, to gain a few extra pennies by violating the laws of the God in Whom you have supposedly placed your trust? So what does this mean? Do you think you can earn God's mercy and blessing with insincere lip service?

So this is where we must concentrate our efforts all year and especially on Yom Kippur. If we want to take upon ourselves just a single area of improvement, this should be the one, to "desist from the *oshek* in our hands." The Torah demands of us honesty and integrity. Before we can approach God with any hope of acceptance, we have to give back all our ill-gotten gains. We have to pay up what we haven't paid or at least negotiate realistic terms that we intend to honor, even if our creditors have completely forgotten about the money owed to them. And we also have to ask their forgiveness for the wrongs we have done to them. Only then can we have a proper *teshuvah*. Only then can we approach God with clean hands.

Sefer Mitzvos haGadol (the *Smag*) also addresses the importance of honesty but from an entirely different perspective (*Mitzvas Asei* 74): "I have already spoken about this," he writes, "to the exiles of Jerusalem in Spain and other places of exile. Now that the exile is stretching far too long, the Jewish people should turn away from useless worldly pursuits and embrace the Holy Blessed One's seal, which is truth. They should not lie to other Jews or to gentiles or deceive them in any way at all. They should sanctify themselves by refraining even from some things that are permitted to them. For it is written (*Zephaniah* 3:13), 'The remnant of Israel will do no evil, nor will they speak falsehood, nor will deceitful tongues be found in their mouths.'"

Before we come to the startling conclusion of his statement, let us just take a few minutes to take note of the *Smag's* profound advice for those that want to achieve the attribute of truth, for those that seek to develop within themselves absolute honesty and integrity. Listen to the connection he makes. "Turn away from useless worldly pursuits and embrace the Holy Blessed One's seal, which is truth."

What does enjoying the pleasures of the world have to do with attaining truth? Why should we turn away from worldly pursuits if we want to be truthful? It is to avoid putting pressure on ourselves, to avoid putting our honesty to the test. Being involved in worldly pursuits awakens the *yetzer hara*, the evil inclination. It makes a person want more and more things that he really doesn't need. If he can't afford those things he desires, he is tempted to turn to *oshek* and *gezel* to help him acquire them. Soon he finds himself spending so much money on luxuries that he is no longer able to afford the basic necessities of life. He cannot put food on the table or pay for the tuition of his children. And this puts even greater pressure on him to cheat and swindle and seek all sorts of dishonest ways to close the gap in his overstretched budget.

How can this be? Doesn't the Gemara tells us (*Beitzah* 16a) that a person's income is determined on Rosh Hashanah and Yom Kippur except for tuition expenses; the more one spends on Torah education for the children, the more one receives? Isn't there a separate account for tuition? Why then do we see that people often do not have the money to pay for the tuition of their children?

People often ask these questions, and I once heard a clever man reply, "God did indeed give you a special account for the tuition of your children, but you've spent it in the department stores!"

If we are accustomed to a life of luxury, there is no end to what we will spend and to the financial difficulties that are likely to arise. And when that happens, it is a short distance to *oshek* and *gezel*. We can only protect ourselves by staying far away from them, by "distancing ourselves from false words." How do we keep our distance? By "turning away from useless worldly pursuits." If we can't afford something, it's not for us. We really don't need all those extra things we have convinced ourselves that we must have. We can manage perfectly well without them. And if we don't want to do without, that is where falsehood begins. That is when there is a grave danger that we may become dishonest. If we want to "embrace the Holy Blessed One's seal, which is truth," we must "turn away from useless worldly pursuits." This is the advice of the *Smag*.

So let us now return to pick up the thread of the *Smag's* argument. Why is it so critical that the Jewish people become scrupulously honest in this seemingly interminable exile? Why is it important that we avoid even those leniencies that are permitted to us? Because, writes the *Smag*, "the remnant of Israel will do no evil, nor will they speak falsehood, nor will deceitful tongues be found in their mouths." This is a reference to Messianic times when only a remnant of the Jewish people will survive. Who will be left over from the great devastation that will precede Messianic times? Who will be there to witness the triumphant arrival of the Messiah? Who will share in that wonderful experience? Only a small remnant of the Jewish people. And who are these people, the worthy remnant of the Jewish people? They are the people that "do no evil nor speak falsehood nor are deceitful tongues found in their mouths." If we want to be part of that remnant, then we too have to be scrupulously honest. Now that Messianic times are approaching, warns the *Smag*, we must prepare by improving our honesty dramatically.

But why is this so? Why will God single out only the honest and truthful people as the survivors of the exile and the witnesses to the Messiah's arrival? What about all the Jews who made great sacrifices to keep Shabbos, to buy *tefillin* and wear them every day? What about the people who moved heaven and earth to find a beautiful *esrog* and *lulav*? What about the people that rose early every morning in the freezing winter and blistering summer and never missed praying with a *minyan*? Why are the people who are honest and truthful so much worthier than all the others who also expressed their devotion and loyalty to God and His Torah?

The answer is that God wants the arrival of the Messiah to be a *kiddush Hashem*, that it should be a sanctification of His holy Name. For this, we need honest and truthful people. The *Smag* explains, "In the future, when the Holy Blessed One will redeem [the Jewish people], the nations of the world will say, 'He has acted justly, for they are truthful people, and the Torah of truth is in their mouths.' But if the Jewish people deal underhandedly with the nations of the world, they will say, 'Look at what the Holy Blessed One has done! He has chosen for Himself thieves and swindlers!'"

When the final redemption arrives, the nations of the world will stand in awe and admiration of God's spectacular revelation on behalf of the Jewish people. So the nations of the world will take a close look at the Jewish people they know, the ones being brought forth from their long exile with such honor and glory. And the nations of the world will wonder, Who are these people? Why should God perform such miracles for them? Why do they enjoy such a special closeness with God? How have they earned it?

Now, where do the nations of the world encounter Jewish people? Do they come into the *yeshivos* and observe them learning the holy Torah with such devotion and enthusiasm? Do they come into the synagogues and see them praying to God three times a day with fervor and intensity? Do they observe them on Rosh Hashanah and Yom Kippur with tears flowing freely as they plead with the Creator for His forgiveness? Do they observe them standing on Succos with *esrog* and *lulav* in hand and expressions of sheer joy on their faces? Do they observe them sitting at the candlelit Shabbos table singing the praises of the Creator and speaking words of Torah?

No, the nations of the world do not regularly see the Jewish people in any of these settings. They only meet Jewish people in the marketplace, and the way these Jews behave in the marketplace determines the opinion of the nations of the world. If the Jews they meet are dishonest, if they cheat and swindle, if they do not meet their obligations honorably and on time, if they cannot be trusted, if they are underhanded and deceitful, if they excel at trickery, then the nations of the world will consider them inferior. And if God works magnificent wonders to bring them forth from exile with fanfare and honor, they will be dismayed. "Look at what the Holy Blessed One has done!" they will say. "He has chosen for Himself thieves and swindlers! For these people, He had to send the Messiah?"

This would be a terrible *chillul Hashem*, a desecration of His holy Name, and God will not allow it. So what will He do? Either He won't bring the Messiah and leave us in exile, Heaven forbid, or He will weed out all the thieves, swindlers and liars so that only an honest "remnant of Israel" is left, people who "will do no evil, nor will they speak falsehood, nor will deceitful tongues be found in their mouths." These are the only people who will emerge triumphantly from exile, because these are the only people whose salvation will bring honor to His holy Name.

But it goes even further than that. If the nations of the world know us only through encounters in the marketplace, then it is not enough to maintain ordinary standards of honesty and integrity. It is not enough to be considered a person of honor and not a thief or a swindler. Because the nations of the world will still be puzzled. They will look at us and say, "All right, these are fine upstanding people. You can't argue with that. But there are many other fine upstanding people in the world. What makes these people so special? Why do they deserve that God should perform such miracles for them?"

The nations of the world, of course, do not see us in the *yeshivos* and the synagogues. They do not see us at the Shabbos table. They have no firsthand knowledge about the sublimity and holiness of life according to the Torah. They only know us in the marketplace.

Therefore, we must be outstanding in the marketplace. We must be so scrupulously honest and truthful with the nations of the world that they will stand in amazement. We must endeavor to make a *kiddush Hashem*, to sanctify His holy Name, with everything we do, even in small ways; if a Jew comes back to a store in the driving rain because he was given too much change and wants to return it, he makes a *kiddush Hashem*. We must use our honesty, integrity and truthfulness to gain the respect of the nations of the world. Then they will understand why God says (*Isaiah* 49:3),

"You are My servant, Israel, in whom I glory." Then they will bow their heads when the Messiah comes and say, "God has acted justly, for the Jewish people are indeed truthful people, and the Torah of truth is in their mouths."

So honesty and the rejection of *oshek* and *gezel* in all their forms are really the keys to our redemption. No matter how much we pray to God and beseech Him to send us the Messiah, we ourselves cannot expect to participate in the final redemption if we are not scrupulously honest. We cannot expect to be numbered among the "remnant of Israel" unless we have made a *kiddush Hashem* in our dealings with the nations of the world. This extends to all sorts of ethical behavior as well, but honesty and integrity in the marketplace are at the very top of the list. And it goes without saying that we behave this way to each other, because that is where it all starts. If we are not genuinely honest and truthful people, if we cheat and swindle each other, it will not help to pretend to the nations of the world that we are people of integrity. We will not be able to fool them. They will see right through our masquerade.

Honesty is also critical in another aspect of our lives. We are completely dependent on prayer. We really cannot expect God to favor us and supply all our needs unless we pray to Him. If we want our prayers to reach Heaven, we have to be honest. The only prayers that are heard are those of people who have returned anything in their possession that doesn't belong to them or those who have never done anything that can be considered *gezel* in the first place.

Job said to his friends (*Job* 16:17), "Because there is no plunder in my hands, and my prayer is pure (*tefillasi zakah*)." The Midrash comments (*Shemos Rabbah* 22:3), "Rabbi Yehoshua the Kohein said in the name of Rabbi Nechemiah, 'Can there be an impure prayer (*tefillah akurah*)? Rather, it means that if someone whose hands are soiled with *gezel* calls out to the Holy Blessed One, He does not answer him. Why? Because he is praying in a state of sin … But Job, having no ill-gotten gains, had a pure prayer.

Therefore, he could say, "Since I have no plunder in my hand, since there is no wrongdoing in my hands, my prayer is pure."'"

Listen to the words of the Midrash. God will not heed the prayer of someone "whose hands are soiled with *gezel*." An interesting phrase. "Whose hands are soiled with *gezel*." Job also speaks about the hands. "There is no plunder in my hands." It seems that ill-gotten gains stick to the hands. It is as if the dishonest person has sticky hands, and when other people's money passes through his hands, some of it remains stuck there. When a person with sticky hands prays, God finds it offensive. The stickiness of his hands is like a sediment of impurities polluting his prayer and making it a murky and tainted *tefillah akurah*, an impure prayer.

This is very worrisome for all of us. We may have fallen into some form of *gezel* quite casually. Perhaps we didn't give it much thought. We may have borrowed something and forgotten to return it. We may have caused someone even a slight damage and not made restitution. But lack of intent does not exonerate us. If we retain money in our possession that is not ours, whether it belongs to someone else or is overdue to be repaid to someone else, we are guilty of *gezel*. And if we stand before God with our sticky hands, He may consider our prayer a *tefillah akurah*, Heaven forbid.

The very first mishnah of *Bava Kama* states, "There are four major categories of damages [for which one is responsible], *shor*, *bor*, *mav'eh* and *hev'er*." Three of these are easily understood. Although *shor* is translated as an ox, it means that the owner is responsible for damages caused by improperly controlling any of his animals. A *bor* is a pit that a person digs or uncovers. A *hev'er* is a fire he sets. But what is a *mav'eh*? This is a very uncommon word. In fact, it is so uncommon that it appears nowhere else. What can it possibly mean?

The Gemara discusses the meaning of *mav'eh* (*Bava Kama* 3b). According to one opinion, it refers to *adam hamazik*, the damages a person inflicts by his own action. A person is responsible for all damages he causes, deliberate or inadvertent. This category of damages is what the mishnah identifies as *mav'eh*. Where do we see that the word *mav'eh* has any connection to a human being?

Although there is no record of this word anywhere else in the Mishnah, the Gemara finds a similar word in the Torah (*Isaiah* 21:12), "The Watchman said, 'Morning has come, and so has night. If you want to beseech, beseech (*im tivayun b'ayu*).'" According to the rules of Hebrew grammar, the action verb *tivayun* changes form to the subject noun *mav'eh* to identify the person who performs the action.

What is Isaiah saying here? *Rashi* explains that the Watchman refers to the Holy Blessed One Who is saying that morning has come for the righteous and night for the evil. If you, the Jewish people, repent and ask for deliverance, you can ask for it. "If you want to beseech, beseech (*im tivayun b'ayu*)." So we see how *mav'eh* can mean a person. Only a person can pray, therefore, only a person can be identified as a *mav'eh*.

But this Gemara is still very puzzling. After all is said and done, why indeed did the mishnah choose to identify the category of damages a person inflicts on his own as *mav'eh*? Throughout *Bava Kama*, this type of damage is identified as *adam*. Why couldn't the mishnah do so as well? Why couldn't the mishnah say quite simply that the four categories are *shor*, *bor*, *adam* and *hev'er*? Why was it necessary to formulate a new, sophisticated and exceedingly enigmatic term to identify a person that inflicts damage? Why *mav'eh*?

Some commentators want to say that the Gemara is telling us that prayer is the essence of a human being. A person is a *mav'eh*, someone who prays, just as King David declares (*Psalms* 109:4), "*Va'ani tefillah*. But I am prayer." This is what he was. A living, breathing prayer. And this is what all people should be. Therefore, the mishnah refers to a person as *mav'eh*.

Be that as it may, why should the Sages of the Mishnah choose to teach us this important truth about the human essence right here in *Bava Kama*? Why in the middle of a list of categories of damage rather than in any of numerous more appropriate places in the vast Talmud? Furthermore, our Sages list ten terms that mean prayer (*Otzar HaMidrashim*, Moshe 27), but *mav'eh*, or any other form of the word, is not on the list. Why doesn't this word appear on that list? And why doesn't the mishnah use one of those ten terms to tell us that the essence of a person is prayer? If anything, the mishnah should have chosen the word *mispallel* to recall King David's "*va'ani tefillah*." Why choose the rare, obscure *mav'eh*?

Actually, if we think into it, the word *mav'eh* is not a general term for prayer. The prophet uses this unusual word to identify a specific type of prayer, and nowhere do we find it used for any other. It refers exclusively to prayer for the *geulah*, for redemption and deliverance, and therefore, it does not appear on the list of general terms for prayer.

When R' Yerucham Levovitz, the great Mashgiach of the Mir, discussed this Gemara, he pointed out that a *mav'eh* must be a very righteous person. If he is identified as a *mav'eh*, he must be a person who prays for the deliverance of the Jewish people all the time. He is not overly concerned with his own personal needs. The focus of his prayer is not his health, safety and livelihood. He is more concerned with the exile of the Jewish people and the distancing of the Divine Presence from Jerusalem. A *mav'eh* seems to be a title of great honor. Why then should the mishnah choose to use this honorable title to describe an *adam hamazik*, a person who inflicts damages?

The mishnah wants to tell us that even the holy *mav'eh*, that great righteous person who spends so much time praying for the redemption of the Jewish people from exile, even he can be an *adam hamazik* if he is not careful in his dealings with other people. Even he may borrow and neglect to repay. Even he may be careless with other people's property and cause scratches and dents. Even he can be guilty of *oshek* and *gezel* if he does not watch his every step. And then what will be with all his holy prayers when he is standing before God with sticky hands? How ironic that by causing damage to others the *mav'eh* may be causing far greater damage to himself by invalidating his own prayers. No matter how holy he is, this *mav'eh*, whose whole essence is the highest form of *tefillah*, can cause himself to lose everything.

Where does the mishnah teach us these lessons? Right at the beginning of the Order of *Nezikin*, which is primarily concerned with fair dealing among people in monetary matters. It is a warning to all of us that disregard of these matters can have terrible repercussions, Heaven forbid. A person that causes damage to another person or to his property, either directly or through neglect, may render his prayers for redemption ineffective. This is the introduction to *Nezikin*. Study these laws carefully and observe them meticulously, because your life and your future depend on them.

So now we understand on another level why the avoidance of *gezel* is such a priority in our prayers on Yom Kippur, why we say, ". . . so that we will desist from the *oshek* in our hands." If we want God to accept our prayers, then we must clean our hands and remove from our possession everything that does not belong to us. Because "if someone whose hands are soiled with *gezel* calls out to the Holy Blessed One, He does not answer him." Dishonesty and deceit create a wall between us and the Creator, a wall that our prayers cannot penetrate. Only by removing all ill-gotten gains from our possession and fulfilling our obligation can we tear down that wall and open the way for our prayers to ascend to Heaven.

CHAPTER TEN

The Power of Speech

Our generation is becoming more and more sensitive to the terrible sin of *lashon hara*, evil speech, a general term that encompasses all sorts of harmful things that people say. We are increasingly aware that such speech destroys people's lives, that it damages or wrecks relationships, that it leads to dissension and strife among the Jewish people.

Why does *lashon hara* lead to all these catastrophic results? The easy answer is that the revelation of hidden facts creates ill will. This is undoubtedly true, but there is a much deeper cause. At the root of all this destruction lies the potentially sinister power of speech. We have to recognize and respect this power if we expect to protect ourselves from its devastation.

Forty years after the Exodus from Egypt, the Jewish people approached the Holy Land and prepared to conquer it. The kingdom of Moav lay directly in the path of the advancing Jewish multitudes, and Balak, king of Moav, feared they would overrun his kingdom. Most fearsome of all was the mighty figure of Moses, the fiery Jewish leader.

In desperation, Balak sent messengers to the elders of Midian. Moses had spent many years in Midian after his escape from Egypt as a young man. He had married a Midianite woman, and his children had been born in Midian. Who would know him better than the elders of Midian?

"What can I do about the Jewish invasion?" he wanted to know. "Their leader Moses appears invincible. What is the secret of his power?"

"*Ein kocho ela bepeh,*" they replied. "His power is in his mouth."

"If so," said Balak, "then I must call for the help of someone whose power is also in his mouth. I will call for Bilaam."

The response of the elders of Midian is a bit puzzling. If anything, one would have expected them to say his power was in his famous staff, the one with which he had administered the plagues in Egypt, with which he had struck the sea and split it apart, with which he had struck the rock to bring forth water. Why did they think Moses' power was in his mouth?

In order to answer this question, we have to go back to the arrival of Moses in Midian many years earlier. On his first day in Midian, he encountered Jethro's daughters at the public well, and he rescued them from a group of troublesome shepherds. They ran back to their father and told him, "An Egyptian man saved us."

Did Jethro's daughters really mistake Moses for an Egyptian?

According to the Midrash, they did not. So what did they mean by "an Egyptian man saved us?" The Midrash explains that the young women thanked Moses for rescuing them, but Moses refused to take any credit for what he had done. He was no more than the agent of divine providence, which had led him to appear at this particular well on this particular day. And then he told them about his history, that he had grown up as a prince in Pharaoh's palace, that he had gone out to see how his Jewish brothers were faring, that he had seen an Egyptian taskmaster beating a Jew, that he had struck down the Egyptian, that he had been forced to flee for his life. He told them how his destiny had led him from place to place until he arrived in Midian on that particular day.

This is what Jethro's daughters meant when they said, "An Egyptian man saved us." The Egyptian taskmaster, by persecuting his helpless Jewish victim, had set in motion a chain of events that led to Moses rescuing them at the well. Most fascinating about this story was that Moses had felled the Egyptian with one of the *sheimos d'kedushah*, the mysterious Names of God that control the forces of holiness. As soon as his lips uttered the holy Name, the Egyptian fell dead on the ground. This sensational story spread through the gossip grapevine of Midian. And so it became known in Midian that Moses possessed great power in his mouth.

After Balak heard what the elders of Midian had to say, he called on his old friend Bilaam who knew the *sheimos hatumah*, the mysterious Names of God that control the unholy forces. Bilaam also had "power in his mouth," and Balak hoped he could neutralize Moses' power.

So here we have the confrontation between the massed Jewish forces on one side and the Moabite defenders on the other. The colossal struggle that looms will be fought between the holy and unholy forces on the battlefield of speech. It pits the power of one mouth against the power of another.

During the Second World War, the world saw a similar phenomenon, where the critical battles in the clash of great powers were fought on the battlefield of speech.

On the side of evil, Hitler was the supreme demagogue. How did he manage to rouse the rabble to such a pitch of frenzy so that they were ready to obey his most malicious and sadistic orders? How did he manage to hoist himself into power and take control of the government? How did he manage to convince the famous German intellectuals to follow him? How did he manage to take a civilized people and turn them into the most despicable barbarians? It was only through the "power in his mouth," in his ability to keep mass rallies of hundreds of thousands of people mesmerized for hours with his hate-filled harangues. More than anything else, Hitler's mouth was the source of his destructive power.

And on the other side, who can forget Winston Churchill's memorable speeches, so eloquent, so inspiring? Who can forget how he reassured his beleaguered people in their darkest hour that they would triumph, that they would "stamp out the evil"?

"We shall fight on the seas and oceans," Winston Churchill declared in a famous speech in 1940. "We shall fight with growing confidence and growing strength in the air, we shall defend our island whatever the cost may be. We shall fight on the beaches. We shall fight on the landing grounds. We shall fight in the fields and in the streets. We shall fight in the hills. We shall never surrender."

This speech and many others like it rallied the reeling British people and gave them the courage to fight. The soldiers in their muddy trenches would huddle over their wireless sets to catch his broadcasts, to hear a few words of encouragement, a spark of hope. This was the most important expression of Churchill's leadership. It was the power of his mouth to bolster the morale of his men and inspire them to fight on to victory.

Rabbeinu Yonah quotes from the *Yalkut*, "The Community of Israel is beloved through its voice and hated through its voice. It is beloved through its voice, as it is written (*Song of Songs* 2:14), 'Let Me hear your voice, because your voice is sweet.' It is hated through its voice, as it is written (*Jeremiah* 12:8), 'She raised her voice against Me, therefore I have hated her.' This is the meaning of that which is written (*Proverbs* 18:21), 'Death and life are in the control of the tongue, and those that love it shall eat its fruit.'"

The tongue controls the power of life and death. One can build with the tongue, and one can destroy with the tongue. One can heal with the tongue, and one can harm with the tongue. One can give life with the tongue, and one can take away life with the tongue. God loves the Jewish people when they use their tongues properly, "because their voice is sweet." And if they do not, He "hates" them, so to speak. Of course, God does not hate the Jewish people. Nonetheless, the prophet employs the harsh word "hate" as a figurative term to show God's extreme displeasure when we abuse the power of speech.

Rabbeinu Yonah focuses on the end of the verse. "And those that love it shall eat its fruit." What does this mean? It refers, he explains, to a person who loves the tongue. In other words, he loves to talk all the time. Indeed, who doesn't like to talk? It is a normal thing. So what is a person to do if he really loves to talk a lot? He should "eat its fruit." He should not satisfy this desire with idle chatter. Instead, he should talk words of Torah, Mussar and wisdom. He should speak about ways to bring people together in peace and harmony. He should speak about ways to raise up the spiritual level of the community. He should praise the good and condemn evil. He should encourage people to seek the truth.

If you like to talk, then talk. That is perfectly fine. No one is stopping you from exercising your power of speech, but you don't have to abuse it. Why do you have to mock people and talk against them? Why wouldn't you rather use your power of speech to bring them together and to raise them up? Be aware that you hold the power of life and death in your tongue. If you feel the natural urge to talk, "eat its fruit." Use it wisely and well.

We find very often in the Torah that a few simple words change the Halachic status of people and articles. One of these is the *mitzvah* of *arachin*, values. If a person says, "*Erki alai*, I accept upon myself my value," he is immediately obligated to donate a sum equivalent to his "value" to the Temple fund. The *Sefer HaChinuch* discusses at length the many aspects of this *mitz-*

vah (§350), but let us focus on his comments regarding its "roots." These are not necessarily the reasons for the *mitzvah*, but rather the channels through which the spiritual sap, so to speak, is drawn into its performance and gives it taste.

"A person can only participate in the higher worlds," writes the *Chinuch*, "through his speech. This is the most distinguished part of the human being. It is what distinguishes him as a person in the verse, 'And the Lord breathed into the person a *nefesh chayah*, a living spirit.' Targum Onkelos translates *nefesh chayah* as '*ruach memalela*, a spirit that speaks.' All the other parts of the body are inanimate [in the higher sense], and if a person were to corrupt [his speech], his body would remain entirely inanimate, a useless vessel. Therefore, a person must keep his word…"

A person "participates in the higher worlds through his speech." What does this mean? Let us understand it on a deeper level.

R' Chaim Volozhiner, in *Nefesh HaChaim*, discusses in depth the concept of *tzelem Elokim*, that a person is created in "the image of the Lord," in order to raise up the sense of self-worth and self-esteem of every single Jew. This long exile in which we find ourselves has brought a steady decline in the physical and spiritual condition of the Jewish people, both as individuals and as a nation. The long decline continues, making us feel increasingly worthless and powerless, as if anything we do, say or think has no real meaning and significance. We don't know our strengths. We don't have goals and a sense of purpose. We don't strive to reach as high as we can. These are the consequences of our exile, and we cannot expect to stop this steady decline unless we gain an appreciation for who and what we are. We can accomplish this, says R' Chaim Volozhiner, by an understanding of the concept of *tzelem Elokim*.

What does it mean to be created "in the image of the Lord"? God has no form and no substance, so how can we be created in His image? Clearly, it is meant only as an expression of a certain similarity. King David writes (*Psalms* 102:7), "I resembled a pelican lost in the desert." Does this mean that he grew wings and a beak? Of course not. It means that he was lonely, forlorn and wandering, like a pelican lost in the desert. When the Torah tells us that humankind was created in God's image, it also means that we were created with a similarity to certain Godly characteristics.

In particular, it refers to the characteristics associated with the Name of *Elokim*, which is translated as "the sole Power in the creation and the control of the world." By saying that we were created *betzelem Elokim*, "in the image of *Elokim*," the Torah is telling us that God gave us the power to control Creation, both in the lower and the higher worlds.

We can more readily relate to the idea of human control of the physical world, but our control also extends to worlds beyond our comprehension and imagination. Just as the unseen puppeteer pulls strings that cause the puppet to move about, so do the actions of the Jewish people in this world pull strings that effect changes in the higher worlds.

Therefore, every person must have *yiras Shamayim*, which is translated as "fear of Heaven." It does not mean that we have to be afraid of Heaven, says R' Chaim Volozhiner. We have to be afraid of God, not of Heaven. Rather, it means that we have to fear the effect of our actions in Heaven. Our every word and deed can build great edifices in the higher worlds.

One day, we will come to Heaven and survey what our lives in this world have wrought in the next. If we are not careful, we may survey a scene of great devastation, with ruins and rubble strewn as far as the eye can see, a scene that would cause us untold pain and anguish. Better to have "fear of Heaven" now, to fear the damage we can do to Heaven, so that when we arrive in Heaven we will find towering spiritual edifices rather than scenes of destruction.

This is R' Chaim Volozhiner's message to every single Jew. No one should say, "What am I? What power do I possess? How can my humble deeds have any influence at all?" On the contrary, he should know and affix in his heart that not one of his deeds, words and thoughts ever goes to waste. If used constructively, they produce eternal edifices, and if used otherwise, one needs to fear the consequences.

We can cause far greater destruction than did Nevuchadnezzar, the Babylonian emperor who destroyed the First Temple, and Titus, the Roman general who destroyed the Second Temple. Nevuchadnezzar and Titus, the archenemies of the Jewish people, are the symbols of destruction, but they had no effect whatsoever on the higher worlds. It was our sins that caused destruction in the higher spheres and undermined the divine support for the Temple in the lower world. The real destruction of the Temple took place in Heaven. The destruction of the wood and stones in Jerusalem was merely the earthly manifestation of the destruction the Jewish people had caused in Heaven with their sinful ways. Nevuchadnezzar and Titus destroyed the wood and stones. We destroyed the Temple. They had no power in the higher worlds, but we do. We have the power to build a Temple, and we have the power to destroy a Temple. Because we were created in God's image.

The prophet declares (*Amos* 4:13), "He forms mountains, creates wind and tells a person about his conversations *(maggid la'adam mah sicho)*." What exactly does "telling a person about his conversations" mean? Does it mean to remind him of the things he said? If so, it should have said *maggid la'adam sicho*. What is the significance of *mah sicho*? R' Chaim Volozhiner explains that it means to tell a person *mah sicho*, "what his conversations are," to show him the far-reaching effects his words have, how they can build and how they can destroy.

Let us take a closer look at the words of the prophet. What do mountains and wind have to do with a person's conversations?

R' Elya Lopian explains that although mountains are massive, solid, immovable, God told the prophet Elijah (*I Kings* 19:11), "A great and powerful wind rips apart mountains and shatters stones." What is a wind? Can you see it? Can you catch it? It is just air. And yet a wind can destroy mountains and shatter stones. That is how God "creates wind." Words can also destroy and shatter, even though they are just air.

Even in this world, the power of speech is far greater than it would appear to us. We understand, of course, that if we say something bad about another person he may lose his job. That is certainly destructive enough. But there is also a destructive side to speech that defies rational explanation. I will give just one example here.

R' Shlomo Wolbe once gave an exceptionally powerful talk to a group of his students in Jerusalem. Afterwards, one of the students came forward. "Thank you, *rebbe*," he said, his eyes wide with reverence and admiration. "This was such a powerful talk. It is so clear that it is the truth that no one could possibly refute it."

"Do you really think no one can refute it?" said R' Wolbe. "I can refute it. And it won't take much, either. Listen: Ha, ha, ha. One word of mockery can counteract one hundred *tochachos*, rebukes."

It is true. A speaker can build up an argument so solid and airtight that he cannot conceive how anyone in his audience will fail to be convinced by the overwhelming logic. And then someone gets up and makes a joke, and the argument loses its entire effect. The precise translation for *tochachah* is "rebuke through the demonstration of the truth." A person may present one hundred logical proofs for the truth, but one word of mockery makes a mockery of it all. How can such a thing be? It is just one example of the awesome power God infused in speech. It cannot be explained rationally.

Why do we use speech so destructively? It all comes down to a lack of faith. We do not have faith in our own importance and significance. We do not have faith in our own power to effect enormous changes both in this world and the next, to build and to destroy.

We can hear a thousand times that the Temple was destroyed because of *sinas chinam*, unjustified hatred, but somehow, deep down in our hearts, we do not believe it. We can hear a thousand times the words of the Chafetz Chaim that if we would stop speaking *lashon hara* about each other we would be redeemed from this long and bitter exile, but somehow, deep down in our hearts, we do not believe it. Why? Because we do not have faith in ourselves.

This then must be our first step to gain control of the power of speech. We have to believe in ourselves. We have to believe that every word we speak leaves its mark in the lower worlds and in the higher worlds. We have to believe that our words can build and they can destroy. We have to recognize the awesome power of speech that God has infused in us, the divine power He has shared with us when He created us in His image. Only if we respect the power of speech can we harness it for the good.

Upreach, Inreach and Outreach

CHAPTER ELEVEN

A Matter of Life and Death

We are standing here one week before Rosh Hashanah.[1] We see the *Yom HaDin*, the Day of Judgment, looming before us. Everything around us proclaims that we are about to be put on trial. The emotional pleas of the Selichos in the early morning hours. The plaintive call of the *shofar* every day after Shacharis. The increase in Torah and Mussar. The heightened tension in the atmosphere. No other time of the year enthralls us so powerfully as do these final days before Rosh Hashanah. No other time cries out

---

1. Adapted from an address delivered in Beth Medrash Govoha on the eve of 23 Elul, 5761 (September 10, 2001), the night before the attack on the Twin Towers.

to us so eloquently, "*Im lo achshav eimasai?* When else if not now?"

Take heed of these penetrating words. *Im lo achshav eimasai?* When else if not now?

There is only a short time left. How we take advantage of it will make a tremendous difference in our lives. It will determine if we are granted spiritual and material success in the coming year. It will determine the course of all things we hold near and dear to our hearts. It can make the difference between life and death. *Im lo achshav eimasai?* When else if not now? If we don't prepare ourselves during these critical days to have a proper Rosh Hashanah, if we don't take a close look at ourselves and make the necessary changes, then all may be lost.

No human being has any assurance about the future. No human being knows what tomorrow will bring, or if he will even live to see tomorrow. All a person knows is that his time on this earth is limited, and that one day he will die.

The theme to which King Solomon returns again and again in the Book of *Koheles* (Ecclesiastes) is that the illusory rewards of this world are not worth pursuing; they are all *haveil havalim*, folly of follies. "Remember your Creator during your youthful years," he writes (*Ecclesiastes* 12:1-5), "before the bad times come, when years arrive of which you will say, 'I have no desire for them.' ... For a person is headed toward his place of eternal rest."

Young person, King Solomon advises, take advantage of your youthful years. It is a time that will never return. You will not stay young forever. You will not live forever. There will come a time when you will lose heart, when you will say, "I have no desire for these years." Whether this means the troubles of the pre-Messianic era or the feebleness of old age or the day of death, you will not be able to rectify the shortcomings of your life; you will lack the morale and the energy. And then it will be too late. Take advantage of your young years, of your vigorous years. Because tomorrow may be too late.

Earlier, King Solomon writes (ibid. 9:10), "Whatever your hand finds the strength to do, do it! For there are no deeds nor calculations nor knowledge nor wisdom in the grave toward which you are headed."

As long as you have the capacity, do something about it. Take control of your life. Fix it. Repair it. For there are no deeds nor calculations nor knowledge nor wisdom in the grave toward which you are headed.

King Solomon is not reminding us about the grave to throw us into a panic. He is doing so to give us perspective. As the Rosh writes in *Orchos Chaim*, "Always keep in mind the day of your death, and prepare provision for your final journey." A faithful Jew does not live with the illusion that this world will last forever. He knows that we are here for only a brief sojourn. He knows that the material pleasures and delights of the world are distractions that can easily divert him from gaining everlasting merit and reward in the next world. He recalls the day of death to remind him that time is short and too precious to be wasted. Because who knows what tomorrow will bring? *Im lo achshav eimasai?* When else if not now?

The Rambam writes (*Mishneh Torah, Hilchos Teshuvah* 3:3), "Just as a person's merits are weighed against his sins on the day of his death, so too are the sins of every person in the world weighed against his merits every year on the holiday of Rosh Hashanah. If he is found to be a righteous person, he is confirmed for another year of life. If he is found to be a transgressor, he is condemned to death. If he is a middling person, his verdict is suspended until Yom Kippur. If he repents, he is confirmed for another year of life. If not, he is condemned to death."

The Rambam draws a comparison. "Just as" a person faces judgment on the day of his death, so too is he judged every Rosh Hashanah. What does he mean to teach us by this comparison?

The point of the comparison is to highlight the focus, the clarity, the truthfulness that are required for a successful Rosh Hashanah. A person on his deathbed is beyond all illusion, beyond confusion. He sees death before his eyes. He knows he is leaving this world behind, and he is completely focused on purifying his soul and repairing as much damage as he can during the last desperate moments of his life.

As we prepare to enter Rosh Hashanah, we must have the same focus and clarity, for we too are not assured that we will live another year. Those who stand before God on Rosh Hashanah and beg for good health and a better livelihood are making a mistake. They think that another year of life is a given, and all they need to negotiate are the terms, the details. But that is not the issue. It is self-delusion. The issue is life itself. Will we live another year? Will we be here tomorrow? We should react to the approach of Rosh Hashanah "just as" we would react to the specter of approaching death. We should gain the same clarity, the same realization of what is meaningful and what is not, the same inspiration. The only difference is that we do not know when our dying day is coming, and it can catch us by surprise. But we do know when Rosh Hashanah is coming, and it is unforgivable to let it catch us by surprise.

We know full well when Rosh Hashanah is coming, and we know what is expected of us. *Im lo achshav eimasai?* When else if not now?

The Rambam writes (*Mishneh Torah, Hilchos Teshuvah* 3:4), "Although sounding the *shofar* on Rosh Hashanah is a Torah decree, it is also symbolic, as if to say, 'Sleepers, awaken from your sleep! Slumberers, shake off your slumber! Scrutinize your deeds, return through repentance and remember your Creator. Those who ignore truth for the foolishness of the moment, who fritter away their years with meaningless folly, useless and ineffective, take a good look at yourselves and improve your ways.'"

Which "truth" is being ignored? To which reality must we awaken? It is the knowledge that life is not endless, that not a single day of it is guaranteed. Therefore, the time to repent and improve is now. *She'im lo achshav eimasai?* Because when else if not now?

Along the same lines, the Meiri writes, "A person should really examine his deeds every day and abandon his sinful ways, as our Sages have said (*Avos* 2:10), 'Repent one day before you die.' In other words, repent today, for you may die tomorrow. Nevertheless, during this time — Rosh Hashanah, that is — a person should be especially inspired. Our Sages have explained this with a parable (*Rosh Hashanah* 16b): 'Three books are open on Rosh Hashanah: one for the righteous, one for the sinful and one for the middling, each of whom is judged according to his deeds.' This is meant to inspire a person to examine his own deeds and to repent from any sins he may have committed. A person that neglects to repent during this time has no part in the Lord of Israel, because the rest of the year does not provide so much inspiration, and the *Midas HaDin*, the Attribute of Strict Justice, takes no notice of him and bides its time until [Rosh Hashanah]."

This is strong language. "A person that neglects to repent during this time *ein lo cheilek b'Elokei Yisrael*; he has no part in the Lord of Israel." Why is this so?

And then the Meiri concludes, "A person should also examine his deeds during troubled times, and also when he endures personal suffering; he should consider that everything comes from God because of sin. Nevertheless, the point of death is the time when everyone who wants to preserve his soul is forced to repent and regret his former rebelliousness, return his ill-gotten gains and confess his sins. *She'im lo achshav eimasai?* Because when else if not now?"

The Meiri makes himself very clear. A person should always be aware that death might be around the corner, not to be plunged into depression, but rather to use this knowledge constructively. Repent one day before you die. Your eventual departure from this world is not a fantasy. It is an important reality, and your awareness of it should have a positive effect on your life.

If you cannot live with the thought of death daily, at least consider it during times of trouble and suffering.

On the day of death, however, everyone who wants to preserve his soul repents. Facing the angel of death, a person knows he has no more choices left. He knows there is no way out. Very soon, he will stand in front of the King of Kings in the Heavenly Court and be asked to give an account of himself. There is no greater inspiration for a human being. Because *im lo achshav eimasai*? When else if not now?

The closest approximation to this inspiration is Rosh Hashanah. God in His mercy holds back the *Midas HaDin*, the Attribute of Strict Justice, all year. But on Rosh Hashanah, when we say that "all the people of the world pass before Him like sheep," how can we avoid thinking about our eventual death? How can we avoid the realization that we need to put our house in order? And if a person still does not repent at such a time, then "he has no part in the Lord of Israel." He is such a cold fish, so completely devoid of human feeling, that even on his deathbed he will not change.

If the mere thought of Rosh Hashanah is not enough to shake us out of our lethargy, God sends us enough messages to remind us that we are not secure with our lives. There is enough going on in the world to throw a fright into us.

Who know if there will even be a world next year?

In every corner of the world, the enemies of the Jewish people are raising up their heads. The Jewish people are not secure everywhere; we are like a lamb among the seventy wolves. We are under attack, threatened from all sides. How can we not take notice? God is talking to us. He is warning us. Forget about material things. Focus on the spiritual. Sleepers, wake up from your sleep! Slumberers, shake off your slumber!

It is comfortable to delude ourselves, but if we open our eyes, we cannot help but see the danger. Just take a look at how many Arabs there are around Boro Park and Flatbush. Thousands! And Heaven forbid, should they ever get it into their heads to make a *jihad* against Jews, I shudder to think of what might happen. What foolish right do we have to feel secure?

There are cities in Europe where thousands of Jews once lived, fine, upstanding Jews and great rabbis and leaders. Go visit these cities today, and you will not find a trace of the vital Jewish communities that once were there. "Imagine if fifty years from now," someone once remarked to me, "they would bring Jews into Boro Park and show them ... that Jews once lived here!"

Can anyone say with certainty that such a thing cannot be? Are we secure? Forget your security. The only security we have is God's protection — if we find favor in His eyes. He is calling out to us. He is telling us to repent, to devote the short time we have left before Rosh Hashanah to soul-searching and improvement. He is saying, "*Im lo achshav eimasai?* When else if not now?"

The fires have not yet been ignited, but everyone who has eyes in his head can see that we are headed for an enormous conflagration. It is up to us, the faithful Jewish people, with our Torah and our prayers, to prevent this fire from consuming the world.

CHAPTER TWELVE

After the Twin Towers

osh Hashanah this year was unlike any we have experienced in a long, long time.[1] We said the same prayers. We read the same portions from the Torah. We sounded the same *shofar*. But it was a different Rosh Hashanah. A very different Rosh Hashanah.

After the passing of the Chazon Ish, the Brisker Rav remarked, "This is more than the passing of a great sage. The world has changed. Until now, we were liv-

---

1. Adapted from an address in Beth Medrash Govoha on the second day of Rosh Hashanah 5762, one week after the attack on the Twin Towers. This chapter also includes elements from related addresses.

After the Twin Towers   ❧ 167

ing in a world with the Chazon Ish, and now, we are living in a world without the Chazon Ish. It is a different world."

I think we can say with certainty that our world has changed as well. Until now, we were living in a world with the Twin Towers. Now, we are living in a world without the Twin Towers. It is a different world. A very different world.

It is hard to look for the positive in a disaster as awful as the terrorist attack on the Twin Towers. It is hard to say that good things may have come out of that morning of utter horror. But as faithful Jews, we recognize the hand of God in all events. We strain to hear the divine messages that speak directly to us in all times and in all forms. We must listen, and if we listen, we will hear and understand.

The Rambam writes (*Mishneh Torah, Hilchos Taanios* 1:3), "If people were to say, 'This thing happened to us in the ordinary course of events; it is just happenstance that we have suffered this calamity,' it would be an act of cruelty ... it would only lead to more calamities." The events of this past week were not happenstance. They were a shattering clap of thunder from the heavens, a call to awakening, a call to introspection, a call to repentance, a call to effect profound changes in our lives.

If we seek out positive messages in this disaster, if we find signs of grace and mercy, if we rummage through the rubble to discover the good that is meant to come out of it, we certainly do not intend to belittle the awful dimensions of the tragedy that has occurred.

There is a saying in the American military that bombing attacks sometimes cause "collateral damage." This means that in order for the primary objectives of a bombing campaign to be achieved there will sometimes be incidental, unintended casualties. Well, acts of God do not cause collateral damage. Divine providence is infinitely complex. Every aspect of every event has a specific purpose, every moment of joy, every bit of suffering is part of the overall divine plan. We believe as an article of our faith that those people who perished in the attack had been inscribed for their fate last Rosh Hashanah, and that all who were spared had their names inscribed in the Book of Life on that very same day. God brought all those people to that place on that day to allow a terrible crime to be committed, so that the entire human race would sit up and take notice. There is no such thing as collateral damage; there are no collateral benefits. Everything is intended. Everything has a message. It is up to us to hear the messages and heed them.

The attack on the Twin Towers was a horrendous crime. It unmasked the face of evil before the world. It caused immeasurable human suffering, thousands of families torn asunder, thousands of widows, widowers and orphans. It spread fear and panic throughout the civilized world. It caused tremendous financial damage; hundreds of businesses failed, and hundreds of thousands of people lost their jobs. It sent shock waves through the international political community and raised tensions in Eretz Yisrael even higher, if such a thing were possible. And then there were the miracles, the thousands of people who should have been there on that day and "just happened" to have stayed away, the forty Hatzalah members given up for dead when the buildings collapsed yet all emerging alive and unharmed. A person would have to be absolutely blind not to discern in these events the divine hand of God steering a world gone awry so that it will right itself and regain its steady course. A person would have to be utterly blind not to see God showing us the stark contrast between good and evil and challenging us to choose.

There is no question in these circumstances about who is the villain and who is the victim. The attack was perpetrated by evil terrorists, cold-blooded murderers who thought nothing of taking planeloads of living, breathing innocent people, defenseless women, children, the elderly, and using them as weapons against thousands of unsuspecting, harmless people. These are the same people who kill innocent Jewish men, women and children almost daily in the streets of Jerusalem, Natanya and all over Eretz Yisrael. They are the angels of death.

America, on the other hand, the victim of this attack, is a wonderful country, the best Gentile nation in the history of the world. It a land of freedom, tolerance and kindness, a safe haven for millions of Jews. But America is not a perfect society. In addition to all its beautiful qualities, it also has its sordid sides. One of the prices of freedom is a decadent, lewd culture, which is unfortunate. Another is the overwhelming sense of *kochi ve'otzem yadi asah li es hachayil hazeh*, "my strength and the power of my hand have produced all this affluence for me" (*Deuteronomy* 8:17).

More than any other people on earth, Americans are inclined to consider themselves masters of their own destiny. They believe in unlimited opportunity, that "the sky is the limit," that "where there is a will there is a way," that there is nothing you cannot do if you set your mind to it. They believe that effort is always rewarded, that if you don't succeed right away, it just means you haven't tried hard enough and often enough.

But where is the Creator in this scheme of things? Where is divine providence? Where are the rewards of goodness and the consequences of sin? Where is the acknowledgment of the Source of all blessings? There is no faith in this world view, no humility, only arrogance and conceit.

Two weeks ago, if one had to choose a single symbol for this American sense of limitlessness, one would undoubtedly have chosen the Twin Towers, these two massive structures reaching halfway to the heavens.

And then they were gone.

In one mind-numbing hour, both of these man-made mountains crumbled and fell, and along with them, American arrogant self-assurance collapsed. The balloon was punctured, and the air hissed out until only a humble, shriveled skin remained. All people were forced to admit they were vulnerable, that they really did not control their own lives, that one streak of fury could undo a lifetime of effort. People recalled that there was a God, and that He ruled the world.

At the very end of *Eichah*, after we have wept bitterly over the ruins of the Temple, we conclude with a wistful prayer (*Lamentations* 5:21), "Bring us back to You, O God, and we will return, renew our days as of old." Tragedy and disaster have brought us to our senses, but it is too late. The Temple is gone. The people are exiled. We have let our good fortune slip through our fingers, and now we mourn. But within the mourning, there is also a glimmer of hope. The gates of prayer are open, and we beseech God to take us back. We plead with Him to bring back our people from exile, to gather us together in peace in Eretz Yisrael and rebuild the Temple. We plead with Him to give us once again the wonderful privilege of bringing sacrifices in the Temple. We plead with Him to "renew our days as of old."

What do we mean by "renew our days as of old"? Which "days of old" are we asking God to recreate for us? For which times do we yearn?

The Midrash explains (*Eichah Rabbah* 5:21), "'Renew our days as of old.' This means the olden times, as it is written (*Malachi* 3:4), 'And the meal offering of Judah and Jerusalem will be as pleasing to God as in bygone days and olden times' ... 'Olden times' refers to the days of Abel, when there was as yet no idol worship in the world."

We are not pleading for the times when the Temple stood in all its glory, when the scent of the sacrifices the Jewish people brought rose up to the heavens. Those times were indeed wonderful, but they were not the best of times. They were not the ultimate. We are pleading for the days of Abel, "when there was as yet no idol worship in the world."

The Jewish people who brought sacrifices to the Temple in Jerusalem were certainly not idolaters. They were fine, upstanding, faithful Jews. Their thoughts and intentions were pure. And yet, their sacrifices were not as "pleasing to God" as the sacrifices Abel brought when there was as yet no idol worship in the world.

Why was this so?

Because when there is idol worship in the world, the very atmosphere becomes contaminated. The spiritual pollution clings to all things, even those that are themselves pure and good. The sacrificial scent that "pleases God" perfectly cannot emanate from the same world that harbors idol worship. And so we pray for days like those of Abel, when the scents of sacrifices rose through pure, unsullied air until they reached the heavens. We pray for days when there will be no idolatry to befoul the pristine air of the earth, to blend its acrid fumes with the holy aroma of our sacrifices.

Today, the air of the earth is somewhat purer than it was two weeks ago. Today, we have learned humility. Arrogance, conceit, self-worship are all forms of idolatry, and they have been greatly diminished. Today, the stench is fainter than it has been in a long time. Amidst all the pain and tragedy, God has handed us an opportunity. Who knows how long this will continue? Who knows how long it will be before people forget that they are not invincible and rediscover their forgotten arrogance? But now the air is fresh and clean. And if we take proper advantage of it, our Torah and *mitzvos* can rise up to the heavens purer than they have ever been.

Fear is another of the unexpected benefits of this great tragedy. Think back to last Rosh Hashanah and Yom Kippur. For what did we pray? *"Uvechein tein pachdecha,"* we beseeched Him. "Please bestow Your fear upon us. Let us be overcome with awe. Let all creatures feel dread." Well, our prayers have been answered. We asked for fear, and we have gotten it.

For many of us, those who are more sensitive to the suffering of our brothers and sisters in Eretz Yisrael, our prayers were already answered in a large measure all through the year. We have been living with fear for many, many months. But now we have all been given such an immense dose of fear that no one can avoid inner trembling. We are all terrified, every single one of us.

So what do we do with this fear? We asked for fear, and God has given it to us. Should we panic? Should we lose our heads in confusion and hysteria? What are we meant to do with this fear? Why did we want it in the first place?

Let us look a little further in the prayers. What did we say after we prayed for fear? We said, "Let all the works revere You. Let all creatures bow down before You. Then they will all become one united group to do Your will wholeheartedly."

This is why we wanted fear. We wanted to use this fear to unite us in our devotion to God. We wanted this fear to bring us to the realization that we are all in God's hands, that we are not in control of our own destinies. We wanted this fear to bring us closer to our Father in Heaven. We wanted this fear to unite all of us, the whole world, all of creation in devotion to the Creator of the Universe.

Well, we have been given the fear. Now we must use it. In Selichos, we pleaded with God to take pity on us for we are *agudim betzarah*, united by sorrow. Now we can also say that we are united by fear. We all share the fear. We are all terrified; that is what God wanted. Now we must unify for Him; that is what He wants.

We fear for our lives, for the safety of our families, but what are we doing about it? Our only hope for refuge and salvation is in God's mercy. That is how we should direct our efforts to allay our fears. That is the only way we will achieve real safety.

People are only people, and in times of crisis, it is only to be expected that they will hunger for every bit of news, every development that may have some relevance to the overall situation. It is understandable that people will be glued to their radios to hear the latest reports. But what is the purpose of listening to the same reports over and over again, repeated from every which angle without adding anything new or meaningful? Is this the best way to calm jittery nerves? If people can find the time in their busy lives to listen to so many redundant, irrelevant reports, surely they can also find time to learn a little more Torah, to do a few more *mitzvos*, to say a few more Psalms, to perform a few more acts of kindness to other people.

Battles, investigations and manhunts will not bring us ultimate safety. "'Not with armies, nor with strength,'" declares the prophet (*Zechariah* 4:6), "'but with My spirit,' said the God of Hosts." We have to bring the spirit of God into our lives. If we want safety, we have to sanctify ourselves, purify ourselves, raise ourselves up, make ourselves more spiritual. We have to pattern our lives after God's ways. We have to be kind and merciful to our families, friends, neighbors, to all people. We have to be compassionate, fair and forgiving. We have to learn the holy Torah and obey its commandments. Armies and strength will not bring us safety. Only closeness to God will protect us. If we dedicate ourselves to being faithful Jews, God will take us under His wings and shield us from all harm.

The wings of an eagle are the metaphor for God's relationship with the Jewish people. He brought us forth from Egypt (*Exodus* 19:4) "on the wings of eagles," and He continues to rescue us and carry us through our perilous history like the mighty king of birds, soaring across the skies and bringing his beloved fledglings to safety.

"Like an eagle," the Torah tells us (*Deuteronomy* 32:11), "He awakens His nest, hovering over His fledglings; He spreads His wings and takes them and carries them upon His wings."

There is so much divine kindness in this description, so much compassion in this comparison to an eagle bearing his fledglings aloft.

Rashi explains that the eagle is a large, heavy bird and its fledglings are tender and frail. Should the eagle land in his nest as other birds do, he would frighten his young. So what does he do? He hovers over the nest but does not land. Instead, he flaps his wings and swoops from tree to tree, shaking the branches and creating so much commotion that his fledglings awake and see him coming, and they prepare themselves to receive this great bird who is their father.

When God comes to judge us and set the course for our future, He does not come upon us all at once. The experience would be too intense. It would be unbearable. So what does He do? He shakes the branches, so to speak. He creates a gathering commotion in the world around us so that we shake ourselves loose from our slumber and take notice. The events that we have witnessed in the last week have caught our attention. The branches and all the trees are still vibrating. We see Him coming. It is time to prepare.

Let us look at the rest of the metaphor. "[Like the eagle,] he carries them upon His wings." Not under his wings but upon them. Unlike other birds that carry their young beneath them, the eagle carries its young upon its wings. Why is this so?

Rashi explains that other birds fear the eagle that flies higher than all of them, and they seek to protect their young from him. But no bird flies higher than an eagle. The eagle's only concern is an arrow shot at him from below. So he carries his young upon his wings to shield them from danger. In the same way, God carries the Jewish people upon His wings, so to speak, and shields from attacks from below.

R' Shamshon Raphael Hirsch makes an additional observation about the comparison to an eagle. The young of all other birds can remain passive and be saved. The father bird grips them in his talons and flies off to safety with them in his grip. But the eagle carries his young upon his wings, and therefore, the young must participate in their own salvation. The eagle comes down low and hovers over its young, and they must jump up onto their father's wings. Otherwise, they will remain right where they are.

The Master of the Universe has come to awaken us from our slumber, we who are the fledglings in His nest. He has stirred the world into an uproar so that we will take notice of His arrival. He has come down to us and spread out His wings.

"Come, My children," He calls out to us. "I have come to carry you to safety. When you are on My wings no harm can come your way. But you must make the effort. You must make the leap. Come, children, jump! Jump higher! Jump as high as you can, and you will finds yourselves upon My wings. Hurry! I am about to carry you aloft!"

CHAPTER THIRTEEN

Ground Zero

Historic events have shaken the world over the past few months,[1] making it a place of uncertainty, fear, danger, where terror lurks around every corner. Many questions are being asked, both among ourselves and in the world at large. What is the role of the Jewish people in these historic world events? How intricately are these events related to us and to what extent do they arise from factors that have nothing to do with us?

It seems to me that these questions should be reversed. It seems to me that all these events are Jewish events, and we must

---

1. Adapted from an address delivered at the Agudath Israel Shabbos of Chizuk in South Florida on January 12, 2002, four months after the attack on the Twin Towers.

ask a different question. What is the role of the world in these Jewish events?

Rashi explains (*Exodus* 7:3) why God displayed so many miracles and wonders in Egypt. God could easily have taken the Jewish people from Egypt anytime, but He chose not to do so. He did not need to conduct a long campaign of plagues to extract Pharaoh's consent. And yet He allowed the process to drag on for months and months until Pharaoh's resistance finally crumbled. Why did He let this happen? Rashi quotes from the Gemara (*Yevamos* 63a) that "the Holy Blessed One brings misfortune to the world so that the Jewish people will take notice and repent." God brought all the plagues on Egypt just to impress the Jewish people with His absolute mastery of the universe.

It was not only in Egypt but also throughout history that God has sought our attention through world events. The Gemara quotes the prophet (*Zephaniah* 3:6-7), "I destroyed nations, their high towers were ruined, I reduced their streets to rubble without passersby, their cities were desolate of people, with no inhabitants. I said, 'Just fear Me, accept reprimand, and her dwellings will not be destroyed, nor everything I laid in store for her, but they rushed to corrupt their deeds.'"

Governments fall. Nations are destroyed. Towers are toppled. Streets are covered with rubble. Cities are depopulated. And all so that the Jewish people will hear God saying, "Fear Me! Hear My reprimand! Then your own dwellings will be spared a similar fate."

The fearsome events we are witnessing on the stage of world events are surely there to send us this message, to teach us lessons we need to learn. So how are we meant to react? What are we supposed to think? What are we supposed to do?

First, let us take a look at how the world reacted and draw a lesson of how not to react. As soon as the Twin Towers were struck, people became frightened and depressed. Many were afraid to walk out of their homes to go the corner store. The marketplaces were virtually deserted, and the economies went into recession.

So what advice did the governments give to the people? "Go back to what was before," they advised. "Go back to normal. Just carry on as if nothing has happened."

This is not our approach. God does not want us to feel insecure. He does not want us to go into recession or depression. But He wants us to grow from the events. He wants us to absorb the messages He has sent us and the lessons He wants us to learn. He wants us to improve and make changes.

The governments say, "Go back to normal." But this is not for us. We are not going back to normal. We are going forward to change.

A new term has entered our consciousness: Ground Zero. It is the term that describes the smoldering patch of rubble where the Twin Towers once stood. But we know that the significance of Ground Zero extends far beyond the scene of the tragedy. It makes us aware that the entire world is really Ground Zero, because all the world bears witness that "*emes Malkeinu, efes zula-so*; our King is truth, there is nothing besides Him." The word *efes* means "zero." We know full well that there is zero in the world other than God. For us, Ground Zero is everywhere.

Certainly, we recognize the dangers around us. Certainly, we are aware of the desperate situations in which our brothers find themselves in different places in the world. But we have responded by putting ourselves in a prayer mode, by accepting that we have nowhere to turn but to our Father in Heaven, that "*ein od milvado,* there in nothing else but Him." Perhaps in the new state of the world, we see it more clearly than we saw it before. And therefore, we also feel more secure. We may feel a little insecurity in ourselves. We may question if we are quite where we should be spiritually. But we are secure in the knowledge that God is with us, that we need only reach out to Him and He will protect us.

In one of his most famous psalms, King David declares (121:1-4), "I lift my eyes to the mountains, from where will my help arrive? My help is from God, the Maker of heaven and earth. He will not allow your feet to falter, your Guardian will not slumber. Behold, He will not slumber nor sleep, the Guardian of Israel."

He lifts his eyes to the mountains and asks, "From where will my help arrive?" Why does he mention the mountains? How do the mountains inspire his question? Our Sages find allusions in the mention of mountains, but what is the *peshuto shel mikra*, the simple meaning of the words?

The Torah refers to God by different Names in different places and situations. All these Names describe His ways and deeds, which is how we perceive His presence. They cannot refer to His essence, because He has no body and no form. We cannot compare Him to any physical being. We can only describe the manner in which He conducts the world, which is reflected by His various names. When He is merciful, we refer to Him by a Name that reflects mercy. When He is strict, we refer to Him by a Name that reflects justice. And so forth.

But there is one exception, one Name that actually uses a physical metaphor to describe God. We refer to Him as *Tzur*, the Rock. Why do we do this? Why do we use a Name that reflects such a confining, physical, material, inanimate object as a rock?

In the highest moments of our prayers, when we come to the connection between Krias Shema and the Shemoneh Esrei, we say, "*Tzur Yisrael, kumah*. Rock of Israel, arise!" Why do we call on the metaphor of God as a rock at this critical juncture of the prayers?

When we reach the Modim prayer in the Shemoneh Esrei, we acknowledge that we are totally dependent on Him, that He holds our lives in His hands, that He is the custodian of our souls, that He performs miracles for us every day, that He performs good and wondrous deeds for us at all times, morning, noon and night. And we begin by saying, "Our Rock, the Rock of our lives!" Again, we use this metaphor of a rock.

And again when we come to the end of the Shemoneh Esrei. We say, "May the expressions of my mouth and the thoughts of

my heart find favor with You, O God, my Rock and Redeemer."
Why do we refer to Him with the metaphor of a rock?

And again on Chanukah in the famous poem known to one and
all. In this poem, we contemplate the history of the Jewish people
through different periods of persecution, and we recall how God
has saved us from danger and destruction every time. And the
poem begins with the famous words, "*Maoz Tzur yeshuasi*. Mighty
Rock of my salvation." Why the metaphor of a rock?

It seems the rock is the only metaphor that can be used to
describe a certain one of God's attributes; if there had been an
abstract metaphor that served the same purpose, it would certainly have been used. What is this extraordinary attribute that only
the metaphor of a rock describes?

In a subsequent psalm, King David speaks about the mountains of Jerusalem (125:2), "As Jerusalem is surrounded by mountains, so does God enfold His people, from now until forever."
God built Jerusalem, the holiest place in the world, with mountains surrounding it on all sides. Why? Because mountains are the
symbol of security, of a blockade that can keep out hostile armies.
Mountains create an air of impregnability.

When the Jewish people came up to Jerusalem and looked at
the mountains, those towering symbols of security, they were
reminded that security ultimately derives from God. They lifted
their eyes to the mountains, and then they asked, "From where
will my help arrive?" They knew that in the end mountains provide only a false sense of security, and they said, "My help is from
God, the Maker of heaven and earth." God enfolds the Jewish
people in the security of His Presence forever and ever.

Nothing gives a person a sense of security like standing behind
a large rock, and what is a mountain if not an immense rock?
When a person gazes upon a mountain, he thinks about security
and stability. He feels he is on sure ground. That is how the
human mind works. Therefore, when we want to focus on the
concept of God as the ultimate source of security, we refer to Him

as our Rock. He is the Rock Who protected us from danger throughout our history. He is the Rock that safeguards our lives and souls every single day, morning, noon and night.

I was once walking in Switzerland with R' Moshe Soloveitchik. We were talking about the mountains, and the conversation turned to King David's question and answer. "I lift my eyes to the mountains, from where will my help arrive? My help is from God, the Maker of heaven and earth." The sequence of the verses had always puzzled me. The speaker of these lines is obviously King David himself. But what about the next lines? "He will not allow your feet to falter, your Guardian will not slumber. Behold, He will not slumber nor sleep, the Guardian of Israel." Who is the speaker of these lines?

The speaker of these lines, R' Moshe told me, is the entire world. Once a person reaches the realization that his "help is from God, the Maker of heaven and earth," the entire world calls out to him, "He will not let your feet lead you to ruin." The mountains set his thought processes in motion, but once he recognizes that his security comes only from God, he sees signs of it everywhere.

During times such as these, when the world wobbles with insecurity, we must turn for reassurance to our Rock, the source of true security. We know what we have to do. We have to raise the level of our prayers and Torah study. We have to strengthen our faith and trust in Him. We have to treat each other with kindness and consideration. If we do all these things, we have no need to become nervous and depressed. We can rely on our Rock, *Maoz Tzur yisheinu*, to protect us from danger, as He has always done.

A rock, however, is not the only thing that reminds us of God's strength. Thunder also does; when we hear thunder, we make a blessing acknowledging that "His strength and power fill the world." But there is a difference. A rock reminds us of God's protective power, while thunder reminds us of the frightening power of His judgment.

Did you ever notice that it usually rains after thunder? Why is this so? The scientists have their explanations and theories. Many years ago, when I was a schoolboy back in England, they told us that thunder is the sound made when two rain-laden clouds bang their heads together and that the crash of the clouds causes them to drop their rain.

R' Elya Lopian disagrees. The sound may very well come from the collision of clouds, as Rashi indicates (*Berachos* 59a). But this collision is not required to stimulate rainfall. God can perfectly well give rain without thunder. The connection is a different one. The Gemara states (ibid.), "Thunder was created for no other reason than to straighten out the creases of the heart." For no other reason! Thunder was not created to shake the rain loose from the clouds. It was created to give people pause and persuade them to correct the flaws of their hearts. So why does it usually rain after thunder?

The world needs rain. It cannot survive without rain. But rain depends on the merit of people. The Torah tells us (*Genesis* 2:5), "For God the Lord did not bring rain onto the earth while there were still no people to work the land." And Rashi explains, "Why did He not bring rainfall? Because there were no people to work the land, and no one to appreciate the goodness of rainfall. But when Adam arrived and understood that the world needs rain, he prayed for rain, and it came down." When there are people who pray and otherwise earn merit, God sends down the rains. Otherwise, He does not.

But what happens when the world, despite its dire need, does not deserve rain? God still wants to bring the rains, but what is He to do? He sends thunder rolling through the world. People are frightened. Somewhere, a few Jews stop and think about the power of the thunder, and it makes them think of God's awesome power. They are humbled, and, trembling with awe, they make the blessing over the thunder, "*Shekocho ugevuraso maleh olam*, that His power and strength fill the world." And in the merit of this recognition of God's mastery, the world is released from its distress, and God sends down the rains.

Every bit of thunder is a forerunner of blessing. It is there to help us "straighten out the creases of our hearts," to remind us that our lives are completely in God's hands and that we are helpless without Him.

Whether it is the thunder of towers that fall, whether it is the thunder of wars that seem imminent, whether it is the thunder of terrorism, whether it is the thunder of sickness in our own families and communities, whether it is the thunder of difficulties with earning a livelihood, the message is the same. All thunders were created to "straighten out the creases of our hearts." The crash of the thunder is meant to awaken fear and awe of God in our hearts and the hearts of the entire community. It is meant to help us open the gates of mercy so that God will rain down blessing upon us.

CHAPTER FOURTEEN

Face
Jerusalem

A t this time in our history, all our hearts are in Eretz Yisrael, especially in Jerusalem, the historical capital of our homeland, the focus of our longing and aspirations. Jerusalem is the heart of the Jewish people, regardless of where they may find themselves.

When the Jewish people were led into exile after the destruction of the First Temple, they sat by the rivers of Babylon and wept, and they made an oath (*Psalms* 137:5-6), "If I forget you, O Jerusalem, may my right hand forget its power. May my tongue adhere to my palate if I fail to remember you, if I do not bring up Jerusalem amidst my greatest joy." In their sorrow, the

Jewish people remembered Jerusalem, and by their oath, they showed how much importance they attached to keeping Jerusalem at the forefront of their thoughts.

What does this mean? What is the special significance of Jerusalem?

The Midrash tells us (*Bereishis Rabbah* 56:10) that the name Jerusalem is a composite of two names. This was the place where Abraham offered up his son Isaac as a sacrifice to God. After the ordeal was over, Abraham built an altar and named the spot May God be Seen (*Yeira'eh*), signifying a place where God's presence is felt and fear of Him is awakened in the human heart. Shem the son of Noah, who ruled over the city under the title Malkizedek, called it *Shalem*, a place of peace and perfection. God took these two names, *Yeira'eh* and *Shalem*, and He put them together to form the name Jerusalem (Yerushalayim). This is the place where peace and perfection can be achieved by encountering the presence of God.

Jerusalem is also the anchor of unity among the Jewish people. As King David writes (*Psalms* 122:2-4), "Our feet marched far and wide to protect the gateways of Jerusalem, a Jerusalem that would reach completion, like the city that is joined in unison, to which the tribes went up, the tribes of God that are a testament to Israel, to praise the Name of God." Jerusalem is the place where all the tribes of Israel congregated. The tribes were very different from each other. Each tribe had its own personality, its own characteristics, its own strengths and talents. But when they all came together to Jerusalem for the common purpose of giving praise to the Name of God, all differences were forgotten. All became one.

Today as well, Jerusalem is, or should be, the focus of unity among the Jewish people, the common ideal that brings all disparate groups together as one indivisible people. What is it about Jerusalem that gives it this special significance? Why is this a place of awe, peace, perfection and unity?

Let us take a look at a *halachah* in *Shulchan Aruch* that for some inexplicable reason is seldom mentioned (*Orach Chaim* 94:1), "When a person stands up to pray, if he is outside of the

Land, he should turn his face toward Eretz Yisrael. He should also direct his heart toward Jerusalem, and the Holy Temple and the Holy of Holies."

Jerusalem is a place that is meant to exist in the heart of every Jew. If we face Israel but do not direct our thoughts through Jerusalem, then we haven't set ourselves in the right frame of mind for prayer, and we haven't established the proper position for prayer.

The *Mishnah Berurah* adds, "Even if he cannot turn his face in that direction, he should imagine himself standing in the Temple in Jerusalem in the Holy of Holies." He supports this statement by quoting King Solomon's prayer at the dedication ceremonies of the First Temple in Jerusalem (*I Kings* 8:46-48). "Should [the Jewish people] transgress against You — for there are no people on earth who never transgress — and You become furious with them and give them to an enemy, and their captors lead them in captivity to the land of the enemy, be it distant or near. And living in the land of their captivity, they reconsider, and they repent and plead with You in the land of their captors, saying, 'We transgressed, we sinned, we were wicked.' And they return to You with all their hearts and souls in the land of their enemies that captured them, and they pray to You through the land You gave to their forefathers, the city You have chosen and the Temple I have built for Your Name. Then You shall hear in Heaven, the place of Your dwelling, their prayers and entreaties, and You shall do justice for them."

King Solomon pleaded with God to accept the prayers offered in the Temple in Jerusalem, and God replied (*I Kings* 9:3), "I have heard your prayers and entreaties that you have pleaded with Me, I have sanctified this Temple that you have built to place My Name there forever, and My eyes and heart will be there for all time." This is one of the few occasions where God specifically states that a prayer has been accepted. God has promised that His eyes and heart will be receptive to prayers that go up to Heaven from the Temple. Therefore, it is important that all prayers, regardless of where we are standing, be directed to Heaven through the Temple in Jerusalem.

Among the many works that flowed from the Chofetz Chaim's prolific pen is a small gem called *Sefer Machneh Yisrael*, a handbook for Jewish soldiers conscripted into the Czar's army. The Chofetz Chaim offers these unfortunate men advice and guidance on how to live as Jews under these trying conditions. Included in this work (ch. 10) is a special prayer the Chofetz Chaim composed for the Jewish soldier to say before he goes out to the battlefield. Facing such immense danger, unsure if he will live to see another day, he must prepare for his possible death, and at the same time, he must pray with all his might for survival. As one can well expect, this very long and deeply moving special prayer is full of confessions of wrongdoing, pleas and supplications and expressions of trust and faith in God.

This prayer, comments the Chofetz Chaim, does not necessarily have to be said in Hebrew. It can be said in any language the soldier understands well. But there are two conditions that are very important.

One, it must be said with absolute sincerity, emanating from the depths of the heart rather than the lips alone. In fact, if the soldier could bring himself to tears it would be even better, since the Gates of Tears are never shut. This condition is easily understandable.

Then the Chofetz Chaim presents his second condition, which is truly astonishing. The soldier should make sure that he directs his prayer through Eretz Yisrael, through Jerusalem, through the Holy Temple, into the Holy of Holies and on to Heaven.

Facing Jerusalem is obviously very serious business. This is not simply a nice refinement or embellishment to prayer. This is what a soldier must keep in mind when he prays to God on what might very well be the last day of his life. Apparently, the advantages of a prayer offered up through Jerusalem are critical.

The Chofetz Chaim goes on to quote King Solomon's plea that God accept prayers that rise to Heaven from the Holy

Temple (*I Kings* 8:33-39), "If Your people Israel are beaten by the enemy when they transgress against You, and they return to You, praise Your Name and pray and plead with You in this Temple, then may You hear in Heaven and forgive the transgression of Your people Israel, and You will bring them back to the land You gave to their forefathers. If the heavens are closed up and there is no rain because they transgressed against You, and they pray to this place and praise Your Name and repent from their transgression when You afflict them, then may You hear in Heaven and forgive... Should there be famine in the land, should there be pestilence... should an enemy besiege them in the land of their gateways, whatever plague and whatever sickness there may be, every prayer and every entreaty that any person among all Your people Israel may have, when each man knows the afflictions of his own heart, and he stretches out his hands to this Temple, then may You hear in Heaven, the place of Your dwelling, and forgive..."

This is what King Solomon accomplished when he built the Holy Temple. He created a point of connection between the physical and spiritual worlds, a conduit for our prayers to rise directly to the Heavenly Throne and be accepted with favor. Whatever plague, sickness or mortal danger a Jew may face, he can send his prayer straight to Heaven if he directs it in his mind and heart through Eretz Yisrael, through Jerusalem, through the Holy Temple, right into the Holy of Holies and upward from there.

Even if he is in a distant land, even if he is shivering with cold and fear on a brutal Russian battleground, the Jew can send his prayers to Heaven though the Holy of Holies. As his prayers travel toward that vortex of holiness before rising to Heaven, they gather holiness as they pass through the Holy Land, the heritage of our forefathers. They gather more holiness as they pass through Jerusalem, the place of fear of God, peace, perfection and unity. They become even more deeply sanctified as they pass though the Holy Temple, the dwelling place of the Divine

Presence. All this takes place in the mind and heart of the Jew who is composing his prayer, and when his prayers finally enter the Holy of Holies, they are so thoroughly sanctified that they rise effortlessly to Heaven.

When we leave a house of mourning, we speak the famous words of consolation, "May God comfort you among the rest of the mourners for Zion and Jerusalem." Who are these mourners for Jerusalem? Who among us mourns for Jerusalem? Who among us appreciates what we are missing? Who among us pleads with God for a rebuilt Jerusalem because he feels an aching need for it? Who among us exclaims in complete sincerity, "If I forget you, O Jerusalem, may my right hand forget its power"?

The Jerusalem for which we long so desperately and whose loss we have mourned for thousands of years — it is not the land and the buildings of Jerusalem that we miss. It is the supreme connection with God that Jerusalem represents. Recreating Jerusalem in our imaginations as a conduit for our prayers is the best available to us right now, but it is no comparison to a rebuilt Jerusalem, crowned with a shining Temple in which the Divine Presence will dwell forever. Only when we appreciate what Jerusalem represents and what we have lost can we grieve over its destruction.

We are all familiar with the words of the prophet (*Jeremiah* 2:2), "Go call out in the ears of Jerusalem, 'So said God, "I remember for you the care of your youth, the love of your betrothal, when you went after Me into the desert, into a land that was unplanted."'"

R' Chaim Volozhiner wonders about the reference to Jerusalem in this prophecy. Since when does Jerusalem have ears? And when was Jerusalem in the desert? And why should he call out only to Jerusalem and not to the rest of the Jewish people?

Jerusalem, says R' Chaim Volozhiner, is a name given to the Jewish people united in the quest for perfection. Corresponding to the terrestrial Jerusalem, he explains, there is the celestial Jerusalem that is described in the mystical terms of the Kabbalah as *makom kenisas hisklalelus neshamos shel Klal Yisrael.* Here on this earth and in Heaven above, Jerusalem is the name given to the unifying force within the Jewish people.

God tells the prophet, "Go call out in the ears of Jerusalem." Go to the Jewish people when they are united together to strive for perfection, when they deserve to be called collectively by the name Jerusalem. And what is the prophet to say to them? How is he to help them in their common quest for spiritual perfection? He is to remind them of their first steps as a nation. He is to say to them in the Name of God, "I remember for you the care of your youth, the love of your betrothal, when you went after Me into the desert, into a land that was unplanted."

How do we understand this? How does the recollection of the desert in particular help the Jewish people rise to higher levels?

The Torah tells us (*Numbers* 14:4) that when things became difficult in the desert some people said to each other, "Let us appoint a leader and return to Egypt." The Steipler Gaon, in *Chayei Olam*, finds this absolutely astonishing. Surely they could not have already forgotten the unspeakable misery and suffering they had endured in Egypt. How could they want to return? Could we imagine someone saying, "Things are so difficult for me here, I would rather return to Auschwitz"?

The answer, says the Steipler Gaon, is that the Egyptian land, fertile, beautiful, blessed with a temperate climate, was the most desirable in the world. "Like the garden of God," the Torah tells us (*Genesis* 13:10), "like the land of Egypt." The problems the Jewish people had were not with the Egyptian land but with Egyptian society. But at this time, when the Jewish people were struggling through the desert, Egyptian society lay shattered by the devastation of the Exodus. Egypt was desolate, depopulated, defenseless and vulnerable. It was the weakest among the nations. A walkover.

After receiving the Torah, the Jewish people could easily have turned around and conquered Egypt. They could have settled down on its fertile plains to live a comfortable Jewish life in accordance with the Torah, just as Jews would do in many places in the Diaspora over the centuries. In the other direction, they faced the hardships and tribulations of the bleak desert, dependent every day on God's miraculous support, always afraid that they might slip and transgress and be left in the desert to their own devices. And what would happen if they managed to survive the journey through the desert? What awaited them beyond? The powerful kingdoms of the seven Canaanite nations awaited them on their steeds and chariots at the borders of the Holy Land. And what if God deemed them unworthy of miraculous intervention? How would they fare on the battlefield against such fierce enemies? Hunger, thirst, war, these were the prospects they faced if they pushed on to Eretz Yisrael. Comfort awaited them in Egypt.

So the Jewish people were faced with a dilemma. What should they do? Should they go establish a Jewish country on the ruins of old Egypt? Should they opt for a life of comfort and safety in a land that would provide all their needs with relative ease and allow them to spend their time learning Torah and fulfilling its *mitzvos*? Should they forgo the fulfillment of the *mitzvos hateluyos ba'aretz,* the commandments relating to the Holy Land, and the higher levels of sanctity that can be attained only in Eretz Yisrael, for the sake of security and comfort in Egypt? Should they opt for a Torah life on a lower standard in Egypt or struggle through the desert and fight wars in the Holy Land in order to achieve Torah life on a higher standard?

The Jewish people united and chose the more difficult path for the sake of an extra closeness to God that can only be found in Eretz Yisrael, in Jerusalem, in Zion. Therefore, it is not surprising that in moments of weakness, when things were difficult, some elements would grumble about the decision that had chosen Eretz

Yisrael over Egypt. It is not surprising that some people would say, "Let us appoint a leader and return to Egypt."

Every step the Jewish people, united in their supreme devotion to God, took through the broiling desert was a reaffirmation of this critical decision. Every step confirmed the willingness of the Jewish people to give up comforts for the sake of spiritual achievement, to give up worldly success for the sake of coming closer to God.

And so whenever the Jewish people unite in this same spirit, whenever we coalesce into an entity that can be called Jerusalem, God recalls for our sake the dedication that characterized the early steps of the Jewish nation when they "went after Me into the desert, into a land that was unplanted." He joins us together with our gallant ancestors who were prepared to walk through the desert and fight wars for the sake of being close to Him.

After the Holocaust, the Jewish people had to reach in, to focus on rebuilding the internal institutions of the communities, the synagogues, the schools, the communal charities. When this was done successfully, we reached out to those of our brothers and sisters who had wandered from the warm embrace of the Torah. Now the time has come to reach up, to rise above the preoccupation with comfort and security and seek higher levels of spiritual achievement for the Jewish people as a whole.

So when we hear the sad news that all too often emanates from Jerusalem, when we feel an instinctive pang and a yearning in our hearts, we must stop and think. For what do we yearn? What does Jerusalem mean to us? Deep in our hearts, we must recreate the exalted idea of Jerusalem, of unity among all Jews in the quest for ever greater closeness to God. If only we can do this, God may just decide to let us see Jerusalem rebuilt speedily in our days.

CHAPTER FIFTEEN

Women in the Workplace

There can be no denying that life in the twenty-first century is a very complicated business. Progress has made things easier in some ways, but much harder in others. The pace and cadences of life are different, and so are our needs. Imagine a family today that has no telephone. It is unthinkable. And that is just the least of it. Drastic changes have been forced on our way of life, and one of the most drastic is the phenomenon of women in the workplace.

Can we say unequivocally that good Jewish women should never step into the workplace? The issues are far too complex for such a simple answer. Many families would be unable to afford their most basic needs — food, shelter, clothing, tuition, medical insurance — without a second source of income. In the yeshivah world, there is even a reversal of roles, where the men go to the *beis midrash* to learn Torah and the women go to work. Is this a good thing? Is it right? What are the benefits, and what price are we paying for those benefits? When must a woman go out to the workplace, and if she does, how should she deal with it?

I would like to begin by putting the woman's role in somewhat sharper perspective. What exactly is expected of her as a mother and a wife?

One of the darkest chapters in the history of the Jewish enslavement in Egypt was Pharaoh's decree of death to all male Jewish newborns. In the Torah's description of the events, two Jewish midwives emerge as heroines who rescued numerous infants. The Torah identifies them as Shifrah and Puah.

Who were these women?

Our Sages tells us that Shifrah was actually Yocheved, the mother of Moses, and Puah was actually Miriam, his sister. Yocheved was called Shifrah, because she was *meshaperes es havlad*; she cleaned, beautified and swaddled the infant after birth. Miriam was called Puah, because she was *po'ah umedaberes vehogah lavlad*; she cooed, murmured and whispered comfortingly to the newborn infant.

Our Sages also tells us that Yocheved and Miriam had the gift of prophecy. What does it take to become a prophet or a prophetess?

Let us listen to the Rambam (*Mishneh Torah, Hilchos Yesodei HaTorah* 7:1): "Prophecy only descends upon a sage who has great wisdom and strong character, whose impulses do not control him in anything whatsoever… He must be a person of extremely wide knowledge …able to understand and to absorb new concepts. He must consistently grow in holiness …and condition himself not to have thoughts about insignificant things… His mind must always be attuned Above …contemplating the wisdom of the Holy Blessed One … Then divine inspiration immediately descends upon him."

If Yocheved and Miriam achieved the gift of prophecy, they must have been on an extraordinarily high intellectual and spiritual level. They had great wisdom, wide knowledge and never any thoughts about insignificant things. And yet, how does the Torah choose to define these prophetesses? As Shifrah and Puah, women who tend to and comfort little infants, as women who take care of babies.

This, explains R' Shmuel Rozovsky, Rosh Yeshivah of Ponevezh, is the primary role of the woman, to take care of the young, to care for them and nurture them and mold them into the people God meant them to be. It is a calling of the highest order, a calling that brings distinction and honor even to women who have attained the gift of prophecy.

Before telling us about the growth and development of Moses, the great leader and prophet of the Jewish people, the Torah first lets us know how a person such as Moses came to be. How does a young Moses gain such a profound sensitivity to other people? Why is it that he cannot tolerate the suffering of his brethren? Why is it that he cannot tolerate the unjust act of driving strangers away from a well?

The answer is Shifrah and Puah. Because these are women with a fine appreciation for the importance of caring for babies, because they do it with absolute devotion, dedication and idealism, a Moses or an Aaron or a Miriam can emerge.

People are born as babies, because their characters have to be developed in stages before they can become adults. We are not like animals that are finished products as soon as they learn how to walk and eat. An adult human being is full of complex emotions and personality traits that need to be molded very carefully. The process starts in the cradle and continues for the rest of his life.

When a mother allows an infant to cry and does not comfort him, he is in danger of growing up a hardened person, a person who feels unloved and rejected, who feels that no one cares. Of course, you don't have to come running every time the child lets out a little peep. But there is a limit to how long you can let him cry. I know there are those who believe a child should be allowed to cry himself out, but I consider it a serious blunder. There must be some sympathy for the child, some mercy. You cannot put the child in another room and let him cry for hours just because you want to go to sleep. That is cruel and insensitive, and the child feels it. He may already be on his way to becoming a dropout. Rejection doesn't necessarily start at fifteen or sixteen years of age. It can and often does start in the cradle.

Rabbeinu Yonah, in *Iggeres HaTeshuvah*, discusses God's instructions to Moses (*Exodus* 19:3), "So shall you say to the house of Jacob [the women] and to the sons of Israel [the men]." Why did God tell Moses to speak to the women first? God wanted Moses to first give the women a synopsis of the Torah, Rabbeinu Yonah explains, because "they are the ones that send off their children to school and see to it that they study the Torah, and they are merciful when their children come home from school."

Let's take a close look at these words. What does it mean that the mothers "send their children off to school"? Does that make them better than the fathers who pay the tuition? And what does it mean that the mothers "are merciful when their children come home from school"?

This seems to be the key to engendering love for Torah in young children. The way the mother sends her children off to school in the morning and the way she welcomes them home when they return will determine how they feel about Torah.

The mothers "are merciful when their children return." Apparently, every child coming home from school needs a good dose of mercy. He has just had a hard day, and he needs his mother to receive him and welcome him and make him feel good.

Imagine a mother greeting her child at the door in a stern teacher's voice, "So what did you learn in school today? Do you know what your homework is? Did you behave yourself today? I want a full report!" This is not what the child needs, an extension of the school he just left. He needs his home to be a place of refuge. He needs his mother to greet him with warmth and kindness, with a reassuring word, a cup of milk and a cookie. He needs his mother to put her arm around his shoulder and ask him how he's feeling. He needs a bit of mercy after a hard day at school, and then he'll be all right.

There isn't a single child that doesn't feel a bit abused by the end of the day. Even if a child enjoys learning, there's a limit. He can sit for one hour, two hours, three, but a whole school day is exhausting and grueling. If he comes home from school to a merciful and understanding mother, it is all bearable. But if he doesn't, the school years are just a sentence to hard labor, from the time he gets up until he goes to sleep. Day after day, a long sentence of hard labor. Who can stand it?

And the way he is sent off to school is just as important. If everything is bedlam, if he is scolded for trying to pour the milk on his cereal and spilling it on the table, if he has one arm in his coat sleeve and the other sleeve is dragging on the floor behind him as he runs out the door, can he come to school in a proper frame of mind? Is it a wonder he ends up hating school? That is not how mothers are meant to "send their children off to school."

There is an art to sending a child off to school, and there is an art to greeting him when he returns. That is what Shifrah and Puah are all about. The role of the mother is to be the merciful one, the one who treats the child with utmost caring and sensitivity and thereby conditions the child to have these feelings as well.

When the father rebukes him with a harsh word or even a judicious slap on the wrist, the child bursts into tears and goes running to his mother, who says, "It's not so bad. Next time you'll do the right thing and your father won't be upset with you." No, this is not a break in the solidarity between father and mother. It is working together, complementing each other. The father provides the strictness, while the merciful mother soothes the child.

This is the ideal situation in a Jewish household. The father earns the family livelihood and sets the standards, and the mother is the merciful one, the safe haven who shelters her children and comforts them when they encounter the harsh realities of life.

Such a mother cannot really go out to the workplace, because by the time she returns, she's the abused one, the one that's had it, the one that is desperately in need of mercy and comforting. When she returns exhausted from the workplace, her child is already waiting for her at the babysitter's, and everything is turned on its head. He is the one who has to welcome and comfort her, rather than the other way around. But which child is clever enough to welcome his overworked mother properly? Instead of soothing her, he is more likely to whine and complain and add to her stress and strain. That is how their day comes to an end. Not exactly an ideal situation.

Unfortunately, however, one of the most debilitating aspects of the dark *galus* in which we presently find ourselves is that ideal situations are hard to come by. Almost no one can live a natural, normal life any longer. Almost no one enjoys a life that is whole and tranquil, with the father and mother fulfilling their specific roles in building the family, establishing the home and raising the children. Everything is artificial and contrived. Even if they may seem superficially prosperous and comfortable, very few households function as ideal Jewish households should.

It used to be that earning a living was not such an overwhelming enterprise. The *Shulchan Aruch* describes (*Yoreh Deah* 146:4) the preferred daily schedule of a working man. He works for three hours and then learns Torah for nine. Not many of us today can earn a living in just three hours, even if we are willing to forego all luxuries and extravagances. Many people cannot make ends meet even if they work ten or twelve hours a day. And that doesn't even take into account travelling time, which is another of the great difficulties of our times.

It used to be that people lived in small towns and villages, and they used to earn their livelihood with small cottage industries. One person may have been the chandler of the community, and all the people bought their candles from him. Another was fishmonger, and everyone bought fish from him. So the chandler and the fishmonger would open their little shops for a few hours a day, and everyone knew that you had to come during those hours if you wanted candles or fish. So three hours a day was more than enough for a man to earn a living for his family, and he was left with enough time in the day to learn Torah for nine hours.

Of course, life was also simpler in those days. People didn't have automobiles, mortgages and medical insurance. They didn't travel, take expensive vacations or send children to summer camp. They stayed at home, lived in simple little houses, ate simple wholesome foods, wore simple, respectable clothes and lived a very good life.

In our times, to our deep regret, it is just about impossible to live such a life. And so serious choices have to be made. If the husband is able to provide a good livelihood for his family so that they are not deprived of their essential needs, then it is certainly right that the wife stay home with the children and be the Shifrah and Puah of the family, the rock of stability, the safe haven, the provider of love and mercy. It would not be right for her to go out into the workplace in order to raise the family's standard of living to keep pace with friends and neighbors and enjoy the luxuries of life.

But what if the husband simply cannot provide the basic necessities for the family? What if he simply cannot earn enough for the mortgage, tuition, food, clothing, medical and dental care and other similar needs? These are not luxuries that we can simply forego. Then it becomes necessary for the wife to get involved and do what she can to supplement the family income, and they must become that bane of contemporary life, the two-income family, an unpleasant term that means everyone in the workplace and no one at home. But what can they do? So they must make plans and adjustments to minimize as much as possible the damage to the family.

Let us also take a look at other circumstances in which this situation often arises. If a man wants to learn Torah very seriously, he cannot expect to do so successfully if he joins the workforce. Where would he find a job that allows him to learn Torah with a fresh mind for nine hours a day? And so that is why we have *kollelim* today; there is no other way to achieve widespread Torah scholarship in Klal Yisrael in our day and age. But in order to learn in a *kollel*, a man must rely on others to support his family, and very often, the one who accepts this burden on her shoulders is his wife.

Is this an ideal situation? No, it is not. But it is a sacrifice a large number of women must make if Torah is to remain a vibrant and vital force among the Jewish people. Many women will decline this honor, preferring that their husbands go to work to earn a living in the conventional manner. That is fine. Many others, however, will embrace it, honored and pleased to make the sacrifice for the merit of Torah study. And so they will go out into the workplace and leave their children with babysitters, and when they come home tired in the afternoon, they will try to be good mothers to their children. This is not the ideal situation by any stretch of the imagination; there is a price to pay. Nonetheless, for those who choose this way of life, it is the correct thing to do; should Torah only be learned by the children of the rich? And if they choose the Torah life, they must make the proper adjustments to compensate for the inevitable shortcomings.

If we stop and think about it, our whole *yeshivah* system is also an adjustment to a less than ideal situation, a compromise for the sake of expediency. The preferred *mitzvah* is for every father to learn with his own son. If he cannot do it himself, he must hire a *melamed*, a teacher for his son. Hiring a *melamed* should be like finding a *shidduch*. You check out the person and try to determine if he would be a proper match for your son in all the different aspects of the relationship. People do this now when they look for special tutors to learn with their children at night. That is what they should do when choosing a *melamed*. But we don't hire a *melamed*. We send them to a school, which simply cannot meet all the needs of all the children all the time. A child may sit through an entire class without learning a word or without connecting to the *rebbe*, and it is no fault of his own. He is simply not made for this *rebbe* nor is this *rebbe* made for him. This can happen for a whole year or even a whole school career. It is the few rather than the majority who connect properly with the *rebbe*, and the rare few who do this throughout their school years. But what can we do? Families have no choice.

When a mother has to enter the workplace, however, the family may indeed have choices. They do not have to settle for the worst-case scenario. They should do their best to compensate for the things that will be missing because of the mother's absence. They should seek out a babysitter with the same scrupulous care and attention they would devote to checking on a *shidduch* or hiring a private *melamed*, a person who is calm and warm and merciful, who will treat the children the way they need to be treated rather than just do it in a perfunctory manner.

It is important to realize what will be missing in the home when she goes out to work. It is not just her presence during the hours she is working and that the children need to be cared for by other people. Even more important, it is the effect on her disposition when she is at home. Instead of being a calm, relaxed person, the Shifrah and Puah of the family, she can come home frustrated and exhausted by the strains and stresses of her work. She may be short-tempered with the children when they don't really deserve it, and the whole rhythm of the household may be affected.

Husband and wife must, therefore, sit down and find a way to create a warm, happy atmosphere for the children even though the conditions do not lend themselves ideally to it. They must literally train themselves to act in ways that do not come naturally to them, to become a new type of mother and father. She must calm down when she walks through the door of her home. Regardless of how distraught she feels, she must get those emotions under control and make herself feel calm and happy so that she can greet her children as a mother should, so that the rest of the day will be a warm, positive and secure experience for them.

As for her husband, he must make arrangements and adjustments in his own life to cover for her as much as possible. Most important, he must appreciate what she is doing and recognize that she is not obligated to do it. It is not her duty to go to work so that he can sit in the *beis midrash* and learn Torah. It is something she is doing out of the goodness of her heart, and he should be very grateful that she is giving him the opportunity to learn and grow in Torah for the benefit of the entire family.

Nowadays, it is accepted in society that women go to work, but I have never yet heard of a woman giving her husband a *kesubah* under the *chupah*. Actually, it is a very strange thing. The husband gives the wife a *kesubah*, and it is read aloud in front of all the assembled wedding guests. Among other things, the husband promises to "work, sustain and support" his wife, and everyone knows — *chassan, kallah*, both families and all the guests — that he has no intention of doing anything of the sort. So what is it all about? Is it just a charade?

It is not. In the *kesubah*, the husband acknowledges that it is his responsibility to work, his responsibility to sustain, his responsibility to support his wife, and if she does it for him, it is a gift. She is doing something she is not obligated to do, and he owes her a tremendous debt of gratitude every single day that she does it. If this point were clear in the marriage from the very beginning, many problems would be avoided. The husband would be ready and eager to do whatever he can to help make the home what it should be, and the wife would feel so appreciated every day that she would come home in much better spirits. The marital relationship would be strong and healthy, and the home would flourish.

There are, of course, many other concerns that must also be addressed. Just as a woman must be concerned about how her absence from the home will affect her home and her children, she must be concerned about how her presence in the workplace will affect her; she is not allowed to expose herself to a work situation in which there is any breach in the barriers of modesty and propriety between men and women. There are no blanket answers to these questions, nor should the people involved answer the questions for themselves. Husband and wife should seek advice and guidance from *gedolim*, the great Torah luminaries of our time, on this as well as on all issues of importance.

Having said all this — that it is not ideal for the woman to earn the family livelihood and that serious adjustments and compensations must be made — let me point out that this applies only to our own times, to the complex, stress-generating society in which we live. In Talmudic times, we actually find that it was quite common for women to earn the family livelihood and let their husbands concentrate on learning Torah.

The most famous example is the story of Rachel who sent off her husband Rabbi Akiva to learn in yeshivah for twelve years and then gladly let him go for an additional twelve years — a total of twenty-four years on her own! That is, of course, how a Rabbi Akiva comes to be, and the credit is all hers. As Rabbi Akiva told his disciples (*Kesubos* 63a), "Everything you and I have achieved belongs to her."

What happened during those twenty-four years Rabbi Akiva was away? Who supported his family? His wife Rachel took care of the home and the children and also earned the livelihood needed to sustain the family.

In fact, it was very common for the Tanna'im and Amora'im to go off to learn Torah in a different city, where they lived on a pittance. Some of them received this pittance from family, some worked a little to earn it. But none took the burden of the family livelihood along with them to yeshivah. Their wives covered for them and gave them the opportunity to concentrate on their learning without any distractions. We cannot say that this was

Women in the Workplace ❧ 205

the normal pattern of life in those days, but we can say that it was an accepted mode to be found among families who lived on a higher level.

The Gemara states (*Berachos* 17a) that women earn merit through their dedication to Torah by "bringing their children to school, sending their husbands to the *beis midrash* and waiting for them to return." At first glance, the Gemara seems to be saying that women earn merit by waiting up until their husbands return from the *beis midrash* late at night.

Encouraging her husband to go learn Torah and waiting up for him to return from the *beis midrash* is certainly a symbol of great *mesiras nefesh* for a woman. What is the meaning of *mesiras nefesh*? It means virtually to give away your life, to sacrifice that which is as dear to you as your very life. Accepting a lower standard of living for the sake of Torah is not really *mesiras nefesh*. It is simply good common sense. It is undoubtedly worthwhile to forego material comforts for the sake of gaining the everlasting rewards of Torah study. Sensible people understand this. But a woman has a powerful need for companionship, especially the companionship of her husband, her life's mate. If she lets her husband go to the yeshivah until late at night, or if her husband is working and she sends him to the *beis midrash* for several hours of solid learning after he comes home, if she is willing to forego her own emotional needs and wait for his company until late at night, that is true *mesiras nefesh*.

Rashi, however, explains this Gemara in a way that reveals an even higher level of *mesiras nefesh*. The women gain merit, according to Rashi, by "giving their husband permission to learn Torah in a different city." They wait for their husbands to return, not late that night, not the next night nor the one after, but weeks, months or even years in the future.

This is what women used to do regularly in the Talmudic era, and this was one of the critical factors that produced the Tanna'im and Amora'im of the Talmud. It is a way of life possible only among people on a very high *madreigah*, who live on an extremely exalted spiritual level. Practically no one in our times can even relate to such a way of life, let alone live it.

The Chasan Sofer interprets this Gemara in a way that is more relevant to our generation. He understands "sending their husbands to the *beis midrash*" to mean that they support their husbands in order to enable them to learn Torah. Furthermore, he states that this is "the main purpose of a woman's creation," that a woman should be a helpmate who takes upon herself the burdens of the household and frees her husband to learn Torah. "These are the ways of the wives of Torah scholars," concludes the Chasan Sofer, who lived in Hungary, "especially in Poland. They are involved in business and allow their husbands to spend their time in the *beis midrash*. How fortunate they are to have such a share in the Torah."

This is perhaps more relevant to our times. Once again, we have to emphasize that the way of life in the Polish towns and villages was simple and the needs of the families were not extravagant. Women were able to do a spot of business from their homes without exhausting themselves to the point where their children suffered. They did not have to run an office and oversee a staff and compete with manufacturers in South America or the Far East. They could do a bit of weaving or make some candles or other minor activities of this nature and sell their products at the door to anyone who needed them. Perhaps they would have to go out to the marketplace once every week or month. But all in all, they could manage it, and they were willing to do so in order to fulfill "the main purpose of a woman's creation," which is to facilitate the Torah of her husband and children and thereby gain her own share in it.

What is a woman's connection to her husband's Torah? Is it simply an arrangement between two people where one learns Torah and the other provides the material support, a sort of Yissachar-Zevulun within the household itself? Or is it something more, something deeper?

The answer lies in a well-known Gemara as illuminated by the profound explanation of the Vilna Gaon. The Gemara states (*Berachos* 61a), "*Mitechilah alah bemachshavah*, at first God had the idea of creating [man and woman] as two separate bodies, but in the end, He created them as one body [and separated them afterward]."

It is ridiculous to think that God vacillates in His thoughts, intending first to do things one way and then changing His mind and doing it another way. Rather, when our Sages use the phrase *mitechilah alah bemachshavah*, they are signaling that this is the goal He wanted to accomplish and that He chose a circuitous path as the best method of achieving that goal. God wanted man and woman to be two separate entities — that was the idea, the goal. How did He go about achieving this goal? By creating them as one body and dividing it into two separate parts. What does this mean?

The Vilna Gaon explains, "God originally created [man and woman] as one body, because He wanted a man to be more attached to his wife than to any of his other relatives. He wanted them to feel so attached to each other because the purpose of a person in this world is to engage in Torah study in order to attain the next world. Had He not formed them from one body, the husband would be compelled to spend his time earning a livelihood; he would not have time for Torah study. God, therefore, formed them from one body so that she would be willing to exert herself for his sake. Only thus would he have the opportunity to devote himself to the Torah. After creating them as one body, however, God split them apart, otherwise nothing would have been accomplished; whenever she went out to market or to take care of other business, he would have had to come along. The original idea is, therefore, fulfilled in the end result." This is a remarkable insight into the husband-wife relationship. God created it in order to facilitate the study of Torah.

God wanted man and woman to be perfect complements to each other — in their personalities, in their aspirations, in their understanding, in their appreciation of each other. And He wanted it to be abundantly clear to the entire world that they are perfect complements rather than separate and distinct entities. Therefore, He created them as one body and divided it into two, so that it would be manifest to all that husband and wife are two complementary parts of one and the same whole. Their attachment to each other is not just for procreation as in the animal world. They are so deeply connected to each other emotionally and spiritually that the needs, concerns and triumphs of the one resonate in the heart and soul of the other.

The role of the woman is to complement and support her husband so that together they are reunited into one perfect whole. God made the man dependent on the woman so that she would be attuned to him and disposed to help him. She is there to encourage him, to compensate for his weaknesses, to inspire and facilitate his efforts to learn Torah. And when he does, his Torah belongs to them both, because it was the combination of both of them that made it happen.

So this is truly the ideal situation. Husband and wife are both content to lead the simplest of material lives. Their needs are minuscule. The husband is a *talmid chacham* who is perfectly happy learning Torah; it is the air he breathes, and he needs nothing else. His wife is perfectly happy with the bare necessities of life, and she is proud and honored to run a small business to support the family while her husband spends his time working hard in the *beis midrash*. The children are happy growing up in a home where both parents are happy, content and fulfilled and in a community environment where everyone lives simply without competition and jealousy. This type of Torah utopia existed in different places and times, but it is clearly not feasible on a wide scale in our generations.

But we can learn values from this virtually unreachable ideal. We can learn that a woman's ultimate fulfillment is when she makes it possible for her husband, and her children to a lesser degree, to learn Torah. We can learn that it is fine and good for a woman to provide or contribute to the family livelihood if this will help her husband learn Torah. And we can apply these lessons to our own times and situations; if we are the planners of our own destiny, we should make this ideal our blueprint. Perhaps it would be exceedingly difficult for a contemporary woman to attempt to do what women were able to do in simpler times. But at least we can learn that it would be worthwhile for the wife to improvise and adjust and seek a way to send her husband to the *beis midrash* while she enters the workplace without causing a disaster to the children in the home. If it cannot be done, then so be it. But if it can be done, if she finds a way to go out into the workplace in order to bring Torah rather than luxury into her home, the rewards are boundless and everlasting.

CHAPTER SIXTEEN

The Mark of Royalty

Freedom is a wonderful thing, but it is a double-edged sword. There was a time when Jewish people were segregated in ghettoes. They were allowed to come out during the day to do a bit of business, but they had to return to the ghetto by nightfall. Living conditions were not particularly pleasant inside the ghetto; it was cramped and dark, and the streets were very narrow. But there was one very good thing about the ghetto walls. They shielded us from the influence of the outside world.

Today, we enjoy the wonderful gifts of freedom. We can live anywhere we please, pursue any lifestyle that suits us, travel and do business anywhere we choose, but in the process, we mingle with the gentiles and are influenced by their ways. Is it any wonder that it has become hard to keep up our standards? Is it any wonder that some of us are somewhat discontented with the Torah way of life, that some of us find it a burden and a restriction, that some of us do not fully appreciate the privilege and pleasure it provides for us every single day?

Our Sages tell us (*Midrash Eichah* 3:2) that before God gave the Torah to the Jewish people He first offered it to the other nations.

The descendants of Eisav asked, "What is written in the Torah?"

And God told them, "You shall not kill."

"Sorry, we can't accept it," they said. "We are warriors. Bloodshed is an important part of our lives. We can't commit to the Torah."

"And how about you?" God said to the descendants of Yishmael.

"What is written in the Torah?" they asked.

And God told them, "You shall not steal."

"Impossible," they said. "We're more or less honest people, but You can't expect us to do business like that, sticking to every detail of honesty. How will we ever make money? No, this Torah is not for us."

"Then how about you?" God said to the descendants of Ammon.

"What is written in the Torah?" they asked.

And God told them, "You shall not commit adultery."

"Oh no, not for us," they said. "Too difficult."

And so it was with all the other nations. They all found some aspect of the Torah that they considered too difficult to fulfill. They all found some excuse that allowed them to turn down God's offer.

Finally, God offered the Torah to the Jewish people.

"Yes! Yes!" they responded. "*Naaseh venishma.* We will do whatever God tells us to do, and we will hear." They didn't ask any questions. They didn't offer any excuses. They just accepted the Torah wholeheartedly, even though they did not yet know what it contained.

God turned to the angels and said, "Who revealed this secret to my children? How did they know that saying '*naaseh venishma*' would place them on the highest spiritual level?"

I would like to ask a bit of a daring question. Were the Jewish people right in neglecting to ask what is written in the Torah? Was it wise to accept the Torah without asking what it contained? One might say that the other nations actually acted quite prudently. They were not about to make a commitment they couldn't keep, so they wanted to know what they were taking on. But what about the Jewish people? Wasn't it rash of them not to ask about what was in store for them? What if God had told them that the Torah forbids one to speak a word of slander or gossip throughout one's entire life? Would they have been just as eager to jump in?

What exactly did the Jewish people want to show by accepting the Torah blindly rather than first asking what it contained? What did they know that the others didn't? What was the secret of *naaseh venishma*?

Actually, these exalted words revealed a profound understanding of the nature of Torah, of the vast power of the Word of God. The Jewish people knew full well that if they would inquire about what the Torah contained they would undoubtedly encounter many rules and prohibitions that would seem too difficult to keep. They knew full well that their capabilities would not measure up to the requirements and demands of the Torah. But they also knew that receiving the Torah would transform them, that it would infuse them with new strengths and powers so that the difficult and the impossible would suddenly become not only possible but a way of life.

So what does this mean? That for the sake of Torah we should be prepared to endure hardships and deprivations? That we should be willing to sacrifice our freedom? We look around us and see gentiles and non-observant Jews living as they please. Yet we must abide by restrictions. We cannot do whatever we choose. We cannot eat wherever we please. We cannot utter vulgar words. We cannot wear immodest clothing. How can we not feel restricted? How can we avoid feeling a pang of jealousy?

Let us consider for a moment. God created people with the ability to experience this wonderful feeling called pleasure. If so, it is inconceivable that He would seek to deprive us of pleasure. If He loved us enough to give us the Torah, would He condemn us to a life devoid of pleasure?

But there are really two levels of pleasure. There are the low pleasures that appeal purely to a person's physical side, the sheer bodily pleasures. And then there are the higher pleasures that appeal to a person's intellect, spirit, artistic sensibilities, sense of honor and dignity. I suppose there is a certain pleasure to be derived from slouching in jeans on the beach, smoking cigarettes and drinking beer. But what if a person were given a chance to meet the president of the United States? Would he gladly toss away the beer and the cigarettes, put on a suit and a clean shirt and even don a tie for the privilege of meeting one of most powerful people on earth? On the day of his visit to the president, would he feel deprived of his ordinary pleasures? Would he feel restricted? Or would he feel the thrill of a much higher pleasure such as he had never experienced before?

And what if the president offered him a position on his staff in the White House in which he would interact with the elite of society — would he turn it down because he would have to wear a suit and tie every day instead of jeans? Or would the higher pleasures of such a position make his ordinary physical pleasures seem trivial and insignificant?

These two sets of pleasures do not live easily together. Usually, the more one experiences the higher pleasures the less one wallows in the lower pleasures, and the more one wallows in the lower the less one is likely to experience the higher pleasures. Most people, except for the coarsest fellows, prefer the higher pleasures, even at the expense of placing limitations on the lower pleasures.

In London, there is a royal residence called Buckingham Palace. It is a famous place; all the tourists make sure to put it on their lists, especially because they want to see the Coldstream

Guards who stand watch outside the palace. These tall, beefy officers are drawn from the families of the aristocracy, and it is a high honor and much sought-after privilege to be chosen. As long as they are on duty, they must stand at attention in their red and black uniforms with their huge bearskin hats held in place by straps on their chins. It is very hot under those hats even in winter, let alone in the scorching summer days, and yet, on days when there are elaborate ceremonies and events, they stand motionless for hours. Sometimes, they faint from heat exhaustion, and they remain on the ground until they are able to stand again. No one is allowed to touch them.

Why would these men want to be guards at Buckingham Palace? Why endure all the difficulty and exertion? Because by their social values, guarding the home of the Queen of England is an honor and a privilege, and the pleasure and satisfaction they derive from doing it far outweigh the discomforts and inconveniences.

Now think about it: would a guard at the palace ever appear for duty in jeans and an exposed midriff? Even more to the point, would the queen herself ever dream of dressing in such a vulgar manner or otherwise behaving like a peasant? Of course not. It would be beneath their dignity.

When God sent Moses to offer the Torah to the Jewish people, He said to them (*Exodus* 19:5-6), "*Vihyisem Li segulah mikol haamim... mamleches kohanim vegoy kadosh.* And you will be dearer to Me than all the peoples... a kingdom of princes, a holy nation." The word *kohanim* here means princes and princesses, God's inner circle. By accepting the Torah, the Jewish people would become royalty. They would rise above the commonfolk of the world by virtue of their close relationship with the King of Kings, the Master of the Universe. They would enjoy this honor every moment of every day. They would live in the palace of the King, so to speak. And so, of course, their pleasure would be of a higher sort. They would experience the finer enjoyments of royal favor, of the ultimate in spiritual, emotional and intellectual fulfillment.

Every Shavuos, we read the story of Ruth. There are many reasons given for this custom, but the simple explanation is that the story reaffirms the privilege of inclusion in the Jewish people and living by the Torah.

Ruth, the daughter of the king of Moab, was married to a Jewish aristocrat. When her husband died in poverty, her mother-in-law left Moab and returned to Israel. Ruth could easily have chosen to return to the royal palace and enjoy the luxuries and pampered lifestyle of a royal princess. Instead, she chose to accompany her penniless mother-in-law and live in Jewish society, speaking the famous words (*Ruth* 1:16), "Your people are my people, your God is my God."

Ruth knew that the royal status she would enjoy in Moab was superficial. Once she perceived the incomparable privilege of being a princess in God's palace, being Moabite royalty was forever meaningless.

Our Sages tell us that Naomi and Ruth could not afford shoes, and they walked back to Israel barefoot; they felt every pebble on the road. Ruth knew all about material comforts and pleasures. How easy it would have been for this daughter of privilege to turn around and run back to her father's palace. How easy it would have been to sink into the lap of luxury for the rest of her life. But that shallow life, even gilded with a veneer of Moabite royalty, no longer held any attraction for her. She wanted to be a princess in God's palace. Now that she was enlightened, only a life of Torah could give her true pleasure and happiness. Only Torah could make her feel content and fulfilled. And in the merit of her great courage and wisdom, she became the ancestress of King David; her descendants would be the royalty of royalty, the Jewish dynasty from whom Mashiach will emerge.

We are all of us princes and princesses; we all bear the mark of royalty. God has honored us by giving us His holy Torah. Every *mitzvah* we do, every word of Torah we study binds us closer to

Him and elevates us to ever higher states of holiness and purity. These are the highest of the high pleasures. No other pleasure on earth can even begin to compare with them.

But we can only experience this pleasure if we recognize the divine privilege we enjoy, if we appreciate the incredible honor God has bestowed upon us, if we are truly delighted when we make the blessing *asher bachar banu mikol haamim venasan lanu es toraso*, "Who chose us from among all the nations and gave us His Torah."

If, however, we do not recognize the Torah for what it is, if we do not value our privileged relationship with God, if we do not view ourselves as His royal retinue, then we will certainly feel burdened and restricted. But the tragedy would be far greater than the loss of some physical low pleasures. The tragedy would be that we were given such a priceless gift and, out of ignorance and folly, did not cherish it properly. The tragedy would be that we had eternity in our grasp and let it slip away. The opportunities lost would be the greatest of tragedies.

CHAPTER SEVENTEEN

Egyptian Milk

H ow do we come close to the Creator of the Universe? How do we become worthy of having His holy Name attached to us, of being His people? It is a process, a progression of steps, each of which is a critical foundation for the one that follows. In our festival prayers, at a time when we rejoice in the celebration of our special relationship with God, we describe the steps that bring us to that point.

"*Atah vechartanu mikol haamim,*" we say. "You chose us from among all the nations. *Ahavta osanu veratzisa banu.* You loved us and favored us. *Veromamtanu mikol haleshonos.* You raised us up above all other languages. *Vekidashtanu bemitzvosecha.* You sanctified us with Your commandments. *Vekeiravtanu Malkeinu laavodasecha*. You drew us close, our King, to serve You. *Veshimcha hagadol vehakadosh aleinu karasa*. And You called us by Your great and holy Name."

This is the progression of steps that cement our special relationship with God. It begins with God choosing us from among all the nations. Having chosen us, He bestows His love and favor on us. He raises us up above all other languages, sanctifies us with His commandments, draws us closer with His service and calls us by His great and holy Name.

Let us take a closer look at the very first step. God chose us from among all the nations. Why did He choose us? Surely this choice was fair and just. There must have been some quality that made Jewish people worthy of being chosen by God. There must have been some quality that set us on the path to sanctification by His commandments. What was this quality?

The Chafetz Chaim explains that what sets us apart from all the other nations of the world is the heritage of *middos tovos*, personal refinement, handed down to us by the *Avos*, the Patriarchs of the Jewish people. The *Avos* were so successful at refining themselves, cultivating within their hearts the finest of personal qualities and characteristics and uprooting their negative tendencies, that these refinements became ingrained in their very being and were passed on to their children and grandchildren. We have inherited these *middos*, these outstanding refinements, and this alone qualified us to be chosen from among all the nations of the world.

This refinement of character, this nobility of the heart, these outstanding *middos*, explains the Chafetz Chaim, are the only environment in which *mitzvos* can thrive and flourish. Without refined *middos*, there can be no *yiras shamayim*, no proper fear of Heaven; there would be no framework, no context. A vulgar person cannot relate to the sublimity of the divine. Without refined *middos*, it would be impossible to perform the *mitzvos* amidst all the ordeals and temptations we must face in the course of our efforts. A vulgar person would be incapable of rising above the obstacles and resisting temptation. Without refined *middos*, it would be futile even to make the attempt.

This is what set the Jewish people apart from the other nations. Our forefathers had this quality, and if we are to remain worthy of their heritage and their chosenness, we must aspire to absorb their *middos*, their refinement, their nobility of character. And this is why God chose us from all the other nations.

The Rambam makes a similar point while discussing the procedure by which a person repents and expiates those sins that are *bein adam lechaveiro*, the sins a person commits against other people. If a person sins against God, *bein adam laMakom*, he has to confess his sin, express his regret for what he has done, promise not to repeat his offense in the future, and he is forgiven. But if he sins against another person, God does not forgive him until he makes amends.

"Neither repentance nor Yom Kippur atones for anything other than sins committed against God…," writes the Rambam (*Mishneh Torah, Hilchos Teshuvah* 2:9). "But those sins that a person commits against another person, such as causing him an injury, cursing him, robbing him and the like, are never forgiven until he makes restitution and appeases [the wronged person]. Even if he returns the money he owes him, he must still appease him and ask his forgiveness. Even if all he did to upset the other person was speak hurtful words, he must appease him and continue to do so until the other person forgives him."

Even when a person has returned his ill-gotten gains or paid for the damage he caused, God will not forgive him until he asks the other person's forgiveness. As long as the hurt and resentment caused by the sin remain, the sin cannot be expiated nor can the slate be wiped clean. Only when there is a reconciliation will God forgive him as well.

As for the victim, should he be ready to forgive easily? Does he have the right to bear a grudge for what was done to him?

The Rambam provides the answer. "It is forbidden for a person to be cruel and not allow himself to be appeased," continues the Rambam (ibid. 2:10). "Rather, a person should be quick to forgive and slow to anger, and when a sinner asks forgiveness, he should forgive him wholeheartedly and with a loving spirit. Even if [the sinner] caused him much pain and harm, he should not seek to exact vengeance."

Isn't it amazing how much is expected of a Jew? A person may have been injured, and his property may have been smashed. He may have suffered great financial losses. He may have been deeply offended and humiliated. And still, when the offender comes forward, sincerely contrite and repentant, and makes restitution and asks forgiveness, he should be quick to forgive. And he should not just mumble the words for form's sake. Instead, regardless of how much he was hurt or offended, he should forgive "wholeheartedly and with a loving spirit." He should accept the apology in the spirit of friendship, good will and peace. He should never bear a grudge or seek vengeance.

Incredible. Can this sort of conduct be expected of ordinary human beings? The answer is yes. It can be and is expected of every single Jewish person. These words of the Rambam appear in the Laws of Teshuvah. They are not just an ideal toward which saints and pious sages aspire. They are Halachah, the practical rulings that apply to all Jews. This is what is expected of all of us.

And then the Rambam concludes with a truly extraordinary statement. "[Wholehearted forgiveness with a loving spirit] is the way of the offspring of Israel with their sincere hearts, but the pagans with their sealed hearts are not like this. They bear a grudge forever."

Here the Rambam clearly defines the dividing line between what is demanded of the Jewish people and the ordinary behavior of other nations of the world. It is not in *emunah*, faith. Although the Jewish concept of faith is far more sophisticated, the nations of the world are also capable of faith; the difference is in the shades and nuances, in the depth of understanding. The dividing line is also not with regard to *mitzvos*. The nations of the world can also relate as a matter of course to commandments. The dividing line is in *middos*.

Only the Jewish people must raise themselves to such a level of refinement, of excellence in character, that they can genuinely forgive and forget, that they can become good friends with those whom they may have considered their worst enemies the day before. This is something that is demanded only of a Jew. As the Rambam writes, "The pagans with their sealed hearts … bear a grudge forever."

Only the descendants and spiritual heirs of Abraham, Isaac and Jacob have within them the potential for such magnificent refinement. And therefore, unfortunately, if the behavior of Jews becomes similar to the behavior of those nations that do not share the legacy of our Patriarchs, if the dividing line between the nations of the world and the Jewish people becomes blurred, we can be sure it is not because the nations of the world are becoming vastly improved in their character refinement. This cannot be expected of people that are not the heirs of Abraham, Isaac and Jacob. If we see the gap closing, it is because the Jews are falling far short of what is expected of them. It is because they are slipping and sliding down to lower levels.

So how do we keep ourselves on a higher level? How do we refine our *middos*? How do we realize the full potential of the Jewish talent for excellence in character?

The answer is by embracing *kedushah*, holiness.

How do we define holiness?

The Rambam in his introduction to the *Mishneh Torah-Yad HaChazakah* gives us important guidelines. The title "*Yad*" is an allusion to the number fourteen, which is the numerical value of the word *yad* (*yod-daled*). The Rambam writes that he chose this title because he had grouped the *mitzvos* and concepts of the Torah in fourteen separate "books," each of which dealt with a distinct area of the Torah. He also gave titles to each of these books to reflect its common theme. Then the Rambam goes on to describe the individual books. Let us see what he writes about the fifth book.

"Within the fifth book," writes the Rambam, "I will include those commandments that relate to forbidden relations and forbidden foods, because these — forbidden relations and forbidden foods — are the two matters by which God has sanctified us and separated us from among the idol worshippers. Furthermore, specifically with regard to these two *mitzvos* the Torah writes respectively (*Leviticus* 20:24), 'And I separated you from among the nations,' and (*Leviticus* 20:26), 'That I separated you from among the nations.'"

There are *taryag mitzvos* in the Torah, six hundred and thirteen of them, and hardly any are described as providing the differentiation between Jews and the nations of the world. All the great *mitzvos* in the Torah do not set us apart definitively from the nations of the world. Only these two sets of *mitzvos*, forbidden relations and forbidden foods, define and, in fact, create the *havdalah bein Yisrael la'amim*, the separation between the Jewish people and the nations of the world.

What is so extraordinary about these *mitzvos*?

The answer lies in the final words of the Rambam's description of the fifth book of the *Yad*, "And I named this book *Sefer Kedushah*, the Book of Holiness." The Book of Holiness! And the only *mitzvos* included in this entire book are forbidden relations and forbidden foods. Of all the *mitzvos* in the Torah, none fall under the category of holiness. Just these two.

Holiness is what challenges the Jewish people to elevate themselves. Holiness is founded on a basis of *middos*, of refinement and nobility, which cause us to turn away from forbidden relations and forbidden foods. This sort of holiness is the hallmark of the Jewish people. And our abstention from acts that contaminate the soul brings us to ever higher levels of holiness and an ever deeper refinement and nobility of character, drawing us ever closer to God.

Let us take another look at the progression that brings us closer to God. *Veromamtanu mikol haleshonos.* You raised us up above all other languages. *Vekidashtanu bemitzvosecha.* And You sanctified us with Your commandments.

What does this mean? What does our language have to do with being sanctified by the commandments?

Our language is called *Lashon HaKodesh*, the Holy Language. In what way is the language itself holy? The Rambam in *Moreh Nevuchim* writes that *Lashon HaKodesh* is the only language that has no words to describe those parts of the human anatomy and those human activities that have to remain private. There are no words in the dictionary of *Lashon HaKodesh* that can be considered obscene. (Of course the Rambam is speaking about *Lashon HaKodesh*, not modern Hebrew, which has created and borrowed words, in order to make it like every other language.) And when it is absolutely necessary to discuss such things, the most *Lashon HaKodesh* provides are oblique references and euphemisms, which serve the purpose perfectly well. Explicitly obscene words do not exist in *Lashon HaKodesh*, and that is what makes the language holy.

Obscene language is the threshold of forbidden relations. Coarseness in speech leads to coarseness in deed. The Torah has set the Jewish people apart from the other nations by the *mitzvos* of forbidden relations. And *Lashon HaKodesh*, the language of the Torah, protects us from contamination by removing the slightest hint of forbidden relations from our vocabulary.

Today, unfortunately, we are a people in exile, living among the nations of the world, most of whom do not share our values. We no longer speak *Lashon HaKodesh*, even among ourselves. But even when we speak other languages, Heaven forbid that the obscenities and vulgarities spoken by the promiscuous peoples among whom we live should pass our lips. Even when we speak English or French or Spanish, we must be careful to keep our words holy.

As long as we maintain the holiness of our speech, even if we are not speaking *Lashon HaKodesh,* we still have the right to say, "You raised us up above all other languages." But if we should ever, Heaven forbid, slip into the speech patterns of our neighbors, we would sink down to their level. If the purity and holiness of our language, no matter which language we speak, should ever be destroyed, damaged or polluted, then we would no longer be able to say, "You raised us up above all other languages." Then how could we ever aspire to say, "You sanctified us with Your commandments"? And we could certainly despair of the next steps, "You drew us close, our King, to serve You," and "You called us by Your great and holy Name."

In *Shulchan Aruch* (*Yoreh Deah* 81:7), the Rema states, "The milk of an Egyptian woman is [as kosher as] the milk of a Jewish woman." If a Jewish child needs natural mother's milk, his own mother is unable to provide it, and there is no Jewish wet nurse to be found, it is permitted in this case to let the child suckle the milk of a pagan woman. It is technically kosher. "Nevertheless," writes the Rema, "a child should not suckle from an Egyptian woman if a Jewish wet nurse is available, because *chalav akum,* the milk of a pagan, dulls the heart and gives rise to immoral tendencies."

That is the way God created the world. The foods we eat affect us, and that is why certain foods are forbidden. Food that is associated with any kind of defilement, whether or not we are aware of it, will cause us to become defiled as well. Even the milk of a pagan wet nurse, which is not quite a forbidden food, should be avoided, because it "dulls the heart and gives rise to immoral tendencies." The milk of a woman encapsulates all her strengths and weaknesses, all her character traits, all her thoughts and impulses. Even a newborn infant should, therefore, drink only the milk of a woman that exemplifies the character traits of our holy ancestors. Otherwise, that pure baby's heart may become dulled and corrupted.

According to the Gra, the source for the Rema's ruling is the Gemara (*Sotah* 12b) that describes what happened when Pharaoh's daughter pulled the infant Moses from the Nile. She saw the infant crying and assumed he was hungry. So she summoned several Egyptian wet nurses to feed him, but he refused to drink. Finally, Miriam arrived and offered to bring a Jewish wet nurse.

Why did Moses refuse to drink? Moses was no more than an infant, and yet he differentiated between an Egyptian wet nurse and a Jewish wet nurse. Clearly, God had instilled in him some kind of a reflex aversion to suckling from an Egyptian woman. Why was that? Because, says the Gemara, "the mouth that would one day speak with the Divine Presence could not suckle from an Egyptian woman."

What does the Gemara mean? At first glance, one might think this was merely a matter of honor, of protocol, that it would not be fitting for a mouth that had suckled from an Egyptian wet nurse to speak with God. But the Rema saw a deeper reason. He understood that by drinking the milk of an Egyptian woman and thereby drawing into himself some of her very essence, Moses would "dull" his heart, tarnish his refined character and open himself up to immoral tendencies. And how could such a person speak with God?

Every single Jew, says the Rema, should also avoid Egyptian milk even though it does not quite extend to the level of forbidden foods. Every Jew should aspire to the highest levels of holiness, to draw ever closer to God through continuous refinement of *middos*, which leads to ever higher levels of holiness. Unless it is absolutely necessary, why should any Jew forfeit the ability to speak with the Divine Presence? What right do we have to make compromises? Of course, we cannot allow a child to starve, and if there is no other choice, then it is permitted to bring an Egyptian wet nurse. But if there is any choice at all, how can we allow the holy heart of a Jewish child to be blunted even in the slightest degree? This is why the Rema wrote that "a child should not suckle from an Egyptian woman."

But why does the Rema refer to "Egyptian milk" instead of using the more generic "pagan milk"? Of course, we could say that he uses this term merely because the source of this rule is the story of Moses and the Egyptian wet nurses. But this really seems insufficient reason for the Rema to refer to pagan milk as Egyptian. He seems to consider that Egyptian milk is more dulling to the Jewish heart than any other, and that the reason all such milk should be avoided is because it also has the Egyptian effect to a certain degree.

I think we may find the explanation in the Torah's warning (Leviticus 18:3), "Do not act in the manner of the land of Egypt where you dwelled, nor shall you act in the manner of the land of Canaan to which I am bringing you." The Torah singles out the Egyptian and the Canaanite as representatives of the highest form of depravity. An Egyptian is more than just an ordinary idolater. He is degenerate, promiscuous and amoral, a product of exposure to the worst spiritual defilement in the world. Anyone who is the least bit familiar with the history of ancient Egypt knows that this is true.

These are the influences that are identified as "Egyptian" milk, the influences that are the essence of a society of lewdness and wanton behavior. These are the influences from which we must protect our children.

With Egyptian milk, you can't expect a child to be sanctified with *mitzvos*. With Egyptian milk, you can't expect him to have refined *middos* and a nobility of character. With Egyptian milk, you can't expect him to learn Torah with relish and delight. With Egyptian milk, you can't expect him to draw ever closer to God.

We look around today at the world in which we live, at the depravity of the modern "street," and we see all the abominations of Egypt and then some. Unfortunately, much as we try to protect ourselves, we are all exposed to this contaminated "street." The videos. The Internet, with all the worst that Egypt ever had to offer available to everyone at the press of a button. There is no need to go into further detail. We all know the situation. We are engulfed in a sea of Egyptian milk.

How can we preserve our pure hearts and spirits? How can we protect the spark of holiness within us? I don't know if in our condition we can appreciate the true meaning of purity and holiness. I don't know if in this corrupt *galus*, this deep spiritual exile in which we find ourselves, we can find our way to the levels of holiness expected of us without tremendous difficulties. But we have to make the effort to establish the *havdalah bein Yisrael la'amim*, that dividing line between us and the world.

Our children must be taught from the very earliest age where to look and where not to look; we cannot wait until it is too late. We must protect ourselves and our children from Egyptian milk. We must make rules and build fences. We must seek advice and devise strategies that will help us become holy in spite of the difficulties we face. Above all, we must send up our tears and our prayers to the Master of the Universe and plead with Him that our homes should be pure and our children should sparkle with holiness.

I want to add a small word of encouragement. We know that the task is difficult. Much more than difficult. We look around at the world, and it seems practically hopeless to create at best more than small islands of holiness. But it really is not so. There is no greater power in the world than *kedushah*, holiness. If we can improve, increase and refine the *kedushah* of our *yeshivos*, our synagogues, our schools and our homes, we can radiate holiness to the entire world and transform and uplift all of humanity.

Before describing the Jewish bondage in Egypt, the Torah states (*Exodus* 1:5), "And all the people that came out of the loins of Jacob were seventy souls, and Joseph was already in Egypt." What is the significance of this information? The commentaries offer a number of explanations, but I would like to focus on an insight that appears in *Be'er Moshe*.

After all the suffering the Jewish people experienced in Egypt, after spending centuries among the Egyptian abominations, they somehow managed to leave with the holiness of their families intact. God Himself bore witness that the Jewish fathers and mothers held themselves pure and holy, that their children were theirs alone, and He sealed this testimony by attaching His holy Name to each and every Jewish family. How was such a thing possible? How did they keep their homes holy despite all the influences to which they were exposed?

The *Be'er Moshe* explains that two factors allowed them to remain holy. One was the influence of Sarah. The Midrash relates that when Sarah was taken to Pharaoh's palace, she was exposed to temptation. She had a *nisayon*, an ordeal. But she braced herself against forbidden relations, and all the Jewish women in the Egyptian exile followed her example and rejected all forbidden relations. By overcoming temptation and establishing standards of holiness, Sarah was able to project her influence hundreds of years into the future to her descendants who would face temptation on the same contaminated soil.

The second factor was Joseph's influence. The Master of the Universe sent Joseph down to Egypt and subjected him to his own terrible *nisayon* with Potiphar's wife. Joseph also overcame that temptation and braced himself against forbidden relations. This was holiness in its highest form. Joseph was able to withstand his *nisayon*, this terrible ordeal he had to face in Egypt, all alone. Under the most trying conditions, he was able to maintain the highest standards of purity and holiness, and thereby, he established a precedent that would protect and preserve the holiness of the Jewish people who would follow him to Egypt and stay there for hundreds of years.

This is what the Torah is telling us when it says, "And all the people that came out of the loins of Jacob." Who were these people that were going down to Egypt?

They were all descended from Jacob, the final and greatest Patriarch who embodied the highest achievements of his parents and grandparents, especially that of Sarah who laid the groundwork for the preservation of holiness among Jewish women even in Egypt. "And Joseph was already in Egypt." Joseph's great achievement when he was alone in Egypt laid the ground for the preservation of holiness among Jewish men.

The *Be'er Moshe* concludes with a sharp observation. After the reunion of Joseph and his brothers, Joseph consoled them and reassured them that what had happened was not really their fault. God had planned it this way. There was a purpose in everything, and now it was becoming clear. And then Joseph adds a strange phrase (*Genesis* 50:20), "And as for you, you had planned evil against me, but the Lord meant it for the good, in order to do as this day (*kayom hazeh*) to sustain numerous people."

What does this mean? How would his coming to Egypt "sustain numerous people"? One might think this simply means that they would be saved from the famine because Joseph had attained power in Egypt. But if so, what is meant by the phrase *kayom hazeh*, "as this day"?

This phrase, explains the *Be'er Moshe*, is a subtle reference to the story of Potiphar's wife. In relating the story of Joseph's strength in overcoming terrible temptation, the Torah uses the same expression (Genesis 39:11), "And it happened as this day (*kehayom hazeh*) ..." In effect, Joseph was saying to his brothers, "Do you know why all this had to happen? Do you know why God wanted me to end up here in Egypt as a lonely, defenseless youth? 'In order to do as this day (*kayom hazeh*).' He wanted to subject me to the temptation and ordeal of Potiphar's wife. Why? In order 'to sustain numerous people.' Because I was able to withstand this ordeal, it will be possible for numerous people, millions of Jewish people that will some day suffer temptation in Egypt, to maintain their standards of holiness. That is why God sent me here."

We all face our own ordeals and temptations. We are all faced with Egyptian milk. It is a matter of serious concern, but we cannot allow a *nisayon* to make us depressed or frightened. Let us consider each *nisayon* as an opportunity to reach the highest levels of purity and holiness. Let us take encouragement from the example of Joseph. And let us take heart in the knowledge that our triumph over temptation will be not only for our own sake, not only for the sake of our families and our children, but also for the sake of hundreds, maybe thousands, of people who will be strengthened by our success. We, too, can "sustain numerous people."

CHAPTER EIGHTEEN

Know the Right Answers

T hat are we supposed to do if a false prophet stands up to speak in the name of some pagan god? The Torah tells us to close our ears and walk away (*Deuteronomy* 13:9). "*Lo sishma eilav*," the Torah states. "Do not listen to him." This is more than just good advice. It is a *mitzvah* in the Torah. We are forbidden to listen to false prophecies.

The *Sefer HaChinuch* reveals to us the roots of this *mitzvah* (§ 467). "People are always making mistakes," he writes. "Their intellects are not powerful enough to reach the ultimate truth in all matters of discussion. Therefore, the Torah is concerned that deceptive arguments, long discussions and debates with this lying scoundrel who prophesies in the name of idols might convince a person to believe him. And even if he is not convinced, he may suspect for a brief moment that there is some truth in these lies. Although we know that his words will have no lasting effect, that the truth will shine out and expose this would-be prophet's words as lies, the Torah nonetheless took pity on us and prevented us from wasting even a brief moment of our lives wavering over this terrible thought."

Apparently, there is no real danger that the false prophet will win us over to his side. The truth will inevitably come to light. And yet we are forbidden to listen to him, because we might consider for a fleeting moment that there is substance to what he is saying. Why is that so terrible? So what if we have a twinge of doubt in our hearts for a moment or two? It will not ruin us. After thinking it over, we will recognize the truth for what it is. So why is it forbidden to listen to him?

The *Sefer HaChinuch's* intriguing response is that the Torah "took pity on us and prevented us from wasting even a brief moment of our lives wavering over this terrible thought." Every moment of life is precious, and the merciful Torah does not want us to waste even one of those precious moments. If a person listens to a false prophet, if he considers even for a few minutes that the false prophecies may be genuine, if he doubts the truth for even the briefest of moments, then he has wrapped that small bit of time in his life in a shroud of darkness and killed it; for that moment in his life, he is not living but dying. The Torah wants us to live, to utilize constructively every moment of the lives we were given and not to destroy willfully even a single one of them.

Very strong words.

And yet we find a seeming contradiction in a famous *mishnah* (*Avos* 2:19), "*Da ma shetashiv l'apikores.* Know how to respond to a heretic." The mishnah seems to imply that it is permitted to conduct discussions with an *apikores,* a heretic. But what happened to the prohibition of listening to the false prophet? If a moment of unnecessary doubt is a tragedy, a little bit of death, why then should we be allowed to converse with heretics? What exactly does the *mishnah* mean by "know how to respond to a heretic"?

Let us take a closer look at the full text of the *mishnah*. "Rabbi Eliezer said, 'Learn Torah continuously. Know how to respond to a heretic. Know before Whom you are laboring and that your Employer can be trusted to reward you.'"

Something seems odd. During competitions, schoolchildren are often asked to find the odd phrase, the statement that seems out of place in the context of the entire quotation. In this *mishnah*, I think any schoolchild would immediately pounce on the statement of "know how to respond to a heretic." What is it doing in this *mishnah*? One easily sees the connection between the first statement regarding diligent Torah study and the third statement regarding eventual reward for our labors. But how does responding to a heretic come in here?

Rabbeinu Yonah enlightens us. "Apply yourself to the study of Torah," he writes, "in order to know how to respond to a heretic. If you don't respond effectively to his arguments and lies, people will accept them. They will drink the vile waters when they see that the heretic has triumphed, and the Name of Heaven will be desecrated."

A person should not learn Torah halfheartedly but with the intensity and clarity that will equip him to respond to a heretic if the situation arises. Otherwise, it is not complete learning. It is not thorough learning. If a person know he may have to respond to a heretic, that if he cannot destroy the heretic's arguments a *chillul Hashem* will result, the Name of Heaven will be desecrated, then he will learn with fire and intensity. That is the type of Torah study that God desires.

The *mishnah* is not suggesting that we enter into discussions with heretics and hope we are going to win. That would be a dangerous thing. What if we are not strong enough to expose all his arguments as utter nonsense? What if the discussion awakens even fleeting doubts in our own minds or in the minds of bystanders and destroys precious moments of our lives? Only a great *talmid chacham* can initiate or participate in such a debate. And when we learn Torah, we should aspire to become such *talmidei chachamim*. Until that time, however, we should avoid such discussions as much as possible, but we should nonetheless know the right answers if circumstances force us to respond.

"The heretic discussed here," Rabbeinu Yonah concludes, "refers to one who denies the truth of *Torah Sheb'al Peh*, the Oral Torah."

The heretic about whom we're speaking here is one that denies that *Torah Sheb'al Peh* was given at Mount Sinai alongside the *Torah Sheb'ksav*, the Written Torah. The heretics in our times, unfortunately, also deny the divine origin of the Written Torah, and therefore, we have to fortify ourselves against this threat as well and be prepared to prove that God gave us both the Written Torah and the Oral Torah from the start. We have to feel that we are the Torah's defenders against those who dare challenge its authority.

There are many proofs of *Torah min Hashamayim*, that both the Written Torah and the Oral Torah are of divine origin. I want to mention four of them here, two for the Written Torah and two for the Oral Torah. Those who study the Torah do not have much need for these proofs. We know it by the impregnable tradition of the Jewish *mesorah*, the chain of transmission, and we experience it in the learning itself. But knowing the internal proofs will nonetheless give us great encouragement and confidence when we face the world. It may also infuse our learning with a new energy and enthusiasm that will enable us to sense its divine origin even more strongly.

One of the better-known proofs of the divine origin of the Torah is the *mitzvah* of *Shemitah*. For six years, the Jewish people in Eretz Yisrael till the fields and reap the harvests. During the seventh year, however, they are required to leave the land fallow. No planting, no harvesting. After seven seven-year cycles comes the time of the *Yovel*, the Jubilee year, and an additional fallow year is added. So now Jewish farmers have to wait two full years before they can get back to work.

The very nature of this *mitzvah* immediately signals to us that it is not of human origin. Eretz Yisrael was an agrarian society; most of the people earned their livelihood through agriculture. Why would the alleged human writers of the Torah propose such a law? It would be sheer folly. Eretz Yisrael was surrounded by enemies throughout its history, and the Jewish people could not have expected to receive food packages from their neighbors. Why would these human legislators want to throw the country into economic crisis every seven years? Only the One Who provides for all the creatures on the face of the earth could have issued such a law.

But the proof goes much further than that. The Torah states (*Leviticus* 25:20), "And should you say, 'What will we eat in the seventh year if we do not plant nor harvest our grain?' Then I shall direct My blessing for you in the sixth year, and [your field] will produce grain for three years."

Would human beings make such a promise? Can human beings hope to deliver on such a commitment? How exactly would they induce the land to produce a threefold crop during the sixth year? And if it didn't the Torah would be discredited. Why would they formulate a law and a promise that would only expose them as frauds? Who asked them to go out on a limb with such an extravagant, unfulfillable promise? It makes no sense.

We know that historically the Jewish people did keep *Shemitah* in Eretz Yisrael and that they survived. The only explanation is that God gave the *mitzvah* and He also made the promise and He kept it. The One Who has the power to give the blessing is the One Who gave the *mitzvah*.

The *mitzvah* of *aliyah leregel*, the obligation to make a pilgrimage to Jerusalem during the festivals, offers a similar proof to the divine origin of the Written Torah. The Torah states (*Exodus* 34:23-24), "Three times a year, all your males must appear before the Master, God, the Lord of Israel ... and no man shall covet your land when you go up to appear before God your Lord three times a year."

A rather strange *mitzvah*, one might say. Three times a year, every male must leave his town or village, make a pilgrimage to Jerusalem and celebrate the festival there. And what about all our enemies? We were never without enemies. All around we had only enemies, and just about no friends. In earlier times, they were called Midian, Edom, Ammon, Moav, Aram. Today, they are called Syria, Jordan, Iraq, Lebanon. That's the way it has always been. The map of Eretz Yisrael showed a small country with the Mediterranean Sea on one side and a sea of enemies on the other.

What kind of security was it to leave every border, every town unguarded three times a year and concentrate all the men in Jerusalem? Our enemies must have caught on after a while that the whole country would be empty during those three particular times, and they had plenty of time to prepare an invasion. All they had to do was walk across the border unchallenged and unmolested, surround Jerusalem, and that would be the end of the country. How could people be expected to make the pilgrimage and leave their homes and fields unprotected?

So the Torah adds a few words, "And no man shall covet your land when you go up to appear before God your Lord three times a year." The Torah promises that no enemies will take advantage of the situation to invade and conquer.

Could human beings have made such a promise and kept it? The idea is preposterous. And yet, people did go on pilgrimage, and the land was not invaded during their absence. Clearly, the One Who controls the world and can make such promises is the One Who gave us the Torah.

Most famous among the proofs to the divine origin of the Oral Torah is the identification of kosher animals. Two characteristic signs identify a kosher animal, *mafris parsah* and *maaleh geirah*, split hooves and chewing the cud. Any animal that does not have these two characteristics is considered unkosher.

The Torah goes on to single out for special mention (*Leviticus* 11:4-7) four animals that have only one kosher sign, the camel, the rabbit and the hare, which chew their cud but do not have split hooves, and the pig, which has split hooves but does not chew its cud. Does this mean that there are no other animals anywhere in the entire world that also have only one kosher sign? The text does not seem to compel us to make this interpretation. The Torah could just as well have been giving four examples of familiar animals that have no more than one kosher sign, but for all we know, there may be hundreds of others.

Not so, says the Gemara (*Chullin* 59a). The wording of each mention of the animals contains the word *hu,* it, which implies a restriction, as if to say, "only this and no other."

What does this mean?

"The One Who controls His world," states the Gemara, "knows that there is no similar animal in His world." Only God knows each of the many thousands of animal species that roam the face of the earth, and He alone can say with certainty that only four animals have a single kosher sign, that the pig is the only animal in the world that has split hooves but does not chew its cud.

This is a very bold statement. The Gemara is going on record as saying that you can travel to the ends of the world, you can climb mountains and cross valleys, you can search through remote jungles and forests, and you will never, ever find a single species other than the pig that has split hooves and does not chew its cud. How could the Sages have discovered such startling information? They obviously knew it by tradition; they learned it through the transmission process of the Oral Torah. Such a statement could not have been made on the basis of an inference from the text alone.

Here then is a daring challenge to the Bible critics and others who deny the divine origin of the Oral Torah. If they want to discredit the Torah, all they have to do is take a trip up the Amazon River or to some other unexplored corner of the world and find a single animal, other than the pig, that has split hooves and does not chew its cud. If they found only one such animal, they would bring all of the Torah into question. And yet, the Sages were not concerned. They knew with absolute certainty that such an animal would not be found, because the Oral Torah said it was so.

Later on (*Chullin* 60b), the Gemara, based on another inference in the text, identifies a species that has a dual spine. How could Moses have known such a thing? "Was Moses a hunter?" asked the Gemara. "Was he an explorer? This provides us with a response to those that deny the divine origin of the Torah." The only way Moses could have known this information is, as the Gemara explains (*Menachos* 29a), that he received it directly from God.

Incidentally, it is worthwhile to note the precise language of the Gemara. "This provides us with a response to those that deny *Torah min HaShamayim*, the divine origin of the Torah." The Gemara does not say that this provides us with proof of *Torah min HaShamayim*, but rather that it provides us with a response to those that deny it. We ourselves do not need these proofs. We have our *mesorah*, our chain of transmission, and we know it from our experience. But what do we do when we meet up with doubters and heretics who do not have our advantages? How do we convince them that the Torah comes to us directly from God? "This provides us with a response." This will open their eyes.

A little-known Midrash provides us with another amazing proof of the divine origin of the Oral Torah. At about the time that he built the First Temple in Jerusalem, King Solomon wrote (*Song of Songs* 2:9), "Behold He stands behind our wall, keeps watch from the windows." What does this mean? About which wall was he speaking?

The Midrash (*Bamidbar Rabbah* 11:2) explains that he was speaking about the *Kosel HaMaaravi*, the Western Wall. " 'Behold He stands behind our wall,' " states the Midrash, "this refers to the Western Wall of the Temple, which will never be destroyed. Why? Because the Divine Presence keeps watch from the windows."

What an incredible statement! The Midrash was written nearly two thousand years ago, at a time when the Romans destroyed the Second Temple. The country was in shambles, with devastation everywhere. The Temple was a smoldering ruin, its treasures carried off to Rome along with many thousands of captives. The future looked black, or bleak at best. And yet, the Sages had the stunning confidence to declare that the Wall would never be destroyed. Never! What could have been the source of such a seemingly irrational conviction? It could only be that they knew it from God Himself. It could only be that the Oral Torah is divine.

History has borne them out. Eretz Yisrael lies at the crossroads of the world. Over the past two thousand years, it has been trampled and ground into the dust by innumerable invasions and wars. It has been devastated again and again until it was left little more than a wasteland and a wilderness. And still, the Wall remained standing in all its ancient majesty. Who could have predicted such a thing? Who could have imagined it?

Just consider what happened in the last half century. The Arabs were incensed against the Zionists over the establishment of the State of Israel. After the partition, the Arabs had control of the entire Old City of Jerusalem for twenty years; the Wall was in their hands. During those twenty years, the Arabs were constantly scheming and plotting against the Jewish people. What could they do to harm us? They knew perfectly well that to destroy the Wall would be like driving a dagger into the heart of every Jew all over the world. Why not?

What would have been the consequences to the Arabs had they destroyed the Wall? At worst, there would have been a vote of condemnation in the Security Council of the United Nations. And in the unlikely event that such a thing did happen, they would have laughed at it. So why didn't they do it? Go ask all the members of the United Nations why the Arabs didn't destroy the Wall when they had it under their control. Why is the Wall still standing? No one will be able to answer.

If you want to know the real answer, it is in the Midrash. Because God promised that the Wall would never be destroyed. There is no other answer.

"This provides us with a response to those that deny *Torah min HaShamayim*, the divine origin of the Torah." The Gemara's bold statement applies here as well. If you encounter people who doubt the divine origin of the Oral Torah, show them the Midrash and point to the Wall.

My *rebbe* R' Elya Lopian, *zt"l,* used to say, when he quoted this Midrash, that people are mistaken. They think that God assured the survival of the Wall because we need a place to pray. This is not true. We need to pray near the hallowed ground on which the Temple once stood. We want to get as close as we can, but we do not need a Wall.

So why do we need the Wall? We need it, says R' Elya, to prove to those of feeble faith that the words of the Sages are *Torah min HaShamayim.* If you could hang a banner from the Wall, it would proclaim, "This place is a response to those that deny *Torah min HaShamayim.*"

Many years ago, R' Chatzkel Levenstein, Mashgiach of Ponovezh, once came hurrying into a meeting of his students in the yeshivah with a large cardboard box tucked under his arm. He put the box on the table and pointed to it excitedly. "In this box is the proof," he declared, "that *Torah min HaShamayim.*"

As his wide-eyed students looked on, R' Chatzkel opened the box and removed packing papers. Then he reached in and pulled out an ordinary food processor.

The students stared at him in bewilderment. What did an ordinary food processor have to do with *Torah min HaShamayim*? True, food processors were still a novelty in those days, a technological marvel. But a proof of *Torah min HaShamayim*?

"Let me explain," said R' Chatzkel. "This morning, when I came home after *Shacharis,* I found the Rebbetzin crying. 'What happened?' I said. 'Why are you crying?'

"She pointed to this box, which was sitting on the table. I took out the shiny machine inside and put it on the table. 'Is this why you were crying?' I asked. 'What is this thing?'

" 'That's exactly why I was crying,' she said. 'A visitor from America came by this morning and left this present for us. He said it is the latest thing from America and that he hopes we enjoy it very much. After he left, I took it out, but I can't figure out what to do with it.'

"I looked at the machine. It did look quite complicated. 'What did you do with the papers that were in the box when you opened it?' I asked. 'It cannot be that someone would manufacture such a machine and not enclose instructions with it.'

" 'I threw them away,' she said.

" 'Can you get them back?' I asked.

"She retrieved the papers, and indeed, there was a booklet that contained diagrams and what looked like instructions. But the Rebbetzin was still frustrated, because the instructions were in English. Neither of us reads English. So we called in a student from England, and he read the instructions and explained everything to the Rebbetzin.

"When the Rebbetzin heard everything the machine does — that it kneads the dough and slices the vegetables and who knows whatever else — that was the end of the crying. She literally lit up with joy. As for me, I grabbed the box and ran to the yeshivah to bring you proof that *Torah min HaShamayim*. It is not possible that the Creator would manufacture such an incredible world and not include instructions with it. It is impossible that He would not reveal to us the purpose of this wonderful machine He has made. Those instructions are found in the Torah."

We are not talking here about people who deny the existence of God. Anyone that takes a look around him cannot help but be over-awed by the intricate design of the natural world. The plants and the animals and the seasons. The human body, which is such a marvel of biological engineering that science keeps studying and studying it down to the molecular level and constantly finding new evidence of near miraculous design. These things could not have happened of themselves. Any rational person instantly sees the hand of God.

But what is the purpose of this incredible machine that is our world? Where are the instructions that tell us why it was created and what we must do with it? They are in the Torah. *Torah min HaShamayim!*

CHAPTER NINETEEN

Our Debt to Russian Jewry

I t is a very great honor for me to be chosen as the *Nasi* of the Vaad l'Hatzalas Nidchei Yisrael,[1] and I can honestly say, without the least bit of false humility, that I do not deserve it. There are many who are far more deserving of this honor, people who have invested years and even decades into the struggle for the rebirth of Torah, first in the Soviet Union and afterwards in the lands of the Former Soviet Union, distinguished people, learned people, courageous people who have literally given their blood, sweat and tears for this holy endeavor. How can I even

---

1. Adapted from the Mashgiach's address at his installation as *Nasi* (President) of the Vaad l'Hatzalas Nidchei Yisrael, an organization working for the rebirth of Torah in the former Soviet Union.

be compared to them? And yet I have accepted this honor. Why would I do such a thing?

The Gemara relates (*Horayos* 10a) that when Rabban Gamaliel heard that his two brilliant disciples, Rabbi Elazar Chasma and Rabbi Yochanan ben Gudgeda, were struggling to make a living, he appointed them to high positions in the rabbinate, but they declined. So he summoned them and said, "*Kimedumim atem she'srarah ani nosein lachem?* Do you imagine for a moment that I am offering you honors? Do you think I am granting you authority, that I am giving you the opportunity to rule over the community and become rich and powerful? Is that why you shy away from these positions with such modesty and humility? If so, you are sadly mistaken. *Avdus ani nosein lachem!* I am offering you servitude, no less. I am calling upon you to toil long and hard for the common good. You have no right to shy away from an opportunity to serve and uplift our people."

In this spirit, I accept the position of *Nasi* of the Vaad. If the members of the Vaad feel that by accepting this title I can make some small contribution to furthering the growth of Torah in the lands of the Former Soviet Union, then how can I decline? If taking on this position will enable me to influence people to take a greater interest in the work of the Vaad, if it will allow me to educate people about the critical work the Vaad is doing, if it will help me draw new people to join us on our periodic visits to these lands where Torah blooms like a flower in the spring after a particularly harsh winter, then how can I refuse?

May God give us all the strength, as long as we are in this prolonged *galus*, as long as we have not yet been deemed worthy of welcoming Mashiach into our midst, to ease the burden of our brethren in that corner of the world. For seventy long years, they have borne the brunt of the *galus* for all the Jewish people. While we in the Western world were enjoying prosperity and safety, they were oppressed, persecuted and downtrodden. While we breathed the air of freedom and built *shuls* and schools for our children, they were struggling to hold on to a small spark of Yiddishkeit. May God help us fan that spark into a flame and that flame into a blaze of fire, the fire of Torah such as once burned brightly in countless cities, towns and villages in those lands.

Just recently, I returned from a short visit to the Former Soviet Union, and even today, a decade after the collapse of communism, an air of depression still hangs over the land. It is rare to see a Jewish face with a broad smile on it. Wherever you turn, you see the bitterness of *galus*. It is a disturbing sight to us who are accustomed to our comfortable homes, who take it for granted that we can walk free in the streets. Even today, when the Jewish people in these blighted lands are supposedly free, a Jew must glance furtively to both sides before reaching out for a bit of Yiddishkeit.

The signs of *galus* are everywhere. I saw an *aron kodesh*, a rough-hewn holy ark of the Torah, hidden away in a corner of a little *shul*. What words would we expect to see displayed on an *aron kodesh* in our communities? Perhaps the verse (*Isaiah* 2:3), "*Ki miTzion teitzei Torah*. For Torah will come forth from Zion." Or perhaps (*Psalms* 19:8), "*Toras Hashem temimah*. God's Torah is perfect." Joyous, exultant verses. But I saw neither of these verses, nor any other like them, on that *aron kodesh* in the inconspicuous little *shul*. Instead, the verse chosen was (*Psalms* 44:18), "*Kol zos ba'asnu velo shechachanucha*. All this has befallen us, and yet we have not forgotten You." The image comes to mind of a small group of oppressed Jews driven underground and proud of themselves that they have not forgotten God. The message they left behind for us, these courageous but piteous words, bespeaks the misery in their hearts.

In St. Petersburg, I saw the great *shul* built in the later eighteenth century during the times of the Czarist regime. It is a magnificent edifice, its spacious grounds hemmed in with an iron gate. On that gate, wrought in words of iron, I read the words, "*Ani maamin be'emunah sheleimah shehaBorei yisbarach Shemo lo levado ra'ui lehis-pallel*. I believe with perfect faith that the Creator, blessed be His Name, is the only One to Whom prayer should be directed." And above that, I read the verse (*Psalms* 90:15), "*Samchenu kimos inisanu shnos ra'inu raah.* Give us joy as lengthy as the days You afflicted us, as the years when we experienced misery." Who would dream that words like these would be chosen to adorn a *shul?*

Again and again, I saw poignant reminders of the hearts of Jews giving expression to their innermost feeling with the *galus* cry, a plaintive lament and a flicker of hope. Again and again, I saw the Jewish spirit repressed and suppressed, afraid to lift up its head.

In the airport, on my way from Moscow to St. Petersburg, I had to make certain changes in my ticket, and I was having trouble communicating with the ticket agent who spoke no English. All of a sudden, a tall, powerfully built man came over. The man was wearing the uniform of a general in the Russian Air Force, and his chest was covered with medals; he was clearly an important personage. Speaking perfect English, he graciously offered to help. In no time at all, everything was arranged, and I thanked him profusely. Somehow, I felt certain that the man was Jewish, but by the time I gathered my papers and turned around, he was gone.

Since my flight was not leaving for a while, I went to the waiting room, and there he was, the general who had kindly helped me. I took a seat next to him and thanked him once again.

"Tell me," I said somewhat audaciously, "are you a Jew?"

"Yes," he said. He shifted his feet ever so slightly. I could sense his discomfort.

I pressed on. "Do you remember anything about Judaism?"

"Not very much."

"But you remember something?"

He frowned and knitted his brows. "I remember my grandfather."

"Your grandfather? Do you remember him well?"

He shook his head. "I hardly remember him at all. I was little more than a child when he died."

"And yet you mentioned that you remember your grandfather. There must have been something about him that stayed in your mind."

He nodded. "There was. My grandfather used to look at me with sad eyes. And he would say, '*Mashiach darf shoin kumen.*'"

He spoke the Yiddish words. *Mashiach darf shoin kumen.* It's about time that Mashiach came already. An old man looking at his young grandson with sad eyes. An old man seeing his grandchildren torn away from everything he held dear and holy. And what could he or anyone else do? There was no other way to survive. All he could do was say, "*Mashiach darf shoin kumen. Mashiach darf shoin kumen.*"

"Do you know what those words mean?" I asked him.

"Yes, I do."

"And do you believe in them? Are they meaningful to you?"

He gave me a long look and said, "In honor of my grandfather, I believe in them."

I couldn't help but smile ruefully at this typically Russian answer.

"Would you tell me your name?" I said, but he refused. A few minutes later, his flight was called, and he left. I never saw him again.

Regardless of how Jewish hearts warm to each other, years upon years of harassment and persecution have ingrained in the hearts of the Jews in these lands such a deep instinctive fear, such a profound distrust, that one Jew is afraid to reveal his name to his brother.

I believe that never in all of history has any other nation succeeded as did the Russians "*lehash'kicham Torasecha ulehaaviram meichukei retzonecha,* to cause the Jewish people to forget your Torah and transgress Your laws." The Germans were mortal enemies of the Jewish people, they had *sinas Yisrael,* and God in His inscrutable wisdom allowed them to wipe out so many of us. But the Communists hated God, they had *sinas Hashem,* and for reasons we cannot fathom, He allowed them to succeed more than any nation that had ever tried before.

Millions of Jews emerging from the shadow of communism know nothing about Torah, nothing about Yiddishkeit. In places where Jewish life once thrived, in places that once teemed with *shuls,* schools and all manner of Torah institutions, in places where great sages, rabbis and scholars once guided vibrant communities, millions of Jews live now in ignorance, oblivious to their heritage and their illustrious past. Communism has fallen, but the tragedy that has befallen our people is not yet a thing of the past. The nightmare may have come to an end, but the time has not yet come when we can finally relax.

I am reminded of a story I once heard from R' Yaakov Galinsky. The story took place in Bnei Brak a few short years after the Second World War. Many young Israelis at that time belonged to an organization called Hashomer Hatzair, the extremely anti-religious youth movement of the Labor Zionists. One day, three Hashomer Hatzair boys walked into Bnei Brak, dressed in their customary short trousers, sandals and caps, and declared that they wanted to learn Torah. In those days, there was not yet a *baal teshuvah* movement such as there is today, with numerous *yeshivos* and organizations and tens of thousands of people returning to Torah. No one knew what to make of these boys nor how to deal with them. So they put the question to the Chazon Ish.

"Do as they ask," said the Chazon Ish. "Teach them Torah."

"But what is this all about?" they asked him.

"I will explain it to you," said the Chazon Ish. "A few generations ago, the grandparents of these boys turned their backs on the Torah and chose the secular life. They left their homes and became communists, socialists, Zionists. In desperation, their parents ran to the *shuls*, threw open the doors of the *aron kodesh* and cried out in anguish, 'Master of the Universe, help us. We are in terrible trouble. We are losing our children. Please, please give us back our children. Our hearts are breaking.' I saw this happen with my own eyes. Rivers of tears flowed from the eyes of brokenhearted parents, and torrents of their prayers assailed the gates of Heaven. But these wayward children had left of their own free will, and their parents' prayers could not bring them back.

"Still, no prayers ever go to waste. God gathered in those tears and prayers and held them for several generations. By then, the grandchildren of these poor parents were all *tinokos shenishbu*, blameless innocents brought up in ignorance. Now, God brought out the tears and the prayers and kindled a spark of Jewish feeling and a hunger for Torah in the hearts of these young boys you see before you. That is why they are here. That is why it is our responsibility to teach them."

And then the Chazon Ish, with his extraordinary wisdom and vision, added a prediction that everyone found incredible at the time, "You will see," he said. "Today, there are only three of them, but one day, they will return in the thousands." And he was right.

When the Communist suppression of Yiddishkeit went into full swing in 1930 and afterward, the Chafetz Chaim and R' Chaim Ozer sent letters to Jewish communities all over the world. These letters are published; anyone who is interested can read them. Full of pain and anguish, they describe the onslaught on the spiritual strongholds of our people. Shuls were being closed, schools shuttered, classes disbanded, rabbis exiled to Siberia, Torah scrolls burned in the streets. Millions of Jews were being torn away from Yiddishkeit. What should be done? "Pray for our people!" they wrote in every letter. "Pray! Pray! Pray!"

And pray we did.

Jewish people poured forth prayers drenched in scalding tears, prayers issuing forth from hearts contorted with pain and compassion for our Jewish brethren in distress. For decades, Jews the world over prayed for Russian Jewry trapped behind the Iron Curtain. In every *shul*, in every school, there were numerous assemblies and innumerable prayers for our Jewish brothers and sisters in Russia. I remember this vividly from when I was a boy in yeshivah. And this is how it was everywhere else as well. We prayed for Russian Jewry, and we cried for them.

So what happened to all those countless millions of prayers?

In the most miraculous way, in the most astounding way, in the most inexplicable way, God used these prayers to bring down the

Soviet Union. When the right time came, the whole rotten, malevolent structure just crumbled into dust. And it was over.

But was it?

Was the collapse of the Soviet Union the answer to all those millions and millions of pure Jewish prayers? Was the fall of the Soviet government the ultimate goal that the Chafetz Chaim and R' Chaim Ozer sought?

Of course not. It was only a small beginning. Now, the harder part would begin, the long struggle to bring back the millions of Jewish people the Soviet Union had estranged from their God and their nation.

By bringing down the Soviet Union, God presented us with the opportunity to complete the fulfillment of all those prayers with our work. God has presented us with a challenge. The walls are down. The people are accessible. So what do we intend to do about it? Are we waiting for it all to happen by itself?

For the last twenty years, the Vaad l'Hatzalas Nidchei Yisrael has been sending *shlichim*, emissaries of Torah, into the Soviet Union and its successor states. One thousand four hundred *shlichim* to date have helped ignite a Torah revolution. In many cities, new *shuls*, *mikvaos*, *yeshivos* and girls' schools are springing up. The sweet sounds of Torah are being heard once again in places where they have been stilled for so many years. In the end, our enemies are defeated, and the Torah triumphs.

In Kishinev, I visited a *shul* that the government allowed the Vaad to acquire for its yeshivah. As I stood in the courtyard, someone told me a bit about the history of this *shul*.

During the War, the German killers rounded up the Jews of Kishinev in a horse market across the way from this *shul* and prepared to slaughter them right then and there. One Jewish man approached the officer in charge and said, "There is a *shul* across the way. Could you grant us permission to go there for one last prayer before we die?" For some unknown reason, the officer granted this request, and hundreds of Jews packed into the *shul* for the final Minchah of their lives. Afterward, they were all taken out to the courtyard of the *shul* and shot to death.

This very ground upon which I stood was soaked with the holy blood of Jewish martyrs. But the *shul* before which I stood once again resounded with the sounds of Torah and prayer. I stepped through the door and stood there for a while watching the eager faces of the young students discovering the beauty and grandeur of the Torah. Born to families that knew nothing about Yiddishkeit, they were poring over the Gemara as their ancestors had done, and enjoying every minute of it. And there were more of them than there had been the year before. And even more than the year before that.

The Jews in these lands are so responsive to everything we do for them. I have seen it everywhere in my travels. Wherever we have opened *shuls* and schools, the people come and say, "Teach us Torah! We want to learn. We want to know. What should we say? What should we do? How should we live?" Their thirst for Torah and Yiddishkeit is incredible. It is the thirst of parched souls who have been denied the life-giving waters of Torah for generations. And now that it is being offered to them once again, they want more and more and more.

But are we doing enough? And are enough of us doing?

We are reaching hundreds, maybe thousands of people, but there are millions that we have not reached. We have started a revolution, but it is only the beginning. We need to make it grow and spread until it takes on a powerful momentum of its own, until it becomes an unstoppable force, until the Jewish people are united and whole once again. We can make it happen.

We have seen the terrible *galus* experiences of Russian Jewry come to an end in our time. Their test is finally over. Now we have ours.

CHAPTER TWENTY

Broadening the World of Torah

Many people in our times are active in *kiruv rechokim*, which means reaching out to Jews distant from our heritage and drawing them nearer. For the most part, these activists are extremely dedicated people working through outreach organizations or through their individual efforts, and they are bringing many tens of thousands of Jews back to their spiritual and religious roots and to the profound pleasures of an authentic Jewish life.

All these people are convinced they are doing God's work, that reaching out to uncommitted Jews is an important *mitzvah*. And they are right. It is indeed a very great *mitzvah*. But which *mitz-*

vah is it? There is no commandment in the Torah that states, "You shall reach out to uncommitted Jews and bring them back." Under which *mitzvah* heading then does outreach fall? Which *mitzvah* do we fulfill when we draw distant Jews nearer to God and His Torah?

Some are of the opinion that outreach is included in the *mitzvah* of *tochachah* (*Leviticus* 19:17), "*Hochei'ach tochiach es amisecha*. You shall surely rebuke your friend." According to this opinion, when we see other Jews transgressing the commandments of the Torah, even if they are only doing so out of ignorance, it is our responsibility to enlighten them and encourage them to mend their ways.

In this day and age, if rebuke means to lecture and reprimand then it is difficult to fulfill the *mitzvah* of *tochachah* by rebuking an uncommitted Jew. Virtually all uncommitted Jews today are *tinokos shenishbu*, blameless innocents brought up in ignorance; the Torah has no more meaning to them than some quaint old parchment scrolls. They have never been taught to recognize the Torah as an authority in their lives. They do not understand that by disobeying the Torah's commandments they are rejecting God's authority. Therefore, informing them that what they are doing transgresses the Torah is not considered an act of rebuke. It is rather an act of futility.

The Chazon Ish essentially makes this point with regard to the laws of *shechitah*, ritual slaughter. A *mumar*, a renegade who transgresses even after being rebuked, is not qualified to perform *shechitah*, even while under strict supervision. However, writes the Chazon Ish, an uncommitted Jew in our times is not considered a *mumar* even if he disregards *tochachah*, because the *tochachah* is meaningless to him. Therefore, he may perform *shechitah* under the watchful eye of a supervisor. An informed Jew who is aware of the Torah's authority and chooses to defy it is considered a *mumar*. An uninformed Jew is not. Therefore, if today's uncommitted Jews are not capable of receiving rebuke in their state of being uninformed, it stands to reason that there cannot be a *mitzvah* to rebuke them.

Where then do we find the *mitzvah* of Jewish outreach?

The Rambam writes (*Sefer HaMitzvos, Asei* 3) that outreach is part of the *mitzvah* of *ahavas Hashem*, loving God. Every day, we say in the Shema (*Deuteronomy* 6:5), "And you shall love God your Lord with all your heart..." But how does one express one's love for God? The Rambam, quoting the *Sifrei*, gives two answers. One of them is to reach out to as many people as possible and draw them closer to God, to inspire them to serve Him and have faith in Him. God calls Abraham (*Isaiah* 41:8) *ohavi*, "the one who loves Me" because of (*Genesis* 12:5) *hanefesh asher asu b'Charan*, "the following they built up in Charan." Abraham was the first outreach activist. He worked to instill faith in God and the concept of His unity in everyone he met, and by doing so he expressed his love for God.

The Rambam explains this with a parable. A person has a friend whom he loves dearly. He sees in this friend many admirable qualities — wisdom, humor, sensitivity, loyalty, generosity, kindness and much more — but to his amazement, other people do not have the same admiration for this friend that he does. His love for his friend does not allow him to accept this state of affairs. If only people knew, he thinks, how wonderful my friend is, they would love him equally well. So he sings the praises of his friend to every person he meets, to every person who will lend him an ear for a few minutes. Don't you see, he says, don't you appreciate, don't you understand? And he doesn't rest until everyone he knows recognizes the worth of this friend and grows to love him as well.

This is the natural reaction, explains the Rambam, of a loving friend. He wants everyone else to have the same appreciation he does for the object of his love. Therefore, if he loves God, he will feel upset that other people do not appreciate God's greatness and infinite kindness. He will find it appalling that other people have no gratitude to God for all the gifts He bestows on them.

He will find it inconceivable that they are unaware of the profound joy inherent in Torah and *mitzvos*. He will find it unbearable that others do not love God as he does. So he will act to correct the situation. He will reach out and teach and cajole and set an example and inspire until he awakens in the hearts of other people a love that burns as brightly as his own. And in this way, in the grand tradition of Abraham, he expresses his love for God. This is the *mitzvah* of outreach.

There is yet another source for the *mitzvah* of Jewish outreach. The Torah tells us (*Deuteronomy* 22:1-3), "You shall not see your brother's ox or his sheep roaming wild and look away from them, you shall surely return them (*hashev tashiveim*) to your brother. And if your brother is not close to you, and you do not know him, then you shall gather it into your house and it shall be with you until your brother seeks it out, then you shall return it to him. So shall you do with his donkey, so shall you do with his garment, so shall you do with any lost object of your brother's that he loses and you find, you shall not be able to look away (*lo suchal lehis'aleim*)."

This commandment is not limited to lost objects. It obligates us to do everything in our power to protect other people's property from damage. We are forbidden to look away when we can do something to help prevent the damage. Rabbeinu Yonah writes in *Shaarei Teshuvah* (3:70), "You shall not be able to look away. This commandment warns us not to be neglectful when it comes to saving someone else's property ... If he sees another's land about to be flooded, he has to raise up a barricade against the floodwaters, just as we are commanded to save another's life and to think of ways to help him in his times of trouble ... Should you say, 'I don't know about this,' [God] recognizes the contents of the heart and knows the hidden thoughts, and He repays each person according to his deeds. If he fails to come to the rescue of another or seek ways to help him, the Holy Blessed One considers him to have caused the damage himself." If we look away, any damage that results is our responsibility.

In these three verses, the Torah uses the words "your brother" five times when once would have been more than enough. The Torah only had to begin with "your brother's" animal. The pronouns "he," "him" and "his" would have been enough for the rest of the passage. It seems that the Torah is emphasizing how we must feel about another Jew. Even if "he is not close to you," even if "you do not know him," he is your brother. If we are all "children of God your Lord," as the Torah states (*Deuteronomy* 14:1), then we are all brothers. And is it possible that a person would stand by idly while his brother's property is being washed away? Is it possible that he would not work long and frantically to save whatever he can? Perhaps that is why the Torah expresses the prohibition as "you shall not be able to look away" rather than as "you shall not look away." The Torah does not just forbid you to look away. The Torah commands you to consider every Jew as your brother so that you will be unable to look away.

The Shelah goes a bit further. "The reason for this commandment," he writes, "is to let us know that if we are responsible for another's monetary loss, we are certainly responsible for his spiritual loss ... The Torah expresses the phrase 'you shall surely return them' as *hashev tashiveim* rather than the more appropriate *hachazor tachzireim*, because *hashavah* intimates that we must stand guard and toil and struggle until our friend does *teshuvah*, until he returns through repentance. Our responsibility does not allow us to look away."

If we truly feel that all Jews are our brothers, if we truly feel connected to all the Jewish people with bonds of love, compassion and brotherhood, then how can we stand by and watch them slip away into spiritual oblivion? How we can stand by without drawing them closer to God and His holy Torah, without inspiring them to *teshuvah*? If they are our brothers and sisters, how are we able to look away?

When a person sets out into the field of outreach motivated by a pure love for God, a sincere desire to lift up His honor in the world and a profound compassion for all Jewish people, there is no limit to what he can accomplish. And there is no limit to his *zechuyos*, the merit he can accumulate in this world.

I once heard a story about a certain *rosh yeshivah* in Eretz Yisrael who was known to be a *baal teshuvah*. This man is a respected *talmid chacham*. His family and household are models of Torah life. His children are learned, refined, accomplished and have extraordinary *middos tovos*, good character. He has produced many disciples over the years, some of whom have since gone out on their own to spread Torah and Yiddishkeit. The community has nothing but admiration for this man.

What was his background? Where did he start? What led him to where he is today? It is an extraordinary story.

This man had grown up on an anti-religious *kibbutz*. He knew nothing about Torah and cared even less. All he cared about was enjoying life. When he was eighteen, he decided to taste every forbidden pleasure the world had to offer, and he set about accomplishing this goal systematically. One day, he heard that in a certain place in Haifa there was a pleasure being offered that he had not yet experienced.

He took a bus to Haifa and set off to find the address he had been given. It was in a neighborhood that was far from respectable. He found the house. It bore a sign advertising the pleasures offered within. Just then he saw a Jew dressed in religious garb coming the other way. As he neared the house, the religious Jew caught sight of the immodest sign and instantly turned his head away, lifting his hand to shield his eyes.

The young *kibbutznik* was shocked. How could someone turn his eyes away from this pleasure being offered? Must be, he reasoned, that this person possessed an even greater pleasure. "That is the pleasure I want!" he declared. On the spot, he turned around and went off to enroll in a yeshivah, where he indeed found the greatest pleasures imaginable. Eventually, he became a *talmid chacham*, raised a family and established his own yeshivah, an entire world of Torah and *mitzvos*.

It is an interesting and inspiring story, but one particular aspect of it struck me when I heard it. This religious Jew, the one who turned his head away from what he shouldn't see, will one day pass away and come before the Heavenly Court to be judged. His sins will be placed on one side of the scale, and his merits on the other. And he will look at the merits piling up in his favor, and he will be confused. "Who are all these people whose *mitzvos* are being counted for my credit?" he will say. "Who are these hundreds of children whose Torah is being placed on my scale? I don't know these people. I've never seen them in my life!"

"Do you remember that day in Haifa," he will be told, "when you turned your head away to avoid seeing something you shouldn't?"

"Vaguely," he will say.

"Well, at that moment, a secular Jew was watching, and what you did inspired him to become a *baal teshuvah*. Therefore, all his Torah and *mitzvos* and all the Torah and *mitzvos* of his children and children's children and disciples and disciples' disciples for all generations are to your credit. And all for that one moment of looking away!"

One moment, one small act of righteousness, and the reward is virtually endless. All the positive results that come out of it for all generations are credited to his account in Heaven. Those in outreach, who perform many great acts of righteousness, are certainly accumulating merit without limit on their own scales. Every person they bring back to God and His Torah represents children and grandchildren for all generations, and if this *baal teshuvah* goes into teaching or outreach himself, the merits are multiplied a hundredfold and a thousandfold as time goes on.

The *Chovos HaLevavos* (*Shaar Ahavas Hashem* 6) writes, "My brother, it is worthwhile for you to know this. A faithful Jew may achieve the ultimate in perfecting himself for God. He may even become like the angels with their superb qualities, their admirable practices, their exertions to serve the Creator and their pure love for Him. But he will never accumulate as much merit as the one who shows people the proper path and reconciles transgressors to the service of the Creator. His merits are multiplied by the merits [of those he has reconciled] and will accumulate for all time.

"Imagine two merchants who come to market, one bearing a single roll of fabric and the other bearing numerous rolls. The merchant who brings only one roll could recover his investment tenfold and still earn only a hundred zuz. The other, however, may only double his investment, but considering the sheer volume of merchandise he has brought to market, he could earn ten thousand zuz.

"In the same way," the *Chovos HaLevavos* concludes, "a person who perfects only himself gains only a limited amount of merit, but a person who elevates not only himself but others as well multiplies his own merit by all the merit of those he has brought closer to God."

Listen to these words. Even if a person perfects himself to the point where he is practically an angel, his merit is minuscule compared to the merit of a person who brings wayward Jews back to their Father in Heaven.

Outreach, however, is no simple matter. Many issues must be considered, questions regarding methods, responsibilities and hazards. Although these issues are of particular relevance to outreach activists, the truth is that each of us should aspire to some form of outreach, even if only in a limited way. And if we do feel a love for God that compels us to reach out to people, we need to consider the issues and seek guidance on the questions that arise. The following are a few brief comments regarding a few of the relevant issues. They are not meant to be definitive rulings, but rather to bring these issues to the attention of those who reach out.

❧The First Step

Since the purpose of outreach is to fulfill the *mitzvah* of loving God, where do we begin? Do we start by showing them the beauty of *Shabbos*? Do we start by teaching them about putting on *tefillin* or keeping a kosher kitchen? How do we teach them to love God? What is the first step?

The answer is actually spelled out quite explicitly in the Gemara (*Yoma* 86a), "It is written (*Deuteronomy* 6:5), 'And you shall love God your Lord with all your heart.' This means that you should cause the Name of Heaven to become beloved among people. A person should learn Torah and Talmud, he should attach himself to Torah sages, and he should deal gently with people. What will people say about him? They will say, 'Fortunate is his father who taught him Torah. Fortunate is his teacher who taught him Torah. Woe to the people who have not learned Torah. This person has learned Torah — and look! How pleasant are his ways, how perfect his behavior!' ... But if a person learns Torah and Talmud and attaches himself to Torah sages but doesn't act in good faith and doesn't speak gently to others, what do people say? They say, 'Woe to him that learned Torah. Woe to his father who taught him Torah. Woe to his teacher who taught him Torah. This person has learned Torah — and look! How corrupt is his behavior, how despicable his ways.'"

The *mitzvos* that attract the uninitiated to Torah and illuminate the path of their return are the *mitzvos bein adam lechaveiro*, the commandments that govern relationships with other people. Be kind to other people. Be thoughtful. Be forgiving rather than vengeful. Do not be quick to anger. Be merciful. All these are *mitzvos* in the Torah as much as *tefillin* and *matzah* are. Even more, these are the *mitzvos* that are most effective in making an impression on other people.

So how do we teach these *mitzvos*?

Only one way: By example.

If we look closely at the quotation from the Gemara, we notice that spreading love of God is accomplished in two parts. We have to learn Torah and Talmud and attach ourselves to Torah sages, and we have to be kind, gentle and faithful in our relations with other people.

The first part establishes our identity in the eyes of the public. They see our strong connection to Torah. They notice that we study the Written Law and the Oral Law and that we seek our guidance from Torah sages. In this way, we become identified with the Torah in the public mind. And then they see how we behave, how meticulous we are in our dealings with other people, how faithful, how gentle, how loving. And it dawns on them that these two things are not a coincidence. They realize that Torah has this wonderful effect on those who embrace it, and they cry out, "Fortunate is the one who learns Torah. Fortunate are his parents and teachers!"

If we can elicit this reaction from the people to whom we are reaching out, we will have ignited in their hearts a spark of love for God and His Torah. Afterwards, all we need to do is fan this spark into a great flame. This, of course, is far from a simple matter, but the first step is the most important and the most difficult.

✿There Can Be No Compromise

Uncommitted Jews will often express interest in the Torah, even though they are not prepared to make a commitment to observance. In such cases, would it be permitted to compromise with them? For instance, would it be all right to tell them to keep Shabbos only at night and carry on as they did before during the day?

In order to answer this question, we have to draw a distinction between compromise, which is absolutely forbidden, and gradualism, which is acceptable and unavoidable.

Every letter of the Torah is inviolate down to the *kutzo shel yod*, a minute part of the letter *yod*; we have no right to adapt or adjust the Torah to different times and situations. At the same time, becoming observant requires drastic changes in a person's life, and in many if not most cases, it must be accomplished gradually, step by step. But you must make it clear to the people that halfway measures are not acceptable as a permanent state. They are no more than intermediate stages on the way to full observance. There is no rush, no pressure. They can take their time and progress at their own comfortable pace. But they must recognize that the goal is full and complete observance of the entire Torah.

R' Yisrael Salanter spent a lot of time in the German port city of Memel. Jewish merchants from Lithuania would often travel to Memel on business, but most of the local Jewish residents were not observant. They did not keep Shabbos, and one can imagine they did many other things they shouldn't have been doing.

It is told that during the first months he spent in Memel, R' Yisrael would get up in *shul* on Shabbos morning after Shacharis, when preachers customarily addressed the congregation, and say, "*Aleh Litvishe Yidden arois.* All Lithuanian Jews, please step out."

After all the Lithuanian Jews had left, he spoke to the German Jews on their level. "My good friends, I know that you are going to leave here when we finish and go to your shops and your businesses. I can't stop you. But I want you to know that certain things are forbidden *mid'Oraisa*, by the Torah itself, while others are only forbidden *mid'Rabbanan*, by Rabbinic decree. At least, try to avoid doing those things that are forbidden by the Torah. You know, you don't have to carry in the street on Shabbos. Leave everything you need in your place of business and walk there with empty pockets. No handkerchief. No money. Nothing at all. Just walk there with empty pockets and do your business."

This was R' Yisrael's message to the non-observant German Jews. He did not want the Lithuanian Jews to hear him say these things, because they would not have reacted well. The more religious ones would have stoned him, and the weaker ones would have followed his advice to the German Jews and conducted their business on Shabbos. But R' Yisrael understood that this was what he had to say to the German Jews. This was the language they had to hear. Don't carry on Shabbos. It was not a compromise, just a

Broadening the World of Torah ❦ 265

small first step. And indeed, in the course of the three years he spent there, he transformed Memel into an observant city.

This important distinction is unfortunately also relevant to situations in observant families. Sometimes, children will fall by the wayside for some reason or another and refuse to do what they know is expected of them. For instance, a young boy may stop praying daily. Should his parents pressure him to go to *shul* three times a day? There really is no point. It won't happen in a constructive way, and nothing will be gained.

It would be much better to say to the boy, "You have to pray three times a day, but you have a difficulty with this. All right, between you and me, for the time being, we'll just do Shacharis and put on *tefillin*. We can do it that way." He is obviously going through a personal crisis. Telling him it is all right to do just a little bit is not a compromise. It is drawing him back gradually, step by step. Be gentle and understanding. He will get there.

❧Two Effective Tools

I have often found the *Sefer HaChinuch* a wonderful key to teaching the *mitzvos* one encounters in the Chumash, because it explains some of the roots and special messages of each individual *mitzvah*. As the author explains in his introduction, he wrote it to get his son together with his friends off the street on the Sabbath. It works today as it did then, because it adds flavor to the otherwise dry study of the *mitzvos*. It makes them fascinating.

For instance, the Torah decrees that a *ganav*, a sneak thief, pays twice the value of the object he stole, while a *gazlan*, a brazen robber who attacks his victim face to face, pays only the value itself. Why is this so? Our Sages tell us that the thief shows that he is afraid of people but not of God. The thief disgraced God, and therefore, he must be penalized. The robber, however, is a fearless person, unafraid of God and unafraid of people. Therefore, he does not deserve an added penalty. Learning the *mitzvos* with their roots brings a deep appreciation for their wisdom, depth and sheer spiritual beauty.

A most effective outreach tool is to invite people to visit a yeshivah where *talmidei chachamim* are learning Torah. The sight and the sound are unlike anything else in the world. It is far more effective than lectures and arguments. People stand mesmerized by the scene. So this is your world! This is Torah! And they become envious, because we have something special that they do not. You can reinforce the experience by telling them stories about the yeshivah world and its great leaders. You can make them hungry by giving them a glimpse of what they are missing.

❧ PROTECTING YOUR CHILDREN

Outreach sometimes presents a danger to one's own children right in the home. How often does it happen — and I speak from experience — that inviting secular people for Shabbos damages the children in the home? Young impressionable children sit at the table and hear all sorts of discussions that are not appropriate for their ears. There may be heated intellectual arguments with a spirited back and forth, which the parents are enjoying immensely. And they may even be getting the better of it and convincing the Shabbos guests. But the child may hear the other side argued strongly and persuasively and think that the parents' response was not so convincing.

If you have babies or older children, you can consider bringing secular people into the home for Shabbos. But if you have children in their formative years, you are taking a great risk — unless you can control the program and limit it to good food, pleasant conversation, *zemiros* and *divrei Torah*. No philosophy.

At the end of the day, you've got to account for your own children. You cannot expose them for the sake of your outreach work. *Kiruv rechokim* has to be *kiruv* all the way. Only attracting, no repelling. What is the good of attracting other people when you are repelling your own children?

Unfortunately, in this day and age, our children are exposed to too many bad influences in too many places. The only place where we hope that they're sheltered is in our own homes. You cannot start bringing the street into your home, even if you have the best intentions.

⚞ PROTECTING YOURSELF

Last but far from least, when you are out there influencing others, how do you protect yourself from being influenced in return? What are the dangers, and what are the guidelines for staying in the safe zone?

Let us listen to the words of the Rambam (*Mishneh Torah, Hilchos Dei'os* 6:1), "It is human nature to be influenced in one's views and actions by one's associates and friends and to adopt the customs of the people in one's country. Therefore, a person must attach himself to righteous people and always live among scholars in order to learn from their deeds. A person must also distance himself from evildoers who walk in darkness in order to avoid learning from their deeds ... Should he find himself in a country whose customs are bad and whose people do not follow the right way, he should move to a place of righteous people who behave properly. If all the countries he has visited or knows by reputation behave improperly, as is the case in our times, or if war or pestilence prevents him from traveling abroad, he should withdraw into his own privacy ... If the people are so evil and sinful that they do not allow him to remain in the country unless he joins the rest of society and adopts their evil practices, he should go dwell in caves, among the thorns or in the wilderness, but he should not behave as the sinful do ..."

The Rambam makes a strong statement. This is human nature. It is the way a person is created. It is normal and to be expected that a person will tend to behave as his friends do and as is common in the environment of the country in which he lives. Therefore, a person must always make sure to live among the righteous and avoid the sinful. In the very first psalm, King David praises the person who avoids the evil, the sinful and the mockers.

If circumstances compel a person to live among the sinful, the Rambam concludes, he is obliged to go into the wilderness and live in a cave. There is no other choice. It doesn't help to say *Tehillim* or devote more time to study and prayer. Nothing helps, because it is human nature to be influenced; it is like a reflex action. The only choice is to head for the caves.

So how do we apply these guidelines to outreach?

We can say straightaway that if a person lives in a strong observant community, such as Lakewood, Monsey, Brooklyn or Baltimore, and goes out for a few hours a day to do outreach work and then comes back to his home, his *beis midrash* and his environment, he is not running a high risk of being adversely influenced. But what if a person spends most of his time doing outreach work in a secular environment? Even more, what if he is offered a position in teaching or the rabbinate that would require his relocating to such an environment? Can it be justified within the Rambam's strict guidelines? Is it possible to avoid the "human nature to be influenced by associates and friends"?

Let us take a closer look at the introductory words of the Rambam. "It is human nature to be influenced in one's views and actions by one's associates and friends and to adopt the customs of the people in one's country." It seems to me that the Rambam makes two distinct statements here, that he identifies two distinct sources of influence. One, a person is influenced by associates and friends. Two, a person is influenced by the environment in his country.

It seems that if a person finds himself "in a country" with a harmful environment, he will resist its influence if his "associates and friends" are strong in their Yiddishkeit, even if they live far away. The only way to counteract the negative influence of his surroundings is to maintain a positive influence through associates and friends.

No matter where he finds himself, no matter how distant it is from the centers of Torah and Yiddishkeit, he must reinforce his feelings of closeness and connection to his associates and friends in the Torah community. He has to feel with profound conviction that he really doesn't belong in this place where he finds himself, that he is only there to awaken a love for God and His Torah in the hearts of his wayward Jewish brothers and sisters. He has to understand that until these people embrace the Torah they cannot be considered more than casual friends; they cannot be counted among his close associates and friends.

In order to remain strong, he must keep his friends in the Torah community uppermost in his heart. He must maintain contact with them, and he must continue to measure himself by their standards. How will they look at me, he must ask himself, the next time we meet in person? Will they see in me the same person they knew so well or will they sense a subtle or perhaps even not so subtle change? Do we still have the same thoughts and interests in common? Do we still share the same values? Will they be proud of me? Or will they be disappointed in what I've become?

As long as he cares profoundly about the opinion of his friends in the Torah community, he will be all right. The positive influence of his friends will protect him from the influence of his place. But if he feels himself drifting apart from his former friends, then he has no armor against the negative influence of his environment. Slowly but surely, subtly and not so subtly, he will change. It is only human nature. He will speak differently, dress differently, act differently, think differently. And one day, he will wake up and not recognize the person he has become.

Another way of insulating oneself from one's environment is mentioned in one of the letters of the Chazon Ish. At issue was whether or not a rabbi could accept a position in a non-observant congregation. How does a person avoid being influenced by the people around him? The Chazon Ish permits him to accept the position but on one condition. He must not attempt to ingratiate himself with them through camaraderie. Instead, he must stake out a higher moral and spiritual ground and thereby set himself apart from the community. He must become its conscience. He must become the opposition. Friendly opposition, but opposition nonetheless.

Nowadays, outreach can take on exceedingly friendly forms. People will say things they do not really believe. They might even make inappropriate compromises. And all this because they want to gain the favor and confidence of the people to whom they are reaching out. So they hide their true intentions, because they are afraid people will say, "You're only interested in converting me!"

The Chazon Ish clearly rejects such an approach. If you try to be their buddy, you will speak their language and take on their interests, and you will begin dropping, dropping, dropping. Because it is human nature to be influenced by friends and the environment.

As for the people's suspicions, it is always best to be honest. "Yes, it is true," you can tell them. "I have come here to transform your lives, to bring you back to God and the Torah. I cannot force you to do anything against your will, nor would I want to do so. But I am patient. I will help you grow and learn until you will want to do it on your own. Does this mean I am not genuinely your friend? Not at all. It just proves my friendship. Because I love you and care about you, my own flesh and blood, my own brothers and sisters, I want you to experience the joy and the fulfillment of loving God."

THE VALUE OF A JEW

In the story of Ruth (2:4), we read that when Boaz went out to the fields he greeted his workers by saying, "*Hashem imachem.* God be with you." And they replied, "*Yevarechecha*

Hashem. God bless you." Our Sages tell us that this was the first time the Name of God was ever used in a personal greeting. Boaz greeted his workers in the Name of God, and they responded in kind. After serious deliberation, Boaz and his court had decided it was permitted to do so.

This was no simple matter.

Imagine if you want to say "Good morning" to someone. So you go into the *shul*, open the *aron kodesh*, the holy ark, and take out the Torah. Then you walk toward him with the Torah on your shoulder, and you say, "Good morning! It's so lovely to see you." Quite unthinkable, one would say.

Using the Name of God in a personal greeting was originally no less scandalous. But Boaz and his court saw a great need. The brotherly feeling among Jews was declining. People were no longer so kind to each other. They did not treat each other with enough respect. So Boaz and his court decreed that the Name of God should be used in greetings, because this would enhance the status of the individual Jew. If the Name of God could be used to greet him, then he certainly deserved to be respected.

Why did Boaz and his court consider it permissible to use the holy Name of God to raise the stature of individual Jews? Because they understood that God loves every single Jew without limit, that He treasures each and every one more than anything else in the world.

In our times, many of the best, brightest and most righteous people of our community, the flower of the Torah world, are investing their time, energy and resources into raising up people who are very, very distant from Torah and Yiddishkeit. It is not a simple thing that they are doing.

But God has shown us that there is no limit to the value of each individual Jew, that it is worthwhile to use the holy Name of God to gain him a little more respect. And if so, it is worthwhile for us to reach out to those Jews who are distant from God and His Torah. Each individual Jewish soul in which the love for God and His Torah is awakened is precious beyond measure. No price is too high to pay. No sacrifice is too great. And the reward is eternal and without limit.

◈ THE MOST EFFECTIVE OUTREACH OF ALL

Before closing, it is important to point out that there is yet another avenue along which the faithful Jew can travel if he wants to reach out to Jews who are distant from the Torah. But it is an avenue available only to those select few whose hearts shine with a profound purity and whose minds and spirits are aflame with a burning passion for the Torah.

The well-known Mishnah in (*Peah* 1:1) lists the commandments — such as honoring parents, being kind to the needy, fostering peace and learning Torah — that bring reward both in this world and the next. The Gemara asks (*Kiddushin* 40a) why *shilu'ach haken*, sending away the mother bird, is not included on this list. And the Gemara answers that a righteous person who is good both with regard to Heaven and with regard to other people is rewarded in this world. A righteous person who is good only with regard to Heaven and provides no benefit to other people does not receive his reward in this world, only in the next.

If so, asks R' Elchanan Wasserman in *Kovetz Maamarim*, why is learning Torah included in this Mishnah as one of the commandments that bring reward in this world as well as the next? True, Torah scholars are useful to the community, but how does the very act of Torah study benefit other people? "Perhaps we can explain it," he writes, "based on [what R' Chaim Volozhiner writes in] *Nefesh HaChaim*. The Gemara states (*Nedarim* 32a) that the world was created because of the Torah, as it is written (*Jeremiah* 33:25), 'If not for My covenant of day and night [the Torah which is studied day and night], I would never have established the design of heaven and earth.' In the same way, the continued existence of the world is also dependent every moment on the study of Torah. If there would be one moment when no Torah is being learned anywhere in the world,

Heaven forbid, all of creation would instantly disintegrate. According to this, we can say that a person that learns Torah has a share in the maintenance of the world, which provides the greatest benefit possible to other people — the benefit of existence."

R' Elchanan Wasserman is talking about a person who learns Torah *lishmah*, for its own sake, not for his own gain or honor but because Torah connects humankind with God, because Torah brings the Divine Presence into the world and thereby enables it to exist.

One of the forty-eight ways through which Torah is acquired, as listed in the Mishnah (*Avos* 6:6), is "love for other people." What does love for other people have to do with growth in Torah learning? If anything, one would think the opposite to be true. The more one loves people, the less one is inclined to sit in a corner and concentrate on Torah study, the less one grows in Torah learning. But according to R' Elchanan Wasserman, we can well understand the connection. The greatest expression of love for other people is intense and dedicated Torah study, which secures the continued existence of the world.

If a person who learns Torah assures the existence of the world, if he creates a connection between God and all of creation, then there can be no outreach greater than learning Torah. What more can we possibly do for our Jewish brothers and sisters than bring them closer to God so that the divine spark of Jewishness in their hearts will burst into flame all by itself? In fact, if enough people would sit in the beis midrash and learn Torah lishmah, that alone could draw all the rest of the Jewish people back to full observance of the Torah.

Who should reach out to other Jews directly and who should do it through Torah study? This is a question each individual must ask his own *roshei yeshivah* and *rabbanim*, people who know him even better than he knows himself. But for those individuals that learn Torah with purity and selflessness, that are driven to bring honor to the Name of God and benefit to His people, that devote all their time and energy to serious Torah study without any thought of personal gain, there is no question that the hours they spend huddled over the Gemara are the most effective outreach of all.